Uncle Art's Bible Favorites

A Study Guide to the Bible

Arthur Perkins

Uncle Art's Bible Favorites: A Study Guide to the Bible

by Arthur Perkins

Signalman Publishing
www.signalmanpublishing.com
email: info@signalmanpublishing.com
Tampa, Florida

Scripture verses are taken from the King James Version of the Bible with straightforward updates made to the more archaic words and phrases, but only where the word or phrase and its replacement was obvious.

ISBN: 978-1-940145-79-2 (paperback)

978-1-940145-80-8 (ebook)

Printed in the United States of America

Dedication

As in the nonfiction work *Marching to a Worthy Drummer* and in my Christian novels *Buddy, Cathy, Jacob* and *Home, Sweet Heaven,* I dedicate this work to my wife Carolyn, the joy of my life who endows it with a richness of love and meaning. We both dedicate this work, above all, to our God, and to our four daughters and their families.

Other Books by Arthur Perkins

Marching to a Worthy Drummer
A Christian Layperson Speaks Out About the Holy Spirit

Buddy
Book 1 of the *Buddy* Series, a Christian novel

Cathy
Book 2 of the *Buddy* Series

Jacob
Book 3 of the *Buddy* Series

Home, Sweet Heaven
Book 4 of the *Buddy* Series

Acknowledgements

I wish to extend a grateful, heartfelt thank-you to the following people who have been instrumental in the production of my books. First, to my God, whose loving character elicits my devotion and the thrill of learning and writing of His beautiful nature. Second, to my wonderful wife Carolyn, whose loving support in all matters of our happy marriage have given me added incentive and the freedom to pursue my writing endeavors. Third, to my brother Jon, whose support has been extremely helpful. Fourth, to my friend and publisher, John McClure of Signalman Publishing, for his enthusiasm and professionalism. I'm truly fortunate to be associated with him. I also wish to thank our pastor, F. David Lambert, ThD., a devoted and knowledgeable Christian. While we don't always agree on every theological matter, we do agree on much, particularly on the divine inspiration and inerrancy of Scripture. I have learned much about God and the Church through his very thorough exposition of Scripture and Church doctrine.

Preface

The Bible Study Guides are intended to be a series of volumes directed toward supporting the Bible study leader or the Sunday School teacher in making insightful presentations to their students on interesting and important Bible topics. Each volume of this series focuses on a particular theme that integrates the stories. Alternatively, the teacher may choose to present chapters among the volumes that are randomly selected, or may implement other integrating themes by extracting chapters from the various volumes that are appropriate to the specific themes chosen by the teacher. The stories themselves were selected on the basis of their innate interest and importance to the understanding of God and our Christian faith. They are truly my favorites.

The topics and their treatment are appropriate for a range of age levels, from early teens through adults, and for precocious preteens as well. Each chapter has been designed to provide sufficient coverage for one typical class session that would include some time for a question and answer period.

Bible verses are taken from the King James Version with straightforward updates applied to the more archaic words and phrases, but only where the word or phrase and its replacement is obvious.

Contents

Volume One *Glimpses of the New Testament Found in the Old* 13

Volume Two *Time and Beyond of God* 69

Volume Three *Delightful Scriptural Appetizers* 137

Volume Four *God's Feminine Side* 183

Volume Five *God's Confections of Love* 235

Volume Six *God's Character* 275

Volume Seven *Israel* 319

Volume One

Glimpses of the New Testament Found in the Old

Contents

Preface 17
One: The Great Commandment 19
Two: Abraham's Sacrifice of Isaac 22
Three: The Story of Joseph 27
Four: The Great I AM 31
Five: The Passover Lamb 34
Six: The Serpent on the Pole 37
Seven: The Father Forsakes Jesus 40
Eight: The Fulfillment of Hannah's Vow 43
Nine: Ruth Foretells the Church 47
Ten: Jesus Quotes the Prophet Isaiah 52
Eleven: Isaiah Foretells Jesus' Agony 56
Twelve: Isaiah Foretells Jesus Wed 59
Thirteen: The Importance of Jonah 62
Fourteen: Jesus' Ride to Destiny 66

Preface

The integrating theme for the present volume, Volume One, is the unity of both Bible Testaments, wherein the Old Testament furnishes vital supporting information for the New Testament, and the New Testament fulfills the promise of the Old Testament. As many people have noted, Jesus Himself regarded the Old Testament as extremely important. After all, the only Scripture available during Jesus first advent, from which He quoted liberally, was the Old Testament. Among His teachings that stress that importance is the following, taken from Matthew 5:17 and 18:

> **Think not that I am come to destroy the law, or the prophets; I am not come to destroy, but to fulfill. For truly I say to you, Till heaven and earth pass, one jot or one tittle shall in no way pass from the law, till all be fulfilled.**

That unity among Testaments works the other way as well. In John 5:45 – 47, Jesus claims that Moses wrote of Him. He repeats that theme elsewhere, particularly on the road to Emmaus, as described in Luke 24:44 and in John 5:45-47:

> **These are the words which I spoke to you, while I was yet with you, that all things must be fulfilled, which were written in the law of Moses, and in the prophets, and in the psalms, concerning me.**
>
> **Do not think that I will accuse you to the Father; there is one who accuses you, even Moses, in whom you trust. For had you believed Moses, you would have believed me; for he wrote of me. But if you believe not his writings, how shall you believe my words?**

I often have marveled at the information regarding Jesus presented in Genesis, to the extent that I personally consider the Book of Genesis to be the first Gospel of Jesus Christ.

One
The Great Commandment

It is a worthwhile endeavor to turn, from time to time, to Exodus 20:1-17 for a review of the Ten Commandments. While it represents law, and many Christians would claim on the basis of Jesus' work on the cross that He rendered the law obsolete, that assessment is too simplistic. A love thing is involved. Jesus also said in John 14:15:

> **If you love me, keep my commandments.**

The New Testament proclaims the law to be valid no longer, primarily because through the indwelling Holy Spirit promised by Jesus, the law is now written on Christians' hearts. But sometimes the cares of daily living turn our hearts far from God. Here are the Ten Commandments of Exodus 20, and we'd all do well to keep them in mind:

> **And God spoke all these words, saying, I am the Lord your God, who have brought you out of the land of Egypt, out of the house of bondage.**
>
> **You shall have no other gods before me.**
>
> **You shall not make to yourself any carved image, or any likeness of anything that is in heaven above, or that is in the earth beneath, or that is in the water under the earth; you shall not bow down yourself to them, nor serve them; for I, the Lord your God, am a jealous God, visiting the iniquity of the fathers upon the children unto the third and fourth generation of them that hate me; and showing mercy unto thousands of them that love me, and keep my commandments.**

> **You shall not take the name of the Lord your God in vain; for the Lord will not hold him guiltless who takes his name in vain.**
>
> **Remember the sabbath day, to keep it holy. Six days shall you labor and do all your work; but the seventh day is the sabbath of the Lord your God; in it you shall not do any work, thou, nor your son, nor your daughter, your manservant, nor your maidservant, nor your cattle, nor the stranger who is within your gates; for in six days the Lord made heaven and earth, the sea, and all that is them is, and rested the seventh day; wherefore, the Lord blessed the sabbath day, and hallowed it.**
>
> **Honor your father and your mother, that your days may be long upon the land which the Lord your God gives you.**
>
> **You shall not murder.**
>
> **You shall not commit adultery.**
>
> **You shall not steal.**
>
> **You shall not bear false witness against your neighbor.**
>
> **You shall not covet your neighbor's house; you shall not covet your neighbor's wife, nor his manservant, nor his maidservant, nor his ox, nor his ass, nor anything that is your neighbor's.**

The essential character of these commandments is the exercise of love. Love is selfless and desires the glory of God and the best for others. This basic feature is encapsulated in Deuteronomy 6:4 and 5:

> **Hear, O Israel: The Lord our God is one Lord: and you shall love the Lord your God with all your heart, and with all your soul, and will all your might.**

This commandment, which the Jews have honored under the title

Shema, and which many Jews recite as a daily prayer, is echoed with the same force by Jesus in Matthew 22:35-38:

> **Then one of them, who was a lawyer, asked him a question, testing him, and saying, Master, which is the great commandment in the law?**
>
> **Jesus said to him, You shall love the Lord, your God, with all your heart, and with all your soul, and with all your mind. This is the first and great commandment.**

Most Christians, when referring to this passage, tend to see it only in association with the next verse, which reads:

> **And the second is like it, You shall love your neighbor as yourself.**

While this next verse is very important and says much about how Christians should behave in the world, the constant pattern of quoting it whenever the earlier verse is mentioned tends to diminish the emphasis that should be placed on the fact that our love toward God is to be our greatest commandment, as is the *Shema* to the Isralites. Both of these verses should be kept in mind often, but sometimes they should be considered separately for the sake of emphasis.

Two

Abraham's Sacrifice of Isaac

Chapter 22 of Genesis describes one of the greatest tests of faith that God would impose upon Abraham or, for that matter, upon any human. In that chapter, God tells Abraham to sacrifice the son whom he dearly loved.

> **And it came to pass after these things, that God did tempt Abraham, and said to him Abraham: and he said, Behold, here I am. And he said, Take now your son, your only son Isaac, whom you love, and get you into the land of Moriah; and offer him there for a burnt offering upon one of the mountains which I will tell you of.**
>
> **And Abraham rose up early in the morning, and saddled his ass, and took two of his young men with him, and Isaac his son, and split the wood for the burnt offering, and rose up, and went to the place of which God had told him. Then on the third day Abraham lifted up his eyes, and saw the place afar off. And Abraham said unto his young men, Stay here with the ass; and I and the lad will go yonder and worship, and come again to you.**
>
> **And Abraham took the wood of the burnt offering, and laid it upon Isaac his son; and he took the fire in his hand, and a knife; and they went both of them together. And Isaac spoke to Abraham his father, and said, My father: and he said, Here am I, my son. And he said, Behold the fire and the wood: but where is the lamb for a burnt offering? And Abraham said, My son, God will provide himself a lamb for a burnt offering: so they went both of them together. And they came to the place which God had told him of;**

and Abraham built an altar there, and laid the wood in order, and bound Isaac his son, and laid him on the altar upon the wood. And Abraham stretched forth his hand, and took the knife to kill his son.

And the Angel of the Lord called to him out of heaven, and said, Abraham, Abraham: and he said Here am I. And he said, Lay not your hand upon the lad, neither do any thing to him: for now I know that you fear God, seeing you have not withheld your son, your only son, from me. And Abraham lifted up his eyes, and looked, and behold, behind him a ram caught in a thicket by his horns: and Abraham went and took the ram, and offered him up for a burnt offering in the stead of his son. And Abraham called the name of that place Jehovah-jireh: as it is said to this day, In the mount of the Lord it shall be seen.

Abraham actually had more than one son, but Isaac was the only son who was born of his wife Sarah, and the Bible carefully showed that it was to be through Isaac's bloodline that the promises of God to Abraham eventually would be realized. It was in the sense that Abraham's seed through Isaac would be the one to bear fruit to God in the bloodline to Judah that Isaac was considered to be Abraham's only son.

Unfortunately, many Christians question why God would command such brutality. They see only God's apparent cruelty in this directive. They don't understand the significance of it in demonstrating the nobility of God's own character, His enormous love toward His Son Jesus and the pain that He would have to endure for our sake in handing Jesus over to the cross for our own salvation. In brief, this episode was a foretelling of God's plan of salvation for mankind in the form of a passion play.

God clearly intended this event in the life of Abraham and Isaac to foretell the sorrow that would be the Holy Father's lot as his only begotten Son Jesus was sacrificed on the cross at Calvary. What God held back from requiring of Abraham, He Himself had to do in this magnificent expression of His sacrificial love toward mankind.

Abraham was blessed for his faith. The importance of it was not just that he was willing to suffer the sorrow of losing his son. The greater part of his faith was that he was willing to represent the drama between the Father and Jesus in the most significant moment in the history of mankind: Jesus' passion on the cross."

Genesis Chapter 24 involves Isaac again, but under considerably happier circumstances. Isaac is now old enough to marry, and his father Abraham is choosy about whom he shall have as a bride. Sarah has died, so the task of selecting the proper wife for Isaac falls on the shoulders of Abraham's trusted servant, who is told to go to the country of Abraham's kinfolk. We pick up the narrative at Genesis 24:10:

> **And the servant took ten camels of the camels of his master, and departed; for all the goods of his master were in his hand: and he arose, and went to Mesopotamia, unto the city of Nahor. And he made his camels to kneel down outside the city by a well of water at the time of the evening, even the time that women go out to draw water. And he said, O Lord God of my master Abraham, I pray you, send me good speed this day, and show kindness to my master Abraham. Behold, I stand here by the well of water; and the daughters of the men of the city come out to draw water: and let it come to pass, that the damsel to whom I shall say, Let down your pitcher, I pray you, that I may drink; and she shall say, Drink, and I will give your camels drink also: let the same be she that you have appointed for your servant Isaac; and thereby shall I know that you have shown kindness to my master.**
>
> **And it came to pass, before he had done speaking, that, behold, Rebekah came out, who was born to Bethuel, son of Milcah, the wife of Nahor, Abraham's brother, with her pitcher upon her shoulder. And she was very fair to look upon, a virgin, neither had any man known her: and she went down to the well, and filled her pitcher, and came up. And the servant ran to meet her, and said, Let me, I**

> **pray you, drink a little water of your pitcher. And she said, Drink, my lord: and she hasted, and let down her pitcher upon her hand, and gave him drink. And when she had done giving him drink, she said, I will draw water for your camels also, until they have done drinking. And she hasted, and emptied her pitcher into the trough, and ran again to the well to draw water, and drew for all his camels. And the man wondering at her held his peace, to wit whether the Lord had made his journey prosperous or not. And it came to pass, as the camels had done drinking, that the man took a golden earring of half a shekel weight, and two bracelets for her hands of ten shekels weight of gold; and said, Whose daughter are you? Tell me, I pray you: is there room in your father's house for us to lodge in? And she said to him, I am the daughter of Bethuel the son of Milcah, which she bare to Nahor. She said moreover to him, We have both straw and provender enough, and room to lodge in. And the man bowed down his head, and worshiped the Lord. And he said, Blessed be the Lord God of my master Abraham, who has not left destitute my master of his mercy and his truth: I being in the way, the Lord led me to the house of my master's brethren. And the damsel ran, and told them of her mother's house these things."**

So Abraham's servant went into the house of Rebekah's brother Laban and told them of his mission to find a wife for Abraham's son Isaac. He related how God had led him directly to Rebekah and had confirmed that she was the one whom he had sought. After this, the servant asked for their consent to take Rebekah back with him and present her to Isaac. Upon receiving their consent, the servant lavished Rebekah and her family with gifts. As he prepared to return home, the family stalled off, asking that Rebekah stay with them for at least ten more days. He, wishing to return immediately, asked them to reconsider the delay, whereupon they called Rebekah into the meeting and asked her for her consent. Having received it from her, the servant then returned home with her and she became Isaac's wife.

At this point, Scripture had already identified Isaac as representing Jesus on the cross. Now, the circumstances of his marriage to Rebekah just as clearly show him as representing Jesus who will wed a very special bride. As the Bible brings out in the New Testament, the bride that Rebekah foretold will be the Church; moreover, Rebeckah's own consent was down in the weeds of apparent importance, but it was there, suggesting that while the lion's share of initiative toward our salvation belongs to God, He did leave a tiny portion of it to us.

Three
The Story of Joseph

The story of Joseph in the Old Testament is long. It begins in Chapter 37 of the Book of Genesis, and goes through Chapter 45. The Bible gives it so much attention because it beautifully shows a very important feature of the Jesus who we'll come to know more fully in the New Testament. There are many such stories in the Old Testament like that, that point directly to Jesus. These tales actually define the Jesus who will later come in the flesh. God's like that. He didn't need to do it that way, but he involved mankind in showing itself just how Jesus would appear when He came down to earth to live among us.

Of the twelve sons of Jacob, whom God renamed Israel, Joseph was the most loved by him. That status of his didn't particularly sit well with the others, and his own actions only made things worse. He was given to telling his father of his brothers' evil deeds, and then when he told them of his dreams in which he was their leader, even over his own father and mother, they'd had it up to their eyeballs with him. They were in a remote field when he came upon them again to check up on them, and, unable to take his attitude any more, they rid themselves of him by selling him to a band of Ishmaelites who were traveling with goods into Egypt. By doing so, they handed him a sentence of lifelong slavery. They covered his coat with the blood of a goat and told their father Jacob that Joseph had been killed by a beast.

This was the beginning of a remarkable adventure of Joseph, one that spanned years of slavery and jail, times of distress in which there was no possibility of freedom except for a miracle from God. But that is just what happened. As God raised up the prophet Daniel many centuries later through the circumstance of dreams, He did the same with Joseph by giving the king of Egypt, who is called Pharaoh, a dream of seven fat and seven emaciated animals. The dream troubled this king greatly, but when he commanded his advisors to explain what it meant, they were unable to do so. But Joseph, still in jail, had already interpreted the dream of a fellow prisoner, Pharaoh's butler, who had been released and restored to his former position as Joseph had predicted would happen. When Pharaoh, the lord of Egypt, had heard of this ability of Joseph, he was released from jail to appear before him and interpret the ruler's own dream. Joseph responded by explaining that the dream foretold of seven future years of plentiful harvest, to be followed by another seven years of drought and famine. He went on to recommend to Pharaoh that he appoint an overseer to supervise the storage of surplus food during the good years to offset starvation during the lean years to follow. Pharaoh, recognizing the hand of God in Joseph's talent, not only released him from jail, but appointed him to be that very supervisor. This commission came in Joseph's thirtieth year, as it was for Jesus when He was baptized for His mission. In a grand demonstration of God's power to raise up the humble, Joseph carried out his assigned duty, in the process becoming a mighty ruler, second in command to Pharaoh over all of Egypt.

As years of plenty passed and were replaced by years of drought, the stores of grain laid up by Joseph began to be used. Now the supervision of Joseph turned to the distribution of food to the needy. Meanwhile, the widespread famine extended outside the borders of Egypt. Other people were beginning to starve, and among these were Joseph's Israelite brothers. Their father Jacob, seeing the plight of his people and the relative ease with which the Egyptians were weathering the drought, sent ten of his sons to Pharaoh to plead for food. Of all his sons, only the youngest, Benjamin, remained behind.

In one of life's great ironies, the Israelites were granted an audience with the Egyptian potentate in charge of distribution, who, of course, was their brother whom they had abused so many long, eventful years ago. Because so much time had passed during which they thought he was dead, they failed to recognize him. As for Joseph, he knew immediately, but declined at that time to make the connection known.

At this point Joseph must have struggled pretty hard with feelings of hurt and anger. He was obviously in control over their very lives. Now Joseph was in the perfect payback position and he knew it. He had the ideal chance to even the score and he began to cash in on the opportunity with harsh words and harsher terms. He did give them some food, but kept Simeon behind as a hostage, refusing to release him unless they brought Benjamin to him as surety that they were not spies. Eventually they were forced by the continuing famine to return for more food, bringing Benjamin with them to the terrible distress of their father Jacob. Joseph played a bit with their fear, framing Benjamin for theft and insisting that he stay behind as his slave. Faced with calamity, they spoke among themselves with shame and guilt of God's retribution for the evil manner in they had treated their brother so long ago. Finally, still not recognizing that it was his brother he was standing before, Judah repented of his evil deeds before Joseph, offering his substitutionary enslavement for the freedom of Benjamin.

Throughout this drama Joseph was beset with mixed feelings of hatred and love. Now, in the wake of Judah's repentance the situation changed dramatically. In one of history's great defining moments, Wisdom was imparted to Joseph such that he understood the events shaping his life in the context of the magnificent loving hand of God. Casting away the temptation to indulge in his petty retribution, he decided to obey his God. I particularly like what Joseph said to his brothers in Genesis Chapter 45:

> **Then Joseph could not refrain himself before all them that stood by him; and he cried, Cause every man to go out from me. And there stood no man with him, while Joseph made himself known to his brothers.**
>
> **And he wept aloud: and the Egyptians and the house of Pharaoh heard. And Joseph said to his brothers, I am Joseph; does my father yet live? And his brothers could**

not answer him; for they were troubled at his presence.

And Joseph said to his brothers, Come near to me, I pray you. And they came near. And he said, I am Joseph your brother, whom ye sold into Egypt. Now therefore be not grieved, nor angry with yourselves, that you sold me here: for God did send me before you to preserve life. For these two years has the famine been in the land: and yet there are five years, in which there shall neither be plowing nor harvesting.

And God sent me before you to preserve you a posterity in the earth, and to save your lives by a great deliverance. So now it was not you who sent me here, but God: and he has made me a father to Pharaoh, and lord of all his house, and a ruler throughout all the land of Egypt. Haste you, and go up to my father, and say to him, Thus says your son Joseph, God has made me lord of all Egypt: come down to me without delay. And you shall dwell in the land of Goshen, and you shall be near unto me, you, and your children, and your children's children, and your flocks, and your herds, and all that you have: and there will I nourish you; for yet there are five years of famine; lest you, and your household, and all that you have, come to poverty.

The importance of Joseph's life, and this story of it, is that Joseph was given the privilege of presenting a very important part of Jesus' character to the world at large. What Joseph did was to suffer on behalf of those who caused his suffering, who hated him. At the end he did it willingly, to save them from starvation and death. Jesus did that very thing – He suffered on behalf of those – us – who, still being in our sins, hated and rejected Him. He did it voluntarily, out of love, for our salvation.

Four
The Great I AM

The Egyptian government was so deep into the oppression of the Israelites when Moses was born that midwives had been commanded to kill the male children at birth. Moses was saved from that fate by the compassion of a succession of women. His mother had waterproofed a basket, placed the three-month-old child in it and put it into the water in the hopes that God somehow would save the baby.

God did. He had big plans for Moses, and for the fulfillment of them, Moses needed to remain alive. Pharaoh's daughter came upon the basket and, having compassion on the baby within, adopted him.

For the first forty years of his life, Moses was a member of Pharaoh's household, enjoying the same privileges and education as a native Egyptian. But he knew that he was an Israelite, and when he saw an Egyptian overseer abusing a slave, he killed him. Rather than appreciating Moses' intervention on their behalf, the Israelites accused him of murder. Pharaoh himself got wind of what Moses had done, and sought to slay him as well. Moses fled Egypt, and for the next forty years of his life led a pastoral existence in the land of Midian, east of the Red Sea. There he married and had a son.

As the second forty years of his life drew to a close, God appeared to him from within a bush that burned without wasting away. Declaring His compassion on the Israelites for the suffering they were experiencing under the harsh hands of the Egyptians, God informed Moses that He had chosen him for the task of delivering his nation from slavery in Egypt and of bringing them into the land that He had promised Abraham, Isaac and Jacob. Being alarmed at the magnitude of this task, Moses questioned whether his people would buy into this plan. He no doubt remembered how he already had been rejected by his people when he had tried to help them, and now God was asking him to do it again, but this time on a vastly larger scale of intervention. As related in Exodus 3:13, Moses peppered God with a series of questions:

> **And Moses said to God, Behold, when I come to the children of Israel, and shall say to them, The God of your fathers has sent me to you; and they shall say to me, What is his name? What shall I say to them?**

In response, God gave him His name, an enigmatic one indeed:

> **And God said to Moses, I AM THAT I AM: and He said, Thus shall you say to the children of Israel, I AM has sent me to you. And God said moreover to Moses, Thus shall you say to the children of Israel, The Lord God of your fathers, the God of Abraham, the God of Isaac, and the God of Jacob, has sent me to you; this is my name forever, and this is my memorial to all generations.**

For the third duration of forty years Moses, having received abundantly of the indwelling Holy Spirit, struggled to fulfill God's plan for him and His people Israel. The journey that followed Moses' encounter with God represents not only Israel's struggle and God's close hand upon that nation and people, but every Christian's path in the hand of Jesus Christ from sin to salvation.

At first glance, this name that God gave Himself seems to emphasize His majesty and power, as if to challenge the right of mere man to question His authority.

Perhaps that is what God intended to convey, but Jesus, when He came in the flesh, took that name for Himself and embellished upon to give it a far different meaning.

That Jesus referred to Himself as the great I AM, and that the Father honored His assertion, is documented in John 8:56-58 and 18:3-6:

> **Then said the Jews to him, You are not yet fifty years old, and have you seen Abraham? Jesus said to them, Truly,**

truly I say to you, Before Abraham was, I am.

Judas then, having received a band of men and officers from the chief priests and Pharisees, came there with lanterns and torches and weapons. Jesus, therefore, knowing all things that should come upon him, went forth, and said to them, Who are you looking for? They answered him, Jesus, of Nazareth. Jesus said to them, I am he. And Judas also, who betrayed him, stood with them. As soon, then, as he had said to them, I am, they went backward, and fell to the ground.

As for Jesus' own interpretation of what this name meant, His descriptions are given in John 6:35, 8:12, 10:7 and 11, 11:25, and 14:6:

And Jesus said to them, I am the bread of life; he that comes to me shall never hunger, and he that believes on me shall never thirst.

Then spoke Jesus again to them, saying, I am the light of the world; he that follows me shall not walk in darkness, but shall have the light of life.

Then said Jesus to them again, Truly, truly I say to you, I am the door of the sheep.

I am the good shepherd; the good shepherd gives his life for the sheep.

Jesus said to her, I am the resurrection, and the life; he that believes in me, though he were dead, yet shall he live.

Jesus said to him, I am the way, the truth, and the life; no man comes to the Father, but by me.

These beautiful self-descriptions depict our God as loving and compassionate, much to our good fortune.

Five
The Passover Lamb

As the fifteenth century B.C. drew to a close, the nation of Israel had been living in Egypt for over four hundred years, the first thirty of which were spent under the favor and protection of Pharaoh, and the following four hundred years – to the day - under a harsher regime. After those first benign years, there had been a progressive descent from friendly relations with the Egyptians, even the elevation of the Israelite Joseph to second in command of Egypt, to slavery under ever more brutal conditions.

God had selected Moses to lead the Israelites out of Egypt, which would take place four hundred thirty years after they came into that land, to the very day. In preparation for that momentous event, which foreshadowed every Christian's exodus from the slavery of sin, God through Moses instituted a custom that has become a tradition observed by Jews and handed from generation to generation down to today.

This observance is called the Passover; it is detailed in Exodus Chapter Twelve:

> **And the Lord spoke to Moses and Aaron in the land of Egypt, saying, This month shall be to you the beginning of months: it shall be the first month of the year to you. Speak to all the congregation of Israel, saying, In the tenth day of this month they shall take to them every man a lamb, according to the house of their fathers, a lamb for a house: and if the household be too little for the lamb, let him and his neighbor next to his house take it according to the number of the souls; every man according to his eating shall make your count for the lamb.**

Your lamb shall be without blemish, a male of the first year: you shall take it out from the sheep, or from the goats. And you shall keep it until the fourteenth day of the same month; and the whole assembly of the congregation of Israel shall kill it in the evening. And they shall take of the blood, and strike it on the two side posts and on the upper door post of the houses, wherein they shall eat it.

And they shall eat the flesh in that night, roast with fire and unleavened bread; and with bitter herbs shall they eat it. Eat not of it raw, nor boiled at all with water, but roast with fire; its head with its legs, and with the inwards parts thereof. And you shall let nothing of it remain until the morning; and that which remains of it until the morning you shall burn with fire. And thus shall you eat it: with your loins girded, your shoes on your feet, and your staff in your hand; and you shall eat it in haste: it is the Lord's Passover.

For I will pass through the land of Egypt this night, and will smite all the first-born in the land of Egypt, both man and beast; and against all the gods of Egypt I will execute judgment: I am the Lord. And the blood shall be to you for a token upon the houses where you are; and when I see the blood, I will pass over you, and the plague shall not be upon you to destroy you, when I smite the land of Egypt.

God through Moses commanded that this observance be a memorial forever. The Israelites left Egypt the next morning, after the Lord had stricken the firstborn of Egypt, passing over without harm those houses which had the blood of the Passover Lamb on their lintels and doorposts.

The significance of this Passover observance is that it is all about Jesus. It foreshadowed Jesus' shed blood on the cross in our behalf. Jesus was crucified at the same time that the religious elite, totally unaware of the custom's significance, killed their Passover lambs as they had done in the same manner every year before. The difference this time was that the real Passover Lamb died once for all for our sins, fulfilling the ritual for which the sacrificial lambs were but a shadow.

John the Baptist knew that this was the very reason that God became a man and lived among us: God Himself in selfless, noble love atoned for our shortcomings, knowing that we were helpless to do it for ourselves. John 1:29 relates John the Baptist's greeting of Jesus as he was baptizing all who came to him in repentance:

> **The next day John saw Jesus coming to him, and said, Behold the Lamb of God, who takes away the sin of the world.**

In Chapter 9, the writer of the New Testament Book of Hebrews explained beautifully this significance of Jesus as the Passover Lamb:

> **But Christ being come a high priest of good things to come, by a greater and more perfect tabernacle, not made with hands, that is to say, not of this building, neither by the blood of goats and calves, but by his own blood he entered in once into the holy place, having obtained eternal redemption for us. For if the blood of bulls and of goats, and the ashes of an heifer sprinkling the unclean, sanctifies to the purifying of the flesh, how much more shall the blood of Christ, who through the eternal Spirit offered himself without spot to God, purge your conscience from dead works to serve the living God? And for this cause he is the mediator of the New Testament, that by means of death, for the redemption of the transgressions that were under the first testament, they who are called might receive the promise of eternal inheritance.**

Six
The Serpent on the Pole

Numbers 21:4-9 speaks of the difficulties that the Israelites faced in the wilderness during their journey from Egypt to the land promised by God. By this time the people had grown tired of eating manna and were beginning to hate it. The way was dangerous as well. Among the hazards were deadly serpents, which had killed a number of people. Moses responded to this threat by having a replica of a snake fashioned in bronze and mounted on a pole, such that those who looked upon the serpent would be healed of snakebite.

> **And they journeyed from Mount Hor by the way of the Red Sea, to compass the land of Edom: and the soul of the people was much discouraged because of the way. And the people spoke against God, and against Moses, Wherefore have you brought us up out of Egypt to die in the wilderness? For there is no bread, neither is there any water; and our soul hates this light manna.**
>
> **And the Lord sent fiery serpents among the people, and they bit the people, and many people of Israel died. Therefore the people came to Moses, and said, We have sinned; for we have spoken against the Lord, and against you; pray unto the Lord, that he take away the serpents from us. And Moses prayed for the people.**
>
> **And Moses made a serpent of bronze, and put it upon a pole, and it came to pass that, if a serpent had bitten any man, when he beheld the serpent of bronze, he lived.**

The serpent on the pole, as representing the serpent of Genesis 3 who deceived Adam and Eve in the Garden, also represented sin.

This episode suggests that in some way a representative of sin can heal people.

The third chapter of John begins with Nicodemus coming to Jesus in the night, probably because he could get away then from the other Pharisees and speak privately with Jesus. Jesus responds with a discourse on spiritual birth, proclaiming that while a person is born in the material world through a natural mother, the Holy Spirit gives birth to a person in the spiritual realm, a necessity for those who are destined for heaven. Jesus continues in verses 14-18 to explain to Nicodemus that He is come in the flesh to point the way to a person's spiritual rebirth through faith in Him.

> **And, as Moses lifted up the serpent in the wilderness, even so must the Son of man be lifted up. That whosoever believes in him should not perish, but have eternal life. For God so loved the world, that he gave his only begotten Son, that whoever believes on him should not perish, but have everlasting life.**
>
> **For God sent not his Son into the world to condemn the world, but that the world through him might be saved. He that believes on him is not condemned, but he that believes not is condemned already, because he has not believed in the name of the only begotten Son of God.**

In this discourse Jesus refers back to the serpent on the pole, through which people who were snakebitten would be healed through fastening their eyes on the brass serpent held up by Moses.

The obvious connection is that the serpent on the pole actually represented Jesus Himself, who indeed became sin on the cross for the purpose of healing mankind from its sinful nature.

Jesus actually became sin, having taken on Himself the sins of every person who ever lived and ever shall live. That is exactly why, in His agony during crucifixion, Jesus uttered the words recorded in the Gospels, as in Matthew 27:46:

> **And about the ninth hour Jesus cried with a loud voice,**

saying, Eli, Eli, lama sabachthani? That is to say, My God, my God, why have you forsaken me?

Unable to look upon sin, the Father, in the grief that was represented by Abraham's attempted sacrifice of Isaac, had to forsake Jesus, covered as He was in the filth of mankind's sin. The words that Jesus spoke, by the way, were first penned by King David a thousand years before Jesus, and went on to describe the effect of crucifixion on a person several hundred years before Crucifixion was known to the Jews.

Seven

The Father Forsakes Jesus

God, knowing that Abraham's beloved son Isaac was precious to him, gave him a terrible commandment, one that would require every last ounce of Abraham's faith, and more so because it didn't make sense. It violated every feature of God that Abraham had known of his Lord.

The awful thing that God had told him to do was to sacrifice Isaac. Why would God do that?

Yet Abraham had the courage and strength of character to trust God, particularly His loving nature. In faith he prepared to carry out the task that God had set before him.

Hundreds of years later, Moses offered healing salvation to those who had been bitten by poisonous snakes during the Israelites' journey through the wilderness. His cure, as directed by God, was to cast a bronze image of a serpent and hold it up on a pole so that those who were bitten could gaze up at it and be healed. Why would God use the image of a serpent, the direct representative of evil from the very beginning at the Garden of Eden, to heal the injured? If this was supposed to represent Jesus on the cross, it was the opposite of Jesus' nature. Again, it just doesn't make sense.

Yet Moses had the courage to obey God's command, and the snake-bitten people were healed through that image.

Both of these events did represent Jesus, as both Abraham and Moses must eventually have come to realize, to their astonishment, the depth of God's love. The fact of the matter was that a grieving Holy Father, unable to look upon sin, had to turn His head away from the sin-covered Jesus on the cross. He had to forsake His own beloved Son to a shame-filled, agonizing death. Jesus, in effect, not only suffered physically on the cross but had to become the filth of sin, taking on Himself all the bad thoughts and deeds of fallen mankind that had been perpetrated throughout history.

A thousand years after Abraham and a thousand years before Jesus came in the flesh, David reigned as king over Israel. During that time, he enjoyed an intimate relationship with God. One might even say that he spoke to God. God certainly spoke to him, as David penned many Psalms, some of which possessed knowledge supernaturally beyond David's time on earth.

One of these Psalms is Psalm 22, which begins with words which Jesus repeated while He was suffering on the cross. According to Matthew 27:46, Jesus uttered these words of Psalm 22 as He suffered:

My God, My God, why have you forsaken me?

It could be that Jesus repeated these beginning words of the Psalm so that readers of the Gospel over the centuries following His crucifixion and resurrection could marvel at David's supernatural picture of crucifixion, a method of punishment that wasn't known until several centuries after David.

Psalm 22:1-18 describes with precision what happens to a person as he is crucified.

My God, my God, why have you forsaken me? Why are you so far from helping me, and from the words of my roaring? O my God, I cry in the daytime, but you hear not; and in the night season, and am not silent.

But you are holy, O you who inhabits the praises of Israel. Our fathers trusted in you; they trusted, and you delivered them. They cried to you, and were delivered; they trusted in you, and were not confounded.

But I am a worm, and no man; a reproach of men, and despised by the people. All they who see me laugh me to scorn; they shoot out the lip, they shake the head, saying, He trusted on the Lord that he would deliver him; let him deliver him, seeing he delighted in him.

> **But you are he who took me out of the womb; you made me hope upon my mother's breasts. I was cast upon you from the womb; you are my God from my mother's belly. Be not far from me; for trouble is near; for there is none to help. Many bulls have compassed me; strong bulls of Bashan have beset me round. They gaped upon me with their mouths, like a ravening and roaring lion.**
>
> **I am poured out like water, and all my bones are out of joint: my heart is like wax; it is melted within me. My strength is dried up like a potsherd, and my tongue cleaves to my jaws; and you have brought me into the dust of death. For dogs have compassed me; the assembly of the wicked have enclosed me; they pierced my hands and my feet. I may count all my bones; they look and stare upon me. They part my garments among them, and cast lots upon my vesture.**

This account of Jesus' crucifixion includes some specific details associated with the event that are profoundly important. Among these are the remarks, as in Isaiah 53, of His reproach and rejection, the specific note of Jesus' hands and feet being pierced with nails, and of lots being cast for His garment, as noted in Matthew 27:35.

Eight
The Fulfillment of Hannah's Vow

The two books of Samuel in the Bible were written over a thousand years before Jesus Christ was born, when Israel was still a young nation. The book of First Samuel opens with a story regarding Hannah, a woman of Israel from the tribe of Ephraim, married to a man named Elkanah.

Hannah wanted to have a son very badly, but she wasn't able to have one. Yet she remained faithful to God, and every year she went with her husband up to a city in Israel called Shiloh to make their yearly worship and sacrifice. Year after year she did this, hoping to have a son by the next year. Finally, one year while she was praying, she broke down and wept in the sight of the priest for her lack of a son. In her misery, Hannah prayed to God, making a promise to Him if He would show His kindness toward her by giving her a son. Her vow went like this:

> **O Lord, of hosts, if you will look on the affliction of your handmaid, and remember me, and not forget me, but will give to your handmaid a male child, then I will give him to the Lord all the days of his life.**

After speaking to God, Eli the Priest blessed her, and she trusted God and was no longer sad when she returned home with her husband.

> **And the Lord remembered Hannah. And she bore a son, and called his name Samuel, saying Because I have asked him of the Lord. And when she had weaned him, she took**

> **him up with her along with sacrifices to the Lord. And they brought the child to the priest Eli. And Hannah said, O my lord, as your soul lives, I am the woman who stood by you here earlier, praying to the Lord. For this child I prayed; and the Lord has answered my prayer which I asked of Him. Therefore also I have lent him to the Lord; as long as he lives he shall be lent to the Lord.**
>
> **And he worshiped the Lord there.**

Hannah did as she had promised God: she left her son Samuel with Eli the priest to live with him and learn the deep things about God from him. Then Hannah prayed again, this time to thank God for His kindness toward her:

> **And Hannah prayed, and said, My heart rejoices in the Lord, my horn is exalted in the Lord; my mouth is enlarged over my enemies, because I rejoice in your salvation. There is none holy like the Lord; for there is none beside you, neither is there any rock like our God. Talk no more so exceeding proudly; let not arrogancy come out of your mouth; for the Lord is a God of knowledge, and by Him actions are weighed. The bows of the mighty men are broken, and they that stumbled are girded with strength. They who were full have hired out themselves for bread; and they who were hungry no longer hungered; so that the barren has born seven; and she who has many children has become feeble. The Lord kills and makes alive; he brings down to the grave and brings up. The Lord makes poor and makes rich; he brings low and lifts up. He raises the poor out of the dust, and lifts up the beggar from the dunghill, to set them among princes, and to make them inherit the throne of glory; for the pillars of the earth are the Lord's, and he has set the world upon them. He will keep the feet of his saints, and the wicked shall be silent in darkness; for by strength shall no man prevail. The adversaries of the Lord shall be broken to pieces; out of heaven He shall thunder upon them. The Lord shall judge the ends of the**

earth; and He shall give strength to his king, and exalt the horn of His anointed.

And Elkanah went to Ramah to his house. And the child did minister to the Lord before Eli, the priest.

Samuel was raised among the priests, where he learned much about God. Then God used him in a mighty way. He became a great prophet, one of the greatest in Israel.

The words that Hannah spoke in thanksgiving to God for His gift of Samuel are significant beyond her time: *'The bows of the mighty men are broken, and they that stumbled are girded with strength.'* The message: God humbles the proud and lifts up the humble.

Hannah was a prophet herself. She foretold in the Old Testament another woman's prayer, far into the future, in the New Testament. This other woman's name was Mary. Hannah's words are echoed in Mary's 'Magnificat' in Chapter 1 of Luke's Gospel, which she spoke after learning that she was to give birth to our Lord Jesus Christ:

And Mary said, "My soul magnifies the Lord, and my spirit has rejoiced in God my Savior. For he has regarded the low estate of his handmaiden, for, behold, from henceforth all generations shall call me blessed. For he that is mighty has done to me great things; and holy is his name. And his mercy is on them that fear him from generation to generation. He has shown strength with his arm; he has scattered the proud in the imagination of their hearts. He has put down the mighty from their seats, and exalted them of low degree. He has filled the hungry with good things; and the rich he has sent empty away. He has helped his servant, Israel, in remembrance of his mercy; as he spoke to our fathers, to Abraham, and to his seed forever."

We can glean something from this. The Old Testament is very important in that it introduces to us the things about God that He describes more fully in the New Testament. Just about everything that Jesus said and did when He came in the flesh was done before in the Old Testament by people of faith who were willing to be directed by the Holy Spirit. The same is true of those who were the closest to Him, like Mary.

We also can learn something else from this. God is our maker, and He loves each of us with a very great passion. But He doesn't like it when we puff ourselves up as important, or when we get upset with ourselves because we don't always win. He made us how He wanted to make us. Perhaps we should think less about how God should make us as perfect as possible and more about how we can be used by God and for His purpose the best that we can with what He has given to us to use.

Nine

Ruth Foretells the Church

The Book of Ruth in the Old Testament is another story that is short, almost the size of the tiny book of Jonah. But it is magnificent in its beauty as it describes the future Marriage of Jesus with His beloved Church.

As the story takes place during the barley harvest in the Fall, the Book of Ruth is traditionally recited in the Jewish community during the Feast of Pentecost, which also occurs during the same time. The subject of the story is much the same as the tale of Rebekah in Genesis 24, but the account also fills in some additional details of the romantic relationship between Jesus and His Church.

The grand design of God that included mankind as an eventual member of the Heavenly Family was foreshadowed in the romantic book of Ruth. From the very beginning of mankind in Adam, God has jealously guarded the bloodline of the Jesus to come. This was well understood by the rulers of this world, from Pharaoh to Herod. At times that were interpreted as Messianic, these secular rulers were given to killing off the male forebears of Mary. They instinctively knew that the bloodline was intended to remain within the Semites, passing down through the Hebrews to the Israelites under Abraham. It was to rest on the specific tribe of Judah, through which came King David, his sons Solomon and Nathan, and, finally, both Mary and her husband Joseph.

But an exception was granted, one of a very few in number. There was a gentile woman named Ruth who, after the untimely death of her first husband, demonstrated a godly loyalty to her mother-in-law Naomi, who had lived in Moab with her Israelite husband. After the death of Naomi's husband Elimelech as well, Naomi decided to move to her husband's homeland of Israel, which God had favored with bountiful crops. Because Ruth was a native of Moab, Naomi thought she would be more comfortable staying there, rather than moving to Israel. Or could she have been testing Ruth?

> **And Naomi said, Turn again, my daughters: why will you go with me? Are there yet any more sons in my womb, that they may be your husbands? Turn again, my daughters, go your way: for I am too old to have a husband. If I should say, I have hope, if I should have a husband also to night, and should also bear sons; Would you wait for them till they were grown? Would you stay for them from having husbands? No, my daughters; for it grieves me much for your sakes that the hand of the Lord is gone out against me. And they lifted up their voice, and wept again: and Orpah kissed her mother in law; but Ruth clave to her.**
>
> **And she said, Behold, your sister in law is gone back unto her people, and to her gods: return after your sister in law.**
>
> **And Ruth said, Intreat me not to leave you, or to return from following after you: for wherever you go, I will go; and where you lodge, I will lodge: your people shall be my people, and your God my God: Where you die, will I die, and there will I be buried: the Lord do so to me, and more also, if ought but death part you and me."**

After making this immortal statement of loyalty, Ruth followed Naomi back to her husband's people, and in poverty gleaned corn in the field of Naomi's relative Boaz.

> **And Naomi had a kinsman of her husband's, a mighty man of wealth, of the family of Elimelech; and his name was Boaz. And Ruth, the Moabitess, said to Naomi, Let me now go to the field, and glean ears of grain after him in whose sight I shall find grace. And she said to her, Go, my daughter. And she went, and came, and gleaned in the field after the reapers; and she happened to come to a portion of the field belonging to Boaz, who was of the family of**

Elimelech. And, behold, Boaz came from Bethlehem, and said to the reapers, The Lord be with you. And they answered him, The Lord bless you. And then said Boaz to his servant who was over the reapers, Whose lady is this?

Ruth, being a pretty woman, obviously had caught Boaz' eye. The attracton was mutual, and out of this first encounter began the first stirrings of a romance. Ruth confided her feelings to Naomi, who advised her to show her interest to Boaz.

And [Ruth] went down to the [threshing] floor, and did all that her mother-in-law told her to do. And when Boaz had eaten and drunk, and his heart was merry, he went to lie down at the end of the heap of grain; and she came softly, and uncovered his feet, and lay down. And it came to pass at midnight, that the man was startled, and turned himself; and, behold, a woman lay at his feet. And he said, Who are you? And she answered, I am Ruth, your handmaid. Spread, therefore, your skirt over your handmaid; for you are a near kinsman.

And he said, Blessed be you of the Lord, my daughter: for you have shown more kindness in the latter end than the beginning, as you followed not young men, whether poor or rich. And now, my daughter, fear not; I will do to thee all that you require; for all the city of my people does know that you are a virtuous woman.

There was a tradition in Israel, instituted by Moses from the Word of God, that if a woman's husband died, a near kinsman was obligated to marry her and raise up children for her. By lying at Boaz' feet, Ruth was claiming that obligation to Boaz. Boaz, in turn, enthusiastically agreed to fulfill that obligation. Ruth conceived a child through this man. His name was Obed:

And Naomi took the child, and laid it in her bosom, and became nurse unto it. And the women her neighbors gave it a name, saying, There is a son born to Naomi; and they called his name Obed: he is the father of Jesse, the father

of David.

Now these are the generations of Pharez: Pharez begat Hezron, and Hezron begat Ram, and Ram begat Amminadab, and Amminadab begat Nahshon, and Nahshon begat Salmon, and Salmon begat Boaz, and Boaz begat Obed, and Obed begat Jesse, and Jesse begat David.

This genealogical record is repeated in the Gospels of Matthew and Luke. As noted in Matthew:

. . .And Salmon begat Booz of Rachab; and Booz begat Obed of Ruth; and Obed begat Jesse; and Jesse begat David the king; and David the king begat Solomon of her that had been the wife of Urias;. . .and Jacob begat Joseph the husband of Mary, of whom was born Jesus, who is called Christ.

It is striking how the Bible can so dramatically convey passion by means of a simple genealogical list. By the grace of this exception that is immortalized in the begats like a medal of honor, the gentiles were permitted to participate in the creation of the physical Jesus. This gentile participation in the bringing forth of the Jewish Messiah is a type of the participation of man in the Godhead.

As Boaz prefigures Jesus Christ, the marriage between Boaz and Ruth also foretells the union between Jesus and His Church. The hint of this relationship is given substance by Paul in Ephesians 5:22-32:

Wives, submit yourselves unto your own husbands, and to the Lord. For the husband is the head of the wife, even as Christ is the head of the church; and he is the savior of the body.

Therefore, as the church is subject unto Christ, so let the wives be to their own husbands in everything. Husbands, love your wives, even as Christ also loved the church, and gave himself for it, that he might sanctify and cleanse it with the washing of water by the word; that he might present it to himself a glorious church, not having spot or

wrinkle, or any such thing; but that it should be holy and without blemish.

So ought men to love their wives as their own bodies. He that loves his wife loves himself. For no man ever yet hated his own flesh, but nourishes and cherishes it, even as the Lord the Church; for we are members of his body, of his flesh, and of his bones.

For this cause shall a man leave his father and his mother, and shall be joined to his wife, and they two shall be one flesh. This is a great mystery, but I speak concerning Christ and the church.

Ten
Jesus Quotes the Prophet Isaiah

The prophet Isaiah, who lived in the eighth century B.C., is a prominent source of Old Testament prophecies that address the Jesus to come. Among these prophecies is the passage in Isaiah 7:14 where the prophet describes Jesus as being born of a virgin, and the passage in Isaiah 9:1 and 2, where Isaiah claims that Jesus will come from Galilee. Because so many of his prophecies depict such accurate facts about Jesus, some would-be Bible scholars attempted to claim that the Book of Isaiah was written after Jesus' first advent. This claim was shown to be false by the discovery of the Dead Sea Scrolls in 1947, the documents of which were dated to before Christ and which contained the complete Book of Isaiah.

Jesus also quoted passages of Isaiah, confirming their authorship. Isaiah 61:1-2a reads as follows:

> **The Spirit of the Lord God is upon me, because the Lord has anointed me to preach good tidings to the meek; he has sent me to bind up the brokenhearted, to proclaim liberty to the captives, and the opening of the prison to those who are bound; to proclaim the acceptable year of the Lord . . .**

Jesus, in Luke 4:16-21, is quoted as saying essentially the same words as Isaiah. And well He should, as He was reading from a scroll.

> **And he came to Nazareth, where he had been brought up; and, as his custom was, he went into the synagogue on the sabbath day, and stood up to read. And there was delivered unto him the book of the prophet, Isaiah. And when he had opened the book, he found the place where it**

was written, The Spirit of the Lord is upon me, because he has anointed me to preach the gospel to the poor; he has sent me to heal the brokenhearted, to preach deliverance to the captives, and recovering of sight to the blind, to set at liberty them that are bruised, to preach the acceptable year of the Lord.

And he closed the book, and he gave it again to the minister, and sat down. And the eyes of all them that were in the synagogue were fastened on him. And he began to say to them, This day is this scripture fulfilled in your ears.

But what adds authority to Jesus' words is that in quoting Isaiah, He didn't finish the entire verse, the rest of which reads:

. . .and the day of vengeance of our God; to comfort all that mourn; to appoint unto those who mourn in Zion, to give them beauty for ashes, the oil of joy for mourning, the garment of praise for the spirit of heaviness, that they might be called trees of righteousness, the planting of the Lord, that he might be glorified.

Isaiah goes on to describe the blessings with which God will endow the nation of Israel.

Why did Jesus break off Isaiah's prophecy in mid-sentence? Because in the synagogue He was describing just what He would accomplish regarding Isaiah's prophecy in His first advent. The remainder of Isaiah's prophecy was related to Jesus' Second Coming, as foretold in the Book of Revelation.

Another passage of Isaiah that was quoted by Jesus is in Isaiah 6:9 and 10:

And he said, Go, and tell this people, Hear you indeed, but understand not; and see you indeed, but perceive not. Make the heart of this people fat, and make their ears heavy, and shut their eyes; lest they see with their eyes, and hear with their ears, and understand with their heart, and are converted, and be healed.

Jesus often spoke of the necessity of having eyes to see and ears to hear what He is teaching. In Mark 4:12, He quotes Isaiah 6:9 and 10 almost verbatim:

> **That seeing they may see, and not perceive; and hearing they may hear, and not understand; lest at any time they should be converted, and their sins should be forgiven them.**

These passages seem to say that God gives a saving knowledge of Him to some people but denies it to others. Is this what He's really saying? There is another passage, in Matthew 11:25-27 that seems so say just that.

> **At that time Jesus answered and said, I thank you, O Father, Lord of heaven and earth, because you have hidden these things from the wise and prudent, and have revealed them to babes.**
>
> **All things are delivered to me by my Father, and no man knows the Son, but the Father; neither knows any man the Father, but the Son, and Him to whomever the Son will reveal Him.**

Why would God deny knowledge of Him to some, as this passage clearly states? In Matthew 13:11-16, Jesus repeats this denial, and gives us an answer as to why, with a commentary similar to that in His Parable of the Talents (Matthew 25).

> **[Jesus] answered and said to them, Because it is given to you to know the mysteries of the kingdom of heaven, but to them it is not given.**
>
> **For whoever has, to him shall be given, and he shall have more abundance; but whoever has not, from him shall be taken away even what he has.**
>
> **Therefore I speak to them in parables, because they seeing, see not, and hearing, they hear not, neither do they understand. And in them is fulfilled the prophecy of Isaiah, which says, By hearing, you shall hear and shall**

not understand, and seeing, you shall see and not perceive; for this people's heart is become gross, and their ears are dull of hearing, and their eyes they have closed, lest at any time they should see with their eyes, and hear with their ears, and should understand with their heart, and should be converted, and I should heal them.

But blessed are your eyes, for they see; and your ears, for they hear.

What Jesus was saying is that some people are so full of selfishness and pride and so caught up in the secular, material world that they don't think of God as even relevant to their lives. They cannot understand, primarily because they don't want to. Paul picked up on this failing of secular-minded people in 1 Corinthians 1:18-25:

For the preaching of the cross is to them that perish foolishness; but unto us who are saved it is the power of God. For it is written, I will destroy the wisdom of the wise, and will bring to nothing the understanding of the prudent. Where is the wise? Where is the scribe? Where is the disputer of this age? Has God not made foolish the wisdom of this world? For after that, in the wisdom of God, the world by wisdom knew not God, it pleased God by the foolishness of preaching to save them who believe. For the Jews require a sign, and the Gentiles seek after wisdom; but we preach Christ crucified, to the Jews a stumbling block, and to the Gentiles foolishness; but to them who are called, both Jews and Gentiles, Christ the power of God, and the wisdom of God. Because the foolishness of God is wiser than men; and the weakness of God is stronger than men.

Eleven

The Prophet Isaiah Foretells Jesus in Agony for Our Sakes

Isaiah 53 is well-known for the detailed accuracy with which the prophet foretold Jesus' mission on Earth as a suffering one to reconcile us to God. It is heart-breakingly descriptive:

> Who has believed our report? And to whom is the arm of the Lord revealed? For he shall grow up before him like a tender plant, and like a root out of a dry ground; he has no form nor comeliness, and when we shall see him, there is no beauty that we should desire him. He is despised and rejected of men, a man of sorrows, and acquainted with grief, and we hid as it were our faces from him; he was despised and we esteemed him not.
>
> Surely he has borne our griefs, and carried our sorrows; yet we did esteem him stricken, smitten of God, and afflicted. But he was wounded for our transgressions, he was bruised for our iniquities; the chastisement for our peace was upon him, and with his stripes we are healed.
>
> All we like sheep have gone astray; we have turned every one to his own way, and the Lord has laid on him the iniquity of us all. He was oppressed, and he was afflicted, yet he opened not his mouth; he is brought like a lamb to the slaughter, and as a sheep before her shearers is dumb, so he opens not his mouth. He was taken from prison and from judgment; and who shall declare his generation? For he was cut off out of the land of the living; for the transgression of my people was he stricken.

And he made his grave with the wicked, and with the rich in his death, because he had done no violence, neither was any deceit in his mouth. Yet it pleased the Lord to bruise him; he has put him to grief. When you shall make his soul an offering for sin, he shall see his seed, he shall prolong his days, and the pleasure of the Lord shall prosper in his hand. He shall see of the travail of his soul, and shall be satisfied; by his knowledge shall my righteous servant sanctify many; for he shall bear their iniquities. Therefore will I divide him a portion with the great, and he shall divide the spoil with the strong, because he has poured out his soul to death; and he was numbered with the transgressors; and he bore the sin of many, and made intercession for the transgressors.

This prophecy reads like an eyewitness account. Beyond that, it describes the purpose of Jesus' first advent on a level of a modern-day preacher who had thoroughly studied both the Gospels and Paul's New Testament Letters.

Moreover, it includes details that represent a transcendence of time. Because of this supernatural characteristic, some would-be theologians attempted to claim that this chapter was written after Jesus' crucifixion. What stopped them in their tracks was the Dead Sea Scrolls, which were scientifically dated to before Jesus' advent, and which contained the complete Book of Isaiah, including this Chapter 53.

Matthew 27:38 and 57-60 show examples of the accuracy of this prophecy, written in the eighth century B.C., which corroborates the phrase:

And he made his grave with the wicked, and with the rich in his death. . .

Then were there two thieves crucified with him, one on the right hand, and another on the left.

When the evening was come, there came a rich man of Arimathea, named Joseph, who also himself was Jesus'

disciple; he went to Pilate, and begged the body of Jesus. Then Pilate commanded the body to be delivered. And when Joseph had taken the body, he wrapped it in a clean linen cloth, and laid it in his own new tomb, which he had hewn out in the rock; and he rolled a great stone to the door of the sepulcher, and departed.

Further corroboration of Isaiah's prophetic accuracy is given in the fulfillment in Matthew 27:26 of the phrase in Isaiah 53:5 *"the chastisement for our peace was upon him, and with his stripes we are healed"*:

Then released he Barabbas unto them; and when he had scourged Jesus, he delivered him to be crucified.

Again, Matthew 27:12-14 matches Isaiah's sentence reading *"He was oppressed, and he was afflicted, yet he opened not his mouth; he is brought like a lamb to the slaughter, and as a sheep before her shearers is dumb, so he opened not his mouth."*

And when [Jesus] was accused by the chief priests and elders, he answered nothing. Then said Pilate unto him, Hear you not how many things they witness against you? And he answered him never a word, insomuch that the governor marveled greatly.

These matches are not coincidental; they reveal an omniscient God who transcends time, knowing the end from the beginning.

Twelve
The Prophet Isaiah Foretells Jesus Wed to His Church

Isaiah 54:1-8 represents a happy, second-advent sequel to the suffering Jesus in the previous chapter, Isaiah 53.

> **Sing, O barren, you who did not bear; break forth into singing, and cry aloud, you who did not travail with child; for more are the children of the desolate than the children of the married wife, says the Lord.**
>
> **Enlarge the place of your tent, and let them stretch forth the curtains of your habitations; spare not, lengthen your cords, and strengthen your stakes; for you shall break forth on the right hand and on the left, and your seed shall inherit the nations, and make the desolate cities to be inhabited.**
>
> **Fear not; for you shall not be ashamed, neither be you confounded; for you shall not be put to shame; for you shall forget the shame of your youth, and shall not remember the reproach of your widowhood any more. For your Maker is your husband; the Lord of hosts is his name; and your Redeemer, the Holy One of Israel; the God of the whole earth shall he be called.**
>
> **For the Lord has called you like a woman forsaken and grieved in spirit, and a wife of youth, when you were refused, says your God. For a small moment have I forsaken you, but with great mercies will I gather you. In a little wrath I hid my face from you for a moment, but with everlasting kindness will I have mercy on you, says**

the Lord, your Redeemer.

One might be tempted to question whether Jesus and His Church are the actual characters in these verses, or whether Isaiah had some other people group in mind. Could He have been referring instead to Israel, and the Jews' relationship with God? But Paul in Galatians 4:27, speaking of the promise and freedom of Christians in Christ, quoted part of this passage in the context of the Church's relationship with Jesus, confirming that this indeed is the correct interpretation:

For it is written, Rejoice, you barren that bear not; break forth and cry, you that travail not; for the desolate has many more children than she who has a husband.

Another New Testament confirmation of Isaiah's prophecy of this promised relationship include the passage in John 2:1-11, the wedding that Jesus attended in Cana of Galilee. This event has the distinction of being the one where Jesus performed His first miracle, signifying its importance to God. The reference to the third day may point to the complete fulfillment of this prophecy upon Jesus' second advent.

And the third day there was a marriage in Cana, of Galilee; and the mother of Jesus was there. And both Jesus was called, and his disciples, to the marriage. And when they lacked wine, the mother of Jesus said to him, They have no wine. Jesus said to her, Woman, what have I to do with you? My hour is not yet come.

His mother said to the servants, Whatever he says to you, do it. And there were set there six waterpots of stone, after the manner of the purifying of the Jews, containing two or three firkins apiece. Jesus said to them, Fill the waterpots with water. And they filled them up to the brim. And he said to them, Draw some out now, and bear it to the governor of the feast. And they bore it.

When the ruler of the feast had tasted the water that was made wine, and knew not from where it was (but the servants who drew the water knew), the governor of the

feast called the bridegroom, and said to him, Every man at the beginning does set forth good wine and, when men have well drunk, then that which is worse; but you have kept the good wine until now.

This beginning of miracles did Jesus in Cana, of Galilee, and manifested forth his glory; and his disciples believed on him.

In Ephesians 5:31 and 32, Paul gives us another strong, direct confirmation of Isaiah's prophecy in Isaiah 54:

For this cause shall a man leave his father and mother, and shall be joined unto his wife, and they two shall be one flesh. This is a great mystery, but I speak concerning Christ and the church.

Thirteen
The Importance of Jonah

The book of Jonah in the Old Testament is tiny, occupying but one or two pages in the Bible. Because his story is so short, Jonah is often mistaken for the most minor of prophets, interesting to us only for his adventure with the fish where he gets swallowed alive and comes out of it still living. But if this is true, why did Jesus refer to him several times in a way that makes Jonah out to be a pretty important person? As a matter of fact, Jesus seems to puff him up out of all proportion to anything that Jonah might have done to deserve this honor. But then, we already appreciate that the Word of God is far deeper than we might see from a quick reading of it.

At first, the story of Jonah makes him out to be anything but noble. Jonah had run away from God after He had told him to preach to the inhabitants of Nineveh to repent of their wickedness. He went aboard a boat that was going in the opposite direction from where God told him to go.

> **But the Lord sent out a great wind into the sea, and there was a mighty tempest in the sea, so that the ship was like to be broken. Then the mariners were afraid, and cried every man to his god, and cast forth the wares that were in the ship into the sea, to lighten it of them . But Jonah was gone down into the sides of the ship; and he lay, and was fast asleep. So the shipmaster came to him, and said to him, What are you about, O sleeper? Arise, call upon your God, if so be that God will think upon us, that we don't die.**
>
> **And they said every one to his fellow, Come, and let us draw straws, that we may know who is responsible for this evil. So they drew straws, and Jonah got the short straw.**

Then they said to him, Tell us, we ask you, why this evil is upon us; What is your occupation? And where do you come from? What is your country? And of what people are you?

And he said to them, I am a Hebrew; and I fear the Lord, the God of heaven, who has made the sea and the dry land.

Then were the men exceedingly afraid, and said to him, Why have you done this? . . .Then said they to him, What shall we do to you, that the sea may be calm to us? for the sea wrought, and was tempestuous.

And he said to them, Take me up, and cast me forth into the sea; so shall the sea be calm to you: for I know that for my sake this great tempest is upon you. . .So they took up Jonah, and cast him forth into the sea: and the sea ceased from her raging.

. . .Now the Lord had prepared a great fish to swallow up Jonah. And Jonah was in the belly of the fish three days and three nights. . .

When Jonah was expelled from the fish he went on to serve the Lord by preaching to the Ninevites. From the king on down they heeded his words, so that to him was attributed the saved souls of the entire city (which now is overlain by the city of Mosul, in Iraq).

The reason for Jesus' promotion of Jonah to the ranks of the great prophets is that Jonah was allowed to represent the sacrificial Jesus who willingly laid down his life for his fellow man. In being swallowed by the sea creature and eventually being vomited out, Jonah also represented the Jesus who descended into the claustrophobic grave for three days before His resurrection.

Jesus recognized Jonah's contribution to His nature and purpose by the most intimate of methods: He re-enacted the essence of Jonah's Old Testament drama in the New Testament, and by so doing notified His disciples that He, too, must die and descend into the grave for three days and three nights. The account is given in the eighth chapter of Matthew's Gospel:

> **And when he was entered into a ship, his disciples followed him. And, behold, there arose a great tempest in the sea, insomuch that the ship was covered with the waves: but he was asleep. And his disciples came to him, and awoke him, saying, Lord, save us: we're about to die.**
>
> **And he said to them, Why are you fearful, O you of little faith? Then he arose, and rebuked the winds and the sea; and there was a great calm.**

As a side point, there are several accounts, some as recent as the past century, in which whalers have been swallowed whole by their quarry and emerged alive through the ordeal, some having been trapped for several days. In one of the modern events of this nature as related in a Readers' Digest story, the seaman was blinded by the gastric juices and remained an albino for the rest of his life. But he lived.

In John 21:15-17, after Jesus' resurrection, He forgave His disciple Peter three times for the three times Peter denied Him. In this instance, Jesus again refers to the prophet Jonah, this time applying the name to Peter.

> **So when they had dined, Jesus said to Simon Peter, Simon, son of Jonah, do you love me more than these? He said to him, Yea, Lord; you know that I love you. He said to him, Feed my lambs. He said to him again the second time, Simon, son of Jonah, do you love me? He said to him, Yea, Lord; you know that I love you. He said to him the third time, Simon, son of Jonah, do you love me? Peter was grieved because he said to him the third time, Do you love me? And he said to him, Lord, you know that I love you. Jesus said to him, Feed my sheep.**

Peter eventually must have figured out that instead of grieving over Jesus' repetitive commands, he should have been very grateful, for in commanding Peter three times to feed His sheep, Jesus was also forgiving him three times, once each for Peter's three denials of Him. As described in Acts, Peter did indeed go on to feed Jesus' sheep three times: in the first incident, given in Acts 2 Peter brought three thousand people to salvation in Jesus; in the second, described in Acts 3, Peter saves five thousand; and in the third, according to Acts 10, Peter through the conversion of the Italian Cornelius, extends salvation to the entire Gentile community.

Why did Jesus label Peter as the son of Jonah? Probably because, like Jonah, Peter feared the anger of those around him if he were to try to fulfill what God wanted to do with him. In Jonah's case, God had told him to preach repentance to the citizens of Nineveh. Jonah tried to duck out of this responsibility by boarding ship and sailing away as far as he could from that business. In Peter's case, he tried to distance himself from Jesus in the face of the crowd's clamor for Jesus' punishment and death. Both Jonah and Peter eventually mustered the courage to complete God's tasks for them, at considerable risk to their lives. Peter himself was eventually crucified for his commitment to the risen Jesus but by then, of course, he had the comfort and guidance of the indwelling Holy Spirit.

As another side note, Nineveh's repentance lasted only a little over a century. The city's debauchery eventually grew to such an awful extreme that God was moved to destroy it through the armies of Nebudchadnezzar in 612 B.C. This sad event was foretold by the prophet Nahum in the book of that name in the Bible. Eerily, this book reads like a modern news account of trends in the United States and God's response to them.

Fourteen
Jesus' Ride to Destiny

Daniel had foretold the appearance of the Messiah around five hundred years earlier in his famous prophecy of the seventy weeks. In Daniel 9:25, the angel Gabriel tells Daniel that from the commandment to restore and rebuild Jerusalem to the coming of the Messiah the Prince would be a total of sixty nine "weeks" of years, or 69 times 7 prophetic years. This duration is equivalent to 483 prophetic years of 360 days per year, which amounts to 173,880 days. When that very day arrived 483 prophetic years from Artaxerxes' command to rebuild Jerusalem in 445 B.C., Jesus presented Himself at Jerusalem as King and Savior. The event is recorded in Matthew 21:1-11, the first three verses of which describe Jesus' acquisition of two asses for His journey into Jerusalem:

> **And when they drew near to Jerusalem, and were come to Bethphage, to the Mount of Olives, then sent Jesus two disciples, saying to them, Go into the village opposite you, and immediately you shall find an ass tied, and a colt with her; loose them and bring them to me. And if any man say anything to you, you shall say, The Lord has need of them, and immediately he will send them.**

It has been said that Jesus rode into Jerusalem on an ass to show His humble nature. But He was following the lead of King Solomon as well, who also came on a mule to receive his kingship over Israel. That earlier event is described in 1 Kings 1:33, 38 and 39:

> **The king [David] also said to them, Take with you the servants of your lord, and cause Solomon, my son, to ride upon my own mule, and bring him down to Gihon . . . So Zadok, the priest, and Nathan, the prophet, and Benaiah, the son of Jehoiada, and the Cherethites, and**

the Pelethites, went down, and caused Solomon to ride upon King David's mule, and brought him to Gihon. And Zadok, the priest, took a horn of oil out of the tabernacle, and anointed Solomon. And they blew the trumpet; and all the people said, God save King Solomon.

Around the middle of the nine hundred or so years between Solomon and Jesus, the prophet Zechariah in verse 9:9 predicted this very event, where Jesus would follow Solomon's lead in riding a lowly animal to be crowned King of Israel.

Rejoice greatly, O daughter of Zion; shout, O daughter of Jerusalem; behold, your King comes to you, he is just, and having salvation; lowly, and riding upon an ass, and upon a colt, the foal of an ass.

The foretelling of this event is one of a large number of prophecies in which the Holy Spirit, through the writings of obedient humans, displayed the character of the Jesus to come. In this case, Jesus showed His humble nature, but also acknowledged His rightful Kingship over Israel and His believers throughout history.

Elsewhere in Scripture the Gospels affirm that Jesus also acknowledged His Godhood and the importance that He placed in the Spiritual domain as opposed to the material world. In John 8, for example, Jesus identified Himself as the God of Abraham who also had spoken to Moses in the burning bush:

Your father, Abraham, rejoiced to see my day; and he saw it, and was glad. Then said the Jews to him, You are not yet fifty years old, and have you seen Abraham? Jesus said to them, Truly, truly, I say to you, Before Abraham was, I AM.

Notice here how the Pharisees were so fixated on the material world that they couldn't comprehend Jesus' pre-existence in the spiritual domain. Yet, through His healing acts, Jesus demonstrated how thoroughly He controlled the material world, showing man that the spiritual world is of far greater significance than the material domain. Jesus constantly told His disciples that a greater life awaits them out of this world that we find ourselves in, a domain that is worthy of a greater allegiance than our material world. Jesus brings this point home in John 17 as He prays to His heavenly Father:

> **And now I come to You; and these things I speak in the world, that they might have my joy fulfilled in themselves. I have given them Your word; and the world has hated them, because they are not of the world, even as I am not of the world. I pray not that You should take them out of the world, but that You should keep them from the evil. They are not of the world, even as I am not of the world.**

Volume Two

Time and Beyond of God

Contents

Preface 73
One: Jesus' Resurrection of Lazarus 75
Two: The Timing of Jesus' Return to Earth 79
Three: Daniel's Prophecy of Jesus' First Advent 83
Four: Jeremiah's Prophecy of Israel's Captivity 87
Five: Ezekiel's Prophecy of Israel's Return 92
Six: The Timing of the Wise Mens' Visit to Jesus 97
Seven: The Ten Periods of Smyrna's Persecution 102
Eight: Forty Days in the Lives of Moses and Jesus 107
Nine: Six Millennia of Mankind's History 111
Ten: The Good Seed 115
Eleven: Perfection in Imperfection 119
Twelve: Daniel's Abomination of Desolation 123
Thirteen: The Time of Daniel's Abomination 127

Preface

The integrating theme for the present volume, Volume Two, is the importance of time to God, and of the supernatural manner in which information in the Bible transcends our own capability of having produced it.

The ability of God, as revealed in the Bible, to transcend time and space, puts our notion of God as omniscient on firm footing. It also puts the Bible itself above other books as the true Word of God, as John in his Prologue (John 1:1-18) so beautifully confirmed in his description of the divine nature of Jesus, linking Him with Scripture in the very first verse of Genesis.

> **In the beginning God created the heaven and the earth.**
>
> **In the beginning was the Word; and the Word was with God, and the Word was God.**

There have been attempts in the past to deny the supernatural character of the Bible, one attempt being to date the source of time information within the Bible to after Jesus' advent. God took care of that handily, in some cases secreting such prescient passages in the Bible until such time as they could be dated accurately to have been written before Christ, and in other cases providing information that wasn't fulfilled until quite recently.

One
Jesus' Resurrection of Lazarus

Chapter 11:1-44 of John's Gospel describes the event of Jesus' resurrection of Lazarus.

> **Now a certain man was sick, named Lazarus, of Bethany, the town of Mary and her sister, Martha. (It was that Mary who anointed the Lord with ointment, and wiped his feet with her hair, whose brother Lazarus was sick.) Therefore, his sisters sent to him, saying, Lord, behold, he whom you love is sick. When Jesus heard that, he said, This sickness is not for death, but for the glory of God, that the Son of God might be glorified by it.**
>
> **Now Jesus loved Martha, and her sister, and Lazarus. When he had heard, therefore, that he was sick, he remained another two days in the same place where he was. Then, after that, he said to his disciples, Let us go into Judea again.**

Jesus' disciples thought at first that Lazarus was merely asleep. They questioned Him as to why, if that were the case, he needed to go to him, along a route they knew was dangerous for Him. Jesus responded directly by telling them that Lazarus was dead. He followed that with an enigmatic statement:

> **And I am glad for your sakes that I was not there, to the intent that you may believe; nevertheless, let us go to him.**

By the time that Jesus got to Lazarus' place, he had already been dead for four days. When Martha and Mary complained about His delay in getting to Lazarus, He reassured them that Lazarus would rise again. Then He made the following statement:

I am the resurrection, and the life; he that believes in me, though he was dead, yet shall he live. And whoever lives and believes in me shall never die. Do you believe this?

When Jesus saw Mary weeping along with Lazarus' friends, He asked where Lazarus had been laid, and wept along with them. The friends marveled at this demonstration of Jesus' love for Lazarus. When Jesus came to the cave where Lazarus was, He asked that the covering stone be removed. Martha responded with horror, reminding Jesus that after four days, Lazarus would have the stench of death. At this, Jesus reminded her that if she would believe, she would see the glory of God. When the covering stone was removed, Jesus lifted up His eyes and, for the sake of the belief of the onlookers, thanked His Father for hearing Him. With that, He commanded Lazarus,

Lazarus, come forth.

Lazarus responded to this command by stepping alive out of the cave, still in his graveclothes.

On the surface, this story is worthwhile for demonstrating Jesus' compassion toward Lazarus, and for His supernatural ability to perform a resurrection. But the story prods us to look for a deeper significance, in the odd circumstance of Jesus waiting for another two days before performing the resurrection. Surely He knew how Mary, Martha and Lazarus' close friends would be grieving, and that his loitering around would serve to prolong their suffering. It would almost seem that Jesus was rather indifferent to the whole business, a thought that clashes with the fact that Jesus made a hazardous journey to reach Lazarus, and that He wept, and that He did perform the resurrection.

The apparent contradictions of motive in the story point out that something else is in play here – that the resurrection was a far more important event than simply reviving Lazarus. Jesus was actually prophesying His own resurrection. Sense can be made that He waited until Lazarus was dead four days before resurrecting him only if there is a significance to the period of four days that is associated with this prophecy.

Verse 4 of Psalm 90 gives us an interesting clue as to what that significance might be.

> **For a thousand years in your sight are but as yesterday when it is past, and as a watch in the night.**

If this was the only passage that presented a specific relationship among specific periods of time, one might be tempted to dismiss the association as reading too much into the verse. But there is another verse, 2 Peter 3:8, that describes that same relationship:

> **But, beloved, be not ignorant of this one thing, that one day is with the Lord as a thousand years, and a thousand years as one day.**

Moreover, the implication of Jesus raising Lazarus after the fourth day is not the only association of four days with Jesus' appearance. There is an even more basic one, the Passover that pointed to Jesus as the Lamb of God. The Passover event, as described in Exodus 12, includes a significant four-day period in verses 3 and 6 just before the killing of the lamb:

> **Speak you to all the congregation of Israel, saying, In the tenth day of this month they shall take to them every man a lamb, according to the house of their fathers, a lamb for a house . . . And you shall keep it until the fourteenth day of the same month; and the whole assembly of the congregation of Israel shall kill it in the evening.**

Here is that same time period, when the lamb has been kept until after the fourth day, after which he was killed. Jesus as the Lamb of God was crucified after the fourth millennium from Creation.

Furthermore, God in Scripture makes other precise relationships among time periods, as in Ezekiel 4:6, where the following sentence may be found:

> **I have appointed you each day for a year.**

In the sense of a day for a thousand years, Jesus came to Earth on the Fourth Day since Creation, confirming that His birth in the midst of a seven-millennium history of man of itself was a prophecy of His own resurrection.

It also confirms God's use of time equivalence in Scripture.

Two

The Timing of Jesus' Return to Earth

This story involves the timing of the end of Jesus' *first* advent as well as His *second.* The primary reason for addressing it now, however, is that it is closely related to the story in the previous chapter, which also dealt with the timing of Jesus' first advent after the fourth millennium after Creation. In that discussion, a day was equated to a thousand years, as suggested in Psalm 90 and 2 Peter 3:8.

In this story, Jesus' resurrection took place three days after His crucifixion. These "days", of course, were actual twenty-four hour periods of time. All four Gospels describe that time, which was a fulfillment of Jonah's prophetic journey inside a great fish, described in Jonah 1:17:

> **Now the Lord had prepared a great fish to swallow up Jonah. And Jonah was in the belly of the fish three days and three nights.**

In Matthew 12:40, Jesus Himself speaks in confirmation of this event's prophetic significance:

> **For as Jonah was three days and three nights in the belly of the great fish, so shall the Son of man be three days and three nights in the heart of the earth.**

This particular passage firmly places the event in the grave. It also suggests that its time duration was three full days and three full nights. Another passage that suggests that Jesus lay in the grave three full days is found in Mark 8:31. Here the implication of complete days is suggested by the word "after."

> **And [Jesus] began to teach them, that the Son of man must suffer many things, and be rejected by the elders, and by the chief priests, and scribes, and be killed, and after three days rise again.**

This point, that Jesus lay in the grave three complete days, is emphasized because there are other passages in the Bible that suggest otherwise, implying that one of these days might not be complete or, indeed, that what took place may have occurred at the very beginning of the third day. Such passages include Matthew 16:21, 17:23, 20:19, Mark 9:31, 10:34, 14:58, Luke 9:22, 13:37, 18:33, 14:46, and John 2:19. A typical passage, in a direct quote of Jesus, is presented in Mark 9:31:

> **For he taught his disciples, and said to them, The Son of man is delivered into the hands of men, and they shall kill him; and after he is killed, he shall rise the third day.**

Many attempts have been made to reconcile these apparently conflicting statements, some quite clever, but all of them trying to demonstrate how a partial day can be considered to be a full day. These reconciliations may have merit. However, there may be a better answer, one that doesn't involve conflict at all. In this alternate explanation, those passages that specify that Jesus lay in the grave three complete days apply to the actual three-day period when Jesus, like Jonah, lay entombed.

Those passages that hint of a partial third day may be describing an entirely different event: Jesus' second advent on the third millennium after His first advent, when He returns for His Church. Revelation 20:4 also speaks of this millennial period, a thousand-year period where Jesus reigns on earth:

> **And I saw thrones, and they sat upon them, and judgment was given unto them; and I saw the souls of them that were beheaded for the witness of Jesus, and for the word of God, and who had not worshiped the beast, neither his**

image, neither had received his mark upon their foreheads, or in their hands; and they lived and reigned with Christ a thousand years.

Significantly, this millennium period would coincide with the third day of Christ after His first advent on the fourth day after Creation, in which it also would coincide with the seventh day after Creation, when God rested from His creative work. This association firmly supports the association made in Chapter 1 regarding the reason that Jesus waited until Lazarus had been dead four days before resurrecting him. It may also impart a meaning to Jesus' words in John 5:15-17 that is not generally appreciated:

The man departed, and told the Jews that it was Jesus who had made him well. And therefore did the Jews persecute Jesus, and sought to slay him, because he had done those things on the sabbath day.

But Jesus answered them, My Father worked hitherto, and I work.

There is yet another passage in Scripture that firmly supports associations of days with millennia. In another suggestion that Jesus will return for His bride, the Church, on the third day after His resurrection, Bible scholar Dr. Scott Hahn has discovered that the first two Chapters of John's Gospel speak of just that connection.

On page 34 of his book *Hail, Holy Queen,* Dr. Hahn notes that the Gospel of John begins with the Prologue, verses 1-18 of Chapter One, and a discussion regarding the identity of John the Baptist. Immediately following that, John opens the scene where Jesus meets the Baptist with the words "The next day . . ." If one takes the initial topic of the discussion as the first day, Dr. Hahn mused, then this passage in John 1:29 would speak of the second day reminiscent of the seven-day Creation period. Then verse 1:35 starts with "Again the next day . . .", implying that this day where Jesus chooses Apostles represents the third day. Again in verse 1:43 John begins with the words "The day following . . ." suggesting that on this fourth day Jesus continues with his pick of Apostles, with

Philip and Nathanael. Chapter One ends with that discussion.

Chapter 2 of John's Gospel starts immediately with the words "And the third day . . .", and proceeds to describe Jesus' first miracle at the wedding in Cana, where He changed water into wine. The entire episode suggests the importance of this event in foretelling Jesus' own marriage to His Church, as Paul declared in Ephesians 5:31 and 32. Dr. Hahn notes that after John wrote of this event, he stopped mentioning days. Dr. Hahn also notes that John couldn't have been speaking of the third day, because the third day had already come and gone in John's narrative. He reasoned that John was talking about the third day after the fourth day, which would have been the seventh day. This meshes perfectly with the accounts in Scripture (e.g. Revelation 19 through 21) where Jesus returns to earth with His bride, the Church, for a thousand-year of period of peace. This would be the seventh millennium of human history.

In Mark 9, Jesus told His disciples that there would be some who would see the kingdom of God come with power before they died, obviously referring to His second coming. The passage then goes on to describe Jesus' transfiguration, which was a preview of that great event to come. Interestingly, verse 2 begins with *"And after six days"*. This, too, in connection with Jesus' transfiguration, is an obvious reference to the end of six millennia of human history, the beginning of the millennium spoken of in revelation.

Three

Daniel's Prophecy of Jesus' First Advent

The angel Gabriel gave Daniel an amazing wealth of prophetic information in response to his supplication to the Lord. More remarkable yet is that it is encapsulated in a mere four verses: Daniel 9:24-27:

> **Seventy weeks are determined upon your people and upon your holy city, to finish the transgression, and to make an end of sins, and to make reconciliation for iniquity, and to bring in everlasting righteousness, and to seal up the vision and prophecy, and to anoint the Most Holy.**
>
> **Know, therefore, and understand, that from the going forth of the commandment to restore and to build Jerusalem to the Messiah, the Prince, shall be seven weeks, and sixty two weeks; the street shall be built again, and the wall, even in troublous times.**
>
> **And after sixty two weeks shall Messiah be cut off, but not for himself; and the people of the prince that shall come shall destroy the city and the sanctuary, and the end of it shall be with a flood, and to the end of the war desolations are determined.**
>
> **And he shall confirm the covenant with many for one week; and in the midst of the week he shall cause the sacrifice and the oblation to cease, and for the overspreading of abominations he shall make it desolate, even until the consummation, and that determined shall be poured upon the desolate.**

Not only is there an abundance of information in those four verses, but some of that prophetic information already has been fulfilled. The timing of its fulfillment is of astonishing accuracy. Of particular interest in this regard is the second of these four verses, Daniel 9:25, which foretells when Jesus will appear in His first advent. This event, which was to take place about five hundred years after the prophecy was written, occurred just as foretold, even to the very day, when Jesus made His triumphal entry on an ass into Jerusalem.

As a side note, Jesus' riding on an ass re-enacted Solomon's riding on a similar animal to be crowned King over Israel. The account is given in 1 Kings 1:38:

> **So Zadok, the priest, and Nathan, the prophet, and Benaiah, the son of Jehoiada, and the Cherethites, and the Pelethites, went down, and caused Solomon to ride upon King David's mule, and brought him to Gihon. And Zadok, the priest, took a horn of oil out of the tabernacle, and anointed Solomon. And they blew the trumpet; and all the people said, God save King Solomon.**

Moreover, Jesus' entry on an ass was specifically foretold in Zechariah 9:9 by that prophet:

> **Rejoice greatly, O daughter of Zion; shout, O daughter of Jerusalem; behold, your King comes to you; he is just, and having salvation; lowly, and riding upon an ass, and upon a colt, the foal of an ass.**

But it was Daniel who had captured the event's timing. According to verse 9:25, there would be a time interval of sixty nine weeks from a certain event to Jesus' appearance. There is no coded equivalence here. A week is simply a group of seven units of time. Here, it is obvious from the prophecy's fulfillment that the unit of time that Daniel was writing of is a year, which is usually understood to be a prophetic year of 360 days' duration. A week in this prophecy, therefore, is a time interval of seven prophetic years.

The event that was to start the prophetic time interval was a commandment to restore and rebuild Jerusalem. The commandment that matches that event was a decree issued by Persian King Artaxerxes Longimanus many decades after the prophecy given in Daniel 9, in 445 B.C., to rebuild the city of Jerusalem. This event is detailed in the Book of Nehemiah. The situation is summarized in Nehemiah Chapter 2:

> **And it came to pass in the month Nisan, in the twentieth year of Artaxerxes, the king, that wine was before him; and I took up the wine, and gave it to the king. Now I had not been sad in his presence. Wherefore, the king said unto me, Why is your countenance sad, seeing you are not sick? This is nothing else but sorrow of heart. Then I was very much afraid. And said to the king, Let the king live forever. Why should not my countenance be sad, when the city, the place of my fathers' sepulchers, lies waste, and its gates are consumed with fire? Then the king said to me, For what do you make request? So I prayed to God of heaven. And I said to the king, If it please the king, and if your servant has found favor in your sight, that you would send me unto Judah, to the city of my fathers' sepulchers, that I may build it. And the king said to me (the queen also sitting by him), For how long shall your journey be? And when will you return? So it pleased the king to send me; and I set him a time.**

The walls were rebuilt in troublous times indeed; in Nehemiah's account, the workers had to have their weapons ready at hand as they worked. The rebuilding project took 49 prophetic years (the first 7 weeks of Daniel 9:25).

Including the additional 62 weeks (434 prophetic years) prophesied in Daniel 9:25, the 69-week time to Messiah from Artaxerxes' decree was 173,880 days, (the product of 483 prophetic years and 360 days per prophetic year), which agrees with astonishing precision with the estimated date of April 6, 32 A.D. for Jesus' triumphal entry into Jerusalem.

For the person who wishes to delve deeper into this prophecy, further details can be obtained by Googling "Jesus' triumphal entry

69 weeks after Artaxerxes' decree."

It is important to keep in mind that the decree of Artaxerxes was made after the decree of Cyrus to end the seventy-year captivity of Judah. The decree of Cyrus was to rebuild the temple in Jerusalem and is covered in the Book of Ezra, while the decree of Artaxerxes, as described in Daniel 9:25, was to rebuild the city of Jerusalem itself and is covered in the Book of Nehemiah.

Four
Jeremiah's Prophecy of Israel's Captivity

A number of prophets concerned themselves with the nation of Judah's progressive rejection of God following King Solomon's reign, and the subsequent carrying away of the people of Judah to Babylon and their captivity there. The major prophetic players were Jeremiah and Daniel, with very interesting contributions by Isaiah and Ezekiel. The prophets Daniel and Ezekiel were contemporaries, their lives occupying approximately the latter half of the seventh century B.C. through the earlier half of the sixth century B.C. and are coincident with Israel's captivity by the Babylonian king Nebudchadnezzar. The prophet Jeremiah also was somewhat contemporary with them but earlier, his life being offset from theirs by perhaps fifty years or so. The prophet Isaiah was earlier yet from Jeremiah, by about a hundred years and about one hundred fifty years earlier than the Babylonian captivity of Judah.

In Jeremiah 25:1-11, that prophet foretold the looming destruction of Jerusalem, its temple, the removal of the inhabitants of Judah and their relocation as captives to Babylon. Jeremiah also specified how long that captivity would last.

> **The word that came to Jeremiah concerning all the people of Judah in the fourth year of Jehoiakim, the son of Josiah, king of Judah, that was in the first year of Nebuchadnezzar, king of Babylon, which Jeremiah, the prophet, spoke to all the people of Judah, and to all the inhabitants of Jerusalem, saying, From the thirteenth year of Josiah, the son of Amon, king of Judah, even to this day, that is the**

twenty third year, the word of the Lord has come to me, and I have spoken to you, rising early and speaking, but you have not listened. And the Lord has sent to you all his servants, the prophets, rising early and sending them, but you have not listened, nor inclined your ear to hear. They said, Turn again now every one from his evil way, and from the evil of your doings, and dwell in the land that the Lord has given to you and to your fathers forever and ever; and do not go after other gods to serve them, and to worship them, and do not provoke me to anger with the works of your hands, and I will do you no harm.

Yet you have not listened to me, says the Lord, that you might provoke me to anger with the works of your hands to your own harm. Therefore, thus says the Lord of hosts, Because you have not heard my words, Behold, I will send and take all the families of the north, says the Lord, and Nebuchadnezzar, the king of Babylon, my servant, and will bring them against this land, and against its inhabitants, and against all these nations round about, and will utterly destroy them, and make them a horror, and a hissing, and perpetual desolations. Moreover, I will take from them the voice of mirth, and the voice of gladness, the voice of the bridegroom, and the voice of the bride, the sound of the millstones, and the light of the lamp. And this whole land shall be a desolation and a horror; and these nations shall serve the king of Babylon seventy years.

God's response to Judah's having turned away from Him is connected to the nation's failure to observe his commandments regarding the Sabbaths. The general requirement to honor the Sabbaths is the fourth of the Ten Commandments, specified by Moses in Exodus 20:8-11:

Remember the Sabbath day, to keep it holy. Six days shall you labor and do all your work; but the seventh day is the sabbath of the Lord your God; in it you shall not do any work, you, nor your son, nor your daughter, your

manservant, nor your maidservant, nor your cattle, nor your stranger that is within your gates. For in six days the Lord made heaven and earth, the sea, and all that is in them, and rested the seventh day; wherefore, the Lord blessed the sabbath day, and hallowed it.

There actually are three sabbaths to be observed in addition to those associated with the feast days. These sabbaths extend in patterns of seven, the first being the seven-day weekly sabbath, the second being the seven-year sabbath, and the third being the seventh seven-year sabbath, or the year-long symbolic Jubilee Year, which overlaps the forty-ninth year of the previous Jubilee period beginning at the seventh month and the first year of the next period extending through the sixth month. The weekly sabbath is described in Leviticus 23, while the seven-year and Jubilee Sabbaths are described in Leviticus 25:

Six days shall work be done; but the seventh day is the sabbath of rest, a holy convocation; you shall do no work therein: it is the sabbath of the Lord in all your dwellings . . . Six years you shall sow your field, and six years you shall prune your vineyard, and gather in the fruit thereof; but in the seventh year shall be a sabbath of rest to the land, a sabbath for the Lord: you shall neither sow your field, nor prune your vineyard . . . And you shall number seven Sabbaths of years to you, seven times seven years; and the space of the seven Sabbaths of years shall be to you forty nine years. Then shall you cause the trumpet of the jubilee to sound on the tenth day of the seventh month, in the day of atonement shall you make the trumpet sound throughout all your land. And you shall hallow the fiftieth year, and proclaim liberty throughout all the land to all the inhabitants thereof: it shall be a jubilee to you; and you shall return every man to his possession, and you shall return every man to his family.

The timing of the jubilee year requires some clarification. I favor the nineteenth century theologian Sir Edward Denny's interpretation of that timing, as he presented in his work *The Seventy Weeks of Daniel.* On page 109 of that book, he presents the following interpretation of Leviticus 25:8-10:

> **Thus the year of Jubilee was a year altogether peculiar, beginning in the midst or in the seventh month of every sabbatic, or forty-ninth year; it was (as shown on plate 2, figures 4 and 6) made up of the last half of one sacred year and the first half of the following.**

In other words, the jubilee year was symbolic, overlapping the forty ninth year of one jubilee period and the first year of the next. In this sense it did not add to actual time, but was spiritual in nature.

In 2 Chronicles 36:19-21 is a record of the fulfillment of Jeremiah's prophecy. This passage also addresses an interesting side issue to the primary one of Judah having turned its back on God. The nation, in its indifference to God, had forsaken the Fourth Commandment, specified in Exodus 20:8-11, to observe the sabbath. Apparently, among the Sabbaths that they had failed to honor was the one that required the land to lay fallow for a year, as specified in Leviticus 25. Their miscreance regarding that commandment matched the duration of their captivity which extended for a period of seventy years from the time that the captivity had begun.

> **And they burned the house of god, and broke down the wall of Jerusalem, and burned all its palaces with fire, and destroyed all its precious vessels. And those who had escaped from the sword [Nebudchadnezzar] carried away to Babylon, where they were servants to him and his sons until the reign of the kingdom of Persia, to fulfill the word of the Lord by the mouth of Jeremiah, until the land had enjoyed her Sabbaths; for as long as she lay desolate she kept sabbath, to fulfill seventy years.**

After the seventy-year period of captivity had ended with the completion of seventy neglected sabbaths, the Persian king Cyrus permitted a number of Jews under Zerubbabel to return to Jerusalem to rebuild the temple. The account of that return is given in the book of Ezra, beginning with Ezra 1:1-3:

> **Now in the first year of Cyrus, king of Persia, so that the word of the Lord by the mouth of Jeremiah might be fulfilled, the Lord stirred up the spirit of Cyrus king of Persia, that he made a proclamation throughout all his kingdom, and put it also in writing, saying, Thus says Cyrus, king of Persia: The Lord God of heaven has given me all the kingdoms of the earth; and he has charged me to build him a house at Jerusalem, which is in Judah. Who is there among you of all his people? His God be with him,, and let him go up to Jerusalem, which is in Judah, and build the house of the Lord God of Israel (he is the God), which is in Jerusalem.**

It is at this point that the prophecy of Isaiah 45:1-4 comes into play, demonstrating God's understanding of time that surpasses our own.

> **Thus says the Lord to his anointed, to Cyrus, whose right hand I have held, to subdue nations before him; and I will loose the loins of kings, to open before him the two-leaved gates; and the gates shall not be shut: I will go before you, and make the crooked places straight; I will break in pieces the gates of bronze, and cut in sunder the bars of iron; and I will give you the treasures of darkness, and hidden riches of secret places, that you may know that I , the Lord, who call you by name, am the God of Israel. For Jacob, my servant's sake, and Israel my elect, I have even called you by your name; I have surnamed you, you who have not known me.**

Isaiah delivered this prophecy about one hundred fifty years before Cyrus was born.

Five
Ezekiel's Prophecy of Israel's Return

According to Bible scholar Dr. Grant Jeffrey, God had foretold in Scripture not only the return of Israel as a nation into her land in 1948, but the exact date of that event. Dr. Jeffrey claims that he was given the ability by God to piece together the items of Scripture by which that event was foretold, thus demonstrating two points: first, that Scripture is supernaturally accurate, and second, that God had everything to do with the return of Israel as a modern nation in bold opposition to those who would claim that Israel is no longer the apple of God's eye.

Before addressing the specifics of Jeffrey's research in this area, we note that his conclusions are corroborated elsewhere in Scripture. The Book of Hosea contains prophecies regarding Israel's lengthy dispersion and her subsequent revival as a nation. While not as precise as the prophecies that Dr. Jeffrey investigated, they are quite remarkable in their own right as to the accuracy of the general timing of Israel's revival after two millennia of dispersion. The dispersion itself is addressed in Hosea 4:4 and 5:

> **For the children of Israel shall abide many days without a king, and without a prince, and without a sacrifice, and without an image, and without an ephod, and without teraphim; Afterward shall the children of Israel return, and seek the Lord, their God, and David, their king, and shall fear the Lord and his goodness in the latter days.**

Hosea 6:2 addresses the general time frame of Israel's return, in which a day is interpreted as a thousand years according to Psalm 90 and 2 Peter 3:

> **After two days will he revive us; in the third day he will raise us up, and we shall live in his sight.**

Returning to Dr. Jeffrey's work regarding Israel's return as a nation, he received his first clue regarding the nature of Israel's return from Ezekiel Chapters 36 and 37, in which the 'dry bones' connect together, are clothed with flesh, and are given life. Many eschatologists view these chapters as applicable to the Jews having been given new life and a return to their homeland after the Holocaust they suffered in Nazi Germany.

As to the timing of their return to their homeland, Dr. Jeffrey received his initial clue regarding that topic from Ezekiel 4:4-6:

> **Lie also upon your left side, and lay the iniquity of the house of Israel upon it; according to the number of the days that you shall lie upon it, you shall bear their iniquity. For I have laid upon you the years of their iniquity, according to the number of the days, three hundred and ninety days; so shall you bear the iniquity of the house of Israel. And when you have accomplished them, lie again on your right side, and you shall bear the iniquity of the house of Judah forty days. I have appointed you each day for a year.**

Here the Word of God specifically laid on Israel a judgment of a year for each day that Ezekiel was commanded to lie on his side. Adding 390 and 40 together, Dr. Jeffrey arrived at a total of 430 years of God's judgment upon Israel. Ezekiel himself was a captive in Babylon, so Dr. Jeffrey assumed that the judgment was to begin at the beginning of Israel's or Judah's captivity. Israel was captured by the Assyrians in the eighth Century B.C., while Judah became captive to Nebudchadnezzar somewhere between 606 and 605 B.C. Dr. Jeffrey attempted to apply the 430 years directly to each of these dates, but came up with no historically meaningful end date.

Pursuing this topic in greater detail, Dr. Jeffrey came to an astonishingly relevant passage in Leviticus 26:17, 18, 27 and 28:

> **And I will set my face against you, and you shall be slain before your enemies; they that hate you shall reign over you, and you shall flee when none pursues you. And if you will not yet for all this listen to me, then I will punish you seven times more for your sins. . . And if you will not for all this listen to me, but walk contrary to me, Then I will walk contrary to you also in fury; and I, even I, will chastise you seven times for your sins.**

Here is where Dr. Jeffrey demonstrates the power of the Holy Spirit and the depth of his knowledge of Scripture. He realized in connection with this passage that during Ezekiel's time, the northern tribes of Israel had been under continuous captivity while Judah was undergoing a punishment that, according to Jeremiah 25:11, would last for precisely seventy years. Jeffrey also realized that the passage in Leviticus quoted above was conditional upon the Jews failing to turn back to God after an initial punishment. Judah's captivity did indeed end after seventy years, when the Persian King Cyrus, who was called by name by Isaiah over a century before his birth (Isaiah 44:28), decreed at some time between 536 and 535 B.C. that Israelites could return to Jerusalem to rebuild their temple. The fulfillment of that prophetic message is recorded in the Book of Ezra. (This prophetic event is not to be confused with the fulfillment of Daniel's prophecy in Daniel 9 regarding the appearance of the Messiah 483 years after the commandment permitting the Jews to rebuild the city of Jerusalem. That prophecy was fulfilled in the beginning event by Artaxerxes Longimanus in 445 B.C. as recorded in the Book of Nehemiah and at the conclusion by Jesus' triumphal entry into Jerusalem in 32 A.D.)

Grant Jeffrey appreciated that the outcome of Leviticus 26 would depend on the behavior of the Jews following the termination of their captivity in Babylon, which meant that the 70-year period of their captivity must be subtracted from the 430-year period of Ezekiel 4 prior to the application of the sevenfold punishment of Leviticus 26. The resulting calculations are:

430 - 70 = 360

360 x 7 = 2520 (prophetic) years x 360 = 907,200 days.

Applying a 907,200-day interval to the assumed earlier date of the end of the Babylonian captivity results, according to Jeffrey, in an end date of 1948, the precise year that Israel became a modern nation in fulfillment of Isaiah 66:7 and 8:

> **Before she travailed, she brought forth; before her pain came, she was delivered of a man-child. Who hath heard such a thing? Who hath seen such things? Shall the earth be made to bring forth in one day? Or shall a nation be born at once? For as soon as Zion travailed, she brought forth her children.**

This calculation may be roughly confirmed first by assuming that the Babylonian captivity ended sometime between 535 and 536 B.C., the two dates most commonly noted by Biblical historians. Multiplying 536 solar years by the number of days in a solar year of 365.25 results in 195,774 days between the end of the Babylonian captivity and the end of the B.C. era. Subtracting 195,774 from 907.200 results in 711,426 days remaining in the A.D. era to the completion of the prophetic time interval. In converting this to years it is noted that the A.D. era starts at A.D. 1 rather than A.D. 0, requiring the addition of 1 to the conversion:

Years A.D. = 1 + (711426/365.25) = 1 + 1947.7782 = 1948.7782

This roughly-calculated date of 1948+ is extremely close to the actual date of the beginning of the modern nation of Israel of May 15, 1948, differing from it at most by less than a year. Indeed, the difference may be brought to zero by assuming an initial day (Cyrus' proclamation) of only a few days later in the year than the end date of May 15.

Dr. Jeffrey, in fact, makes that very claim, asserting that the precise date of Cyrus' proclamation results in the founding of the nation of Israel May 14, 1948, the exact day when she became a modern nation. Until I have been able to verify that claim, I will refrain from making the same assertion. Nevertheless, having a prediction actually come to pass within a year over 25 centuries after it was made is entirely sufficient to demonstrate beyond all doubt the supernatural origin of the prophecy.

Nevertheless, the rough verification made above, viewed in the context of the remarkable prophecy of Hosea 6:2 noted earlier and the equally remarkable prophecy of Israel's return as a nation made in Ezekiel Chapters 36 and 37, is more than sufficient to demonstrate both the supernatural source of Scripture and God's continuing love of Israel.

Six

The Timing of the Wise Men's Visit to Jesus

This discussion of the timing of the Wise Men's visit to Jesus includes a reconciliation between the alleged inconsistency between the Gospels of Matthew and Luke in their accounts of Jesus' birth.

At first glance, the story of Jesus' birth in the Gospel of Matthew appears to conflict with the account given in the Gospel of Luke. The event, in Matthew's account, is accompanied by violence against the young males in Bethlehem, danger for Jesus, and the flight of Jesus' family into Egypt to escape the wrath of Herod. Luke, on the other hand, presents a peaceful scenario surrounding the birth of Jesus.

According to Matthew 2:1-16:

> **Now when Jesus was born in Bethlehem of Judea in the days of Herod the king, behold, there came wise men from the east to Jerusalem saying, Where is he that is born King of the Jews? For we have seen his star in the east, and are come to worship him. When Herod the king had heard these things, he was troubled, and all Jerusalem with him. And when he had gathered all the chief priests and scribes of the people together, he demanded of them where Christ should be born. And when they said to him, In Bethlehem of Judea: for thus it is written by the prophet [Micah in Micah 5:2], And you Bethlehem, in the land of Judah, are not the least among the princes of Judah: for out of you shall come a Governor, that shall rule my people Israel.**

> **Then Herod, when he had privately called the wise men, enquired of them diligently about what time the star appeared. And he sent them to Bethlehem, and said, Go and search diligently for the young child; and when you have found him, bring me word again, that I may come and worship him also.**
>
> **When they had heard the king, they left him; and, lo, the star, which they saw in the east, went before them, till it came and stood over where the young child was.**
>
> **When they saw the star, they rejoiced with exceeding great joy. And when they were come into the house, they saw the young child with Mary his mother, and fell down, and worshiped him: and when they had opened their treasures, they presented to him gifts; gold, and frankincense, and myrrh.**

Keep in mind two items from the above account: first, to enquire diligently is to ask for details. The details were such that Herod must have suspected that Jesus was up to two years old at the time of the Wise Men's visit.

Second, the wise men came into Jesus' house, not the manger. Both of these facts point to the visit of the Wise Men having taken place at some time after His birth.

The corresponding account of the event of Jesus' birth from Luke's perspective is presented in Chapter 2 of his gospel:

> **And she brought forth her firstborn son, and wrapped him in swaddling clothes, and laid him in a manger; because there was no room for them in the inn. And there were in the same country shepherds abiding in the field, keeping watch over their flock by night.**
>
> **And, lo, the angel of the Lord came upon them, and the glory of the Lord shone round about them; and they were sore afraid. And the angel said to them, Fear not: for, behold, I bring you good tidings of great joy, which shall**

be to all people. For to you is born this day in the city of David a Savior, who is Christ the Lord. And this shall be a sign to you: You shall find the babe wrapped in swaddling clothes, lying in a manger.

And suddenly there was with the angel a multitude of the heavenly host praising God, and saying, Glory to God in the highest, and on earth peace, good will toward men.

And it came to pass, as the angels were gone away from them into heaven, the shepherds said one to another, Let us now go even to Bethlehem, and see this thing which is come to pass, which the Lord has made known unto us. And they came with haste, and found Mary, and Joseph, and the babe lying in a manger. And when they had seen it, they made known abroad the saying which was told them concerning this child. And all they that heard it wondered at those things which were told them by the shepherds. But Mary kept all these things, and pondered them in her heart. And the shepherds returned, glorifying and praising God for all the things that they had heard and seen, as it was told to them.

And when eight days were accomplished for the circumcising of the child, his name was called JESUS, which was so named of the angel before he was conceived in the womb.

And when the days of her purification according to the law of Moses were accomplished, they brought him to Jerusalem, to present him to the Lord; (As it is written in the law of the Lord, Every male that opens the womb shall be called holy to the Lord;) and to offer a sacrifice according to that which is said in the law of the Lord, A pair of turtledoves, or two young pigeons.

Luke's account, unlike that of Matthew's, paints a peaceful scenario, one in which the family of Jesus makes an uneventful return from Bethlehem, one that includes the presentation of

Jesus to the Lord at Jerusalem. But Mary also had to wait until her purification was completed before Jesus was presented at the temple. The Mosaic law that specifies the post-birth purification is given in Leviticus 12:

> **And the Lord spoke to Moses, saying, Speak to the children of Israel, saying, If a woman has conceived seed, and born a man child: then she shall be unclean seven days; according to the days of the separation for her infirmity shall she be unclean. And in the eighth day the flesh of his foreskin shall be circumcised. And she shall then continue in the blood of her purifying thirty three days; she shall touch no hallowed thing, nor come into the sanctuary, until the days of her purifying are fulfilled.**

According to this purification rite, Mary had to wait at least forty one days, and possibly longer, depending on her health, before presenting Jesus to the temple. During this time, there is no suggestion in Luke's account of any violence or effort of Herod's attempt on Jesus' life. Rather, in harmony with the details of Matthew's account, this peaceful interlude points to the likelihood that the visit of the Wise Men didn't occur until after Mary's purification period, and possibly years after.

The distance that the Wise Men had to travel after seeing the star in their homeland also suggests a lengthy time duration between their first sight of the star and their arrival at Bethlehem, which would place their arrival well after Jesus' birth. But why would the Wise Men associate that star with the birth of Jesus? Bible scholar Hal Lindsey has suggested that the Wise Men were members of a cadre of Persian mystics whose Chaldean forbears had access to the teachings of Daniel during his captivity in Babylon. The information imparted to them by Daniel may well have included the prophecy of seventy weeks in Daniel 9:24-27, which would have given the Wise Men an understanding with virtually pinpoint accuracy of when Jesus would appear. When the star appeared to them, its timing must have identified it with Jesus as well as pointing to the direction of Jesus' birth from their location.

The Wise Men's wisdom consisted in their faith in Daniel's prophecy and their diligence in observing the sky for confirmation and direction.

Seven

The Ten Periods of Smyrna's Persecution

In Revelation Chapters 2 and 3 Jesus dictated messages to John regarding seven Churches located in what is now Turkey. At that time John was in exile on the Island of Patmos, having been banished there by the Roman emperor Domitian for placing his Christian belief above the worship of the emperor. John's vision occurred toward the end of the first century, before John was released from his exile at Domitian's death in A.D. 96.

These Churches are, in the sequence that Jesus presented them, Ephesus, Smyrna, Pergamos, Thyatira, Sardis, Philadelphia, and Laodicea. The messages generally followed the same seven elements: Church name, the name Jesus chose for Himself in addressing them, a commendation, a concern over a matter that needed correction, an exhortation, a promise to the overcomer, and a closing statement. The closing statement was identical for all seven Churches: He that hath an ear, listen. Two Churches were singled out for having no commendation: Sardis and Laodicea; another two Churches were singled out for having no concern: Smyrna and Philadelphia.

These seven Churches are variously identified as seven Churches representative of Christianity at the time that Jesus delivered the message, as well as Churches that typified the prevailing character of the Church over seven sequential eras of Christianity, and Churches representative of Christianity throughout the entire Christian era from the first Pentecost to the Second Coming of Christ. In actuality, the three views are not mutually exclusive; they all have some validity. Corresponding to the sequential view, Christian theologians have associated an identification and time period for each Church, as follows:

Ephesus: Apostolic, first through fourth centuries

Smyrna: Persecuted, first through fourth centuries

Pergamos: Heretical, first through fourth centuries

Thyratira: Post-Constantine, fifth through ninth centuries

Sardis: Medieval, tenth through sixteenth centuries

Philadelphia: Missionary, sixteenth through nineteenth centuries

Laodicea: End-Time, twentieth century to the return of Jesus Christ to earth

The specific message given to Smyrna is presented in Revelation 2:8-11:

> **And to the angel of the church in Smyrna write: These things say the first and the last, who was dead, and is alive. I know your works, and tribulation, and poverty (but you are rich); and I know the blasphemy of them who say they are Jews, and are not, but are the synagogue of Satan. Fear none of those things that you shall suffer. Behold, the devil shall cast some of you into prison, that you may be tried, and you shall have tribulation ten days; be you faithful to death, and I will give you a crown of life. He that has an ear, let him hear what the Spirit says to the churches: He that overcomes shall not be hurt of the second death.**

Over the years many Christians have wondered what Jesus meant by the ten days of persecution. I favor the opinion given by John Foxe in *Foxe's Christian Martyrs of the World.* During the time interval ranging from A.D. 64 under the reign of Nero to A.D. 313 under Diocletian, Foxe in Chapters 1 and 2 of his work identified ten separate periods when persecution was particularly violent and widespread, typically a result of the Christian refusal to worship the Roman emperor as god. During these and subsequent persecutions, Christians remained nonviolent, holding fast to Jesus' Sermon on the Mount, particularly His Word in Matthew 5:43-48 regarding the treatment of enemies:

> **You have heard that it has been said, You shall love your neighbor, and hate your enemy; but I say to you, Love your enemies, bless them that curse you, do good to them that hate you, and pray for them who despitefully use you, and persecute you. That you may be the children of your Father, who is in heaven; for he makes his sun to rise on the evil and on the good, and sends rain on the just and the unjust. For if you love them who love you, what reward have you? Do not even the tax collectors the same? And if you salute your brothers only, what do you more than others? Do not even the heathen so? Be you, therefore, perfect, even as your Father, who is in heaven, is perfect.**

In fact, as a rule Christians under persecution have, in the spirit of Titus 3:1, generally attempted to follow the dictates of the governments of which they have been subjects. It only has been under a direct conflict of loyalty between God and the government that Christians have practiced civil disobedience. An example of that is given in Acts 5:26-29:

> **Then went the captain with the officers, and brought [the apostles] without violence; for they feared the people, lest they should have been stoned. And when they had brought them, they set them before the council; and the high priest asked them, Saying, Did not we strictly command you that you should not teach in [Jesus Christ's] name? And, behold, you have filled Jerusalem with your doctrine, and intend to bring this man's blood upon us.**
>
> **Then Peter and the other apostles answered, and said, We ought to obey God rather than men.**

Persecution typically is not unexpected in the Christian community, except, perhaps, in those Churches having the Laodicean character. Jesus Himself gave Christians plenty of warning about it, typical examples being given in Matthew 5:10-12 and John 15:18-20:

Blessed are they who are persecuted for righteousness' sake; for theirs is the kingdom of heaven. Blessed are you, when men shall revile you, and persecute you, and shall say all manner of evil against you falsely, for my sake. Rejoice, and be exceedingly glad; for great is your reward in heaven; for so persecuted they the prophets who were before you.

If the world hates you, you know that it hated me before it hated you. If you were of the world, the world would love its own; but because you are not of this world, but I have chosen you out of the world, therefore the world hates you. Remember the word that I said to you, The servant is not greater than his lord. If they have persecuted me, they will also persecute you; if they have kept my saying, they will keep yours also.

It is an interesting fact that the persecution of the early Christians didn't harm the Church in the least, but rather helped it grow. It strengthened those Christians who held fast in its wake and in the scattering of those who fled, it served to propagate the Gospel to lands that otherwise would not have known of Jesus Christ and the salvation that He offered.

A summary of Foxe's take on the ten "days" of Smyrna's persecution is presented in the table below.

PERIOD	DATES	PERSECUTOR	COMMENT
1	54-68	Nero	Peter and Paul killed
2	95-96	Domitian	John Exiled to Patmos
3	104-117	Trajan	
4	161-180	Marcus Aurelius	Polycarp martyred
5	200-211	Septimus Severus	
6	235-237	Maximus	
7	249-251	Decius	
8	257-260	Valerian	
9	270-275	Aurelian	
10	303-313	Diocletian	worst persecution

After Diocletian's persecution, Constantine became Emperor of Rome and legitimized Christianity, which led to growing complacence thereafter, a condition that continued to worsen until the Reformation, of which Martin Luther played a major part. The persecutions that occurred during the Middle Ages were largely associated with the Catholic Inquisition. Modern persecutions are primarily the result of the Muslim hatred toward Christians and the attempt of morally weak governments to maintain an uneasy peace between themselves and the Muslim communities within their borders.

Eight
Forty Days in the Lives of Moses and Jesus

After Moses' return from the top of mount Sinai with the stone tablets upon which God had written the Ten Commandments, he found that the people had returned to worshiping a golden calf cast from jewelry. In his intense anger, he broke the tablets. In His mercy, God allowed Moses to return to the mountain, where God would inscribe a second set of tablets with the Ten Commandments. The episode is recorded in Exodus 34:1-10 and 27-29:

> **And the Lord said to Moses, Hew you two tables of stone like the first; and I will write upon these tables the words that were in the first tables, which you did break. And be ready in the morning, and come up in the morning to Mount Sinai, and present yourself there to me in the top of the mount. And no man shall come up with you, neither let any man be seen throughout all the mount; neither let the flocks nor herds feed before that mount. And [Moses] hewed two tables of stone like the first; and he rose up early in the morning, and went up to Mount Sinai, as the Lord had commanded him, and took in his hand the two tables of stone.**
>
> **And the Lord descended in the cloud, and stood with him there, and proclaimed the name of the Lord. And the Lord passed by before him, and proclaimed, The Lord, the Lord God, merciful and gracious, long-suffering, and abundant in goodness and truth, keeping mercy for thousands, forgiving iniquity and transgression and sin, and who**

will by no means clear the guilty, visiting the iniquity of the fathers upon the children, and upon the children's children, to the third and to the fourth generation.

And Moses made haste, and bowed his head toward the earth, and worshiped. And he said, If now I have found grace in your sight, O Lord, let my Lord, I pray you, go among us; for it is a stiff-necked people; and pardon our iniquity and our sin, and take us for your inheritance. And [the Lord] said, Behold, I make a covenant: Before all your people I will do marvels, such as have not been done in all the earth, nor in any nation: and all the people among whom you are shall see the work of the Lord; for it is an awe-inspiring thing that I will do with you.

And the Lord said to Moses, Write you these words; for after the tenor of these words I have made a covenant with you and with Israel. And [Moses] was there with the Lord forty days and forty nights; he neither ate bread nor drank water. And he wrote upon the tables the words of the covenant, the ten commandments.

Moses' time spent on Mount Sinai had a prophetic element, as the forty days and forty nights of his stay on the mountain in the presence of the Lord pointed to Jesus Christ and the identical time He spent in the wilderness as His first act after being baptized. The account is given in all the synoptic Gospels (Matthew, Mark and Luke). The following is Matthew's version of the event, Matthew 3:16 and 17, and 4:1-11:

And Jesus, when he was baptized, went immediately out of the water; and, lo, the heavens were opened to him, and he saw the Spirit of God descending like a dove, and lighting upon him. And, lo, a voice from heaven, saying, This is my beloved Son, in whom I am well pleased. Then was Jesus led up by the Spirit into the wilderness to be tested by the devil. And when he had fasted forty days and forty nights, he was afterward hungry.

And when the tempter came to him, he said, If you are the Son of God, command that these stones be made bread. But [Jesus] answered and said, It is written, Man shall not live by bread alone, but by every word that proceeds out of the mouth of God. Then the devil took him up to the holy city, and set him on a pinnacle of the temple, and said to him, If you are the Son of God, cast yourself down; for it is written, He shall give his angels charge concerning you, and in their hands they shall bear you up, lest at any time you dash your foot against a stone. Jesus said to him, It is written again, You shall not put the Lord, your God, to the test. Again, the devil took him up to an exceedingly high mountain, and showed him all the kingdoms of the world, and the glory of them, and said to him, All these things will I give you, if you will fall down and worship me. Then said Jesus to him, Begone, Satan; for it is written, You shall worship the Lord, your God, and him only shall you serve. Then the devil left him, and behold, angels came and ministered to him.

Shortly after this forty-day period of trial, Jesus started His ministry. The Gospels don't mention the number of days that passed between the two events, so one cannot dogmatically assume that it was ten. Nevertheless, it is a possibility that fifty days passed from the time of Jesus' baptism to the beginning of his active ministry.

If that is indeed the case, the pattern of forty plus ten days continues beyond Jesus. In John 12:26 and 14:12, Jesus indicates that His disciples will follow His lead:

If any man serve me, let him follow me; and where I am, there also shall my servant be: if any man serve me, him will my Father honor.

Verily, verily, I say unto you, He that believeth on me, the works that I do shall he do also; and greater works than these shall he do, because I go to my Father.

In John 20:22, apparently on the day following His resurrection,

Jesus breathes on His disciples, conferring on them the Holy Spirit. He remained with them for forty days. From the time of Jesus ascension until the Pentecost ten days later, the disciples didn't appear to have responded to the indwelling Holy Spirit. Their power from God came at the Pentecost, as described in Acts 2. Could that forty-plus-ten-day period have been a time of testing and strengthening for the disciples, as it may have been for Jesus?

The number forty is common in Scripture. Moses communed with God with a backdrop of terrifying violence while Jesus as God communed with His Word with a backdrop of terrifying evil. Both of them fasted for the duration. God granted Nineveh through Jonah forty days to get its act together.

The Israelites wandered in the wilderness for forty years; both David and his son Solomon reigned as kings for forty years.

Nine

Six Millennia of Mankind's History

Like the number forty in Scripture, the number seven also appears often, and actually is the most prominent of numbers. The multiple associations of a day with a millennium as presented earlier in Chapters One, Two and Five of this Part suggests that God has taken seven days of Creation and stretched them out into seven thousand years of human history.

It is clear from Psalm 90 and 2 Peter 3:8 that the Lord stretched His days of creation into a thousand years each. Beyond those direct equations of days to millennia is God's obvious equation of the first day to a millennium in Genesis 2:17:

> **But of the tree of the knowledge of good and evil, thou shalt not eat of it; for in the day that thou eatest thereof thou shall surely die.**

As P.J. Hanley remarked in Chapter Five in his book *The Seven Lost Keys of End-Time Prophecy*, Adam died before the end of a millennium at the age of 930 years. In fact, no human has ever lived to be a thousand years old. Given that limitation of Adam's life to just under a thousand years, the "day" intended by God in Genesis 2:17 must have been a millennium. Hanley also asserts that the association of a day with a thousand years of human history was a common interpretation among the Jewish prophets and rabbis.

Further confirmation of this is abundant: the four days of keeping the Passover Lamb; the four days Jesus waited to resurrect Lazarus; the fourth millennium that had passed before Jesus' first advent; the third day after the fourth day that Jesus referred to multiple times regarding His return to earth, the third day after the fourth day according to John:1 and 2 that brought Jesus to the wedding at Cana in anticipation of His marriage to His Church; Hosea's prophecy in Hosea 6:2 of the restoration of Israel after two days; and the final millennium specified in Revelation.

A number of ideas were spawned around the middle of the nineteenth century that had a large effect on our perception of Scripture. Many of these ideas arose from our successes in technology and science. Some of them attempted to toss God away as no longer necessary, while others displayed a growing awareness that the time of Jesus' return to earth may be approaching.

The latter half of the nineteenth century produced two men of exceptional intellect, vision and devotion to God, and who possessed a glimpse of the closure of this age. Their names were Sir Edward Denny, who wrote *The Seventy Weeks of Daniel* in 1849, and Henry Grattan Guinness, who published *The Approaching End of the Age* in 1878. Both of them pictured human history as occupying six millennia prior to the return of Christ on earth with His Church for the final millennium of Revelation. Each of them constructed cyclic representations of the six millennia of human history, but on very different logical bases and with equally different numbers. Astonishingly, they ended up at the same place. Just as amazingly, they were complementary, one cycle displaying the prominence of the number twelve, and the other of the number seven.

The numbers twelve and seven are both Scripturally significant, one being associated with Israel and the other with the Church.

Israel had twelve tribes; Jesus had twelve apostles; when Jesus fed the five thousand, Luke 9:10 tells us that the event took place near Bethsaida on the north shore of the Sea of Galilee, a locale consisting primarily of Jews; from that event there were twelve baskets of leftovers. In His feeding of the four thousand, however, Jesus performed that miracle on the Decapolis side of the Sea of Galilee, according to Mark 7:31. That is the south side of the sea where the population was mostly Gentile, prominently associated with the Church, as confirmed by Jesus in Revelation 1. In His feeding of the four thousand, there were seven baskets of leftovers.

Taking his cue from Daniel 9:24, Sir Edward Denny split his seven millennia of human history into twelve periods of 490 years each.

> **Seventy weeks are determined upon your people and upon your holy city, to finish the transgression, and to make an end of sins, and to make reconciliation for iniquity, and to bring in everlasting righteousness, and to seal up the vision and the prophecy, and to anoint the most Holy.**

Daniel's weeks were periods of seven years each; seventy of them amount to 490 years. A period of 490 years also can be derived from the Books of Exodus, Deuteronomy and Joshua. Exodus 12:40 and 41 is very specific regarding the length of the Israelites' stay in Egypt:

> **Now the sojourning of the children of Israel, who dwelt in Egypt, was four hundred and thirty years. And it came to pass at the end of the four hundred and thirty years, even the selfsame day it came to pass that all the hosts of the Lord went out from the land of Egypt.**

After that 430-year duration, 400 of which were spent under increasingly hostile Pharaohs, the Israelites wandered in the wilderness for forty years, and then spent the next thirteen years, according to the Jewish historian Josephus, in conquering the Promised Land. These three durations add up to 483 years, or sixty-nine weeks of years. A final seven years is assumed for a period where the Israelites settled into their new home in peace. Denny himself constructed a 490 period somewhat differently than Josephus, using the 430-year duration of the Israelites' stay in Egypt as the final segment of that period.

Each 490-year interval of Denny's cycles, consisting of seven seventy-year periods, also introduces the number seven into his system. His twelve cycles amount to five thousand eight hundred and eighty years, which seem to be rather random until one realizes that each period of 490 years also includes ten symbolic Jubilee years. If these are added together, they amount over the twelve cycles to one hundred twenty years. Adding these 120 years to the 5880 years yields a total of six thousand years, or six millennia of human history.

Henry Grattan Guinness constructed his cycles from an entirely different perspective. He noted from Genesis 25:7-11 that Abraham died at the age of one hundred seventy five years, during which some important events in his life, like the birth of Isaac, occurred at twenty-five year intervals. From that, Guinness perceived that Abraham's lifetime, in seven cycles of twenty five years, might represent the entire six-thousand-year sweep of human history. Dividing six thousand by seven, he came up with a figure of 857 and a lot of numbers past the decimal place. But then he may have noted that in six millennia there would be 120 Jubilees. If he subtracted these 120 symbolic years from the six thousand, he would arrive at a number of 5880 years. In dividing that number by seven, he found that it came out exactly to 840 years, furnishing a firm basis for his seven cycles. Furthermore, if he divided the number 840 by seven again, he came up with the number of 120, or twelve times ten. Attempting next to expand the 25-year duration of each cycle to 840 years, he came up with the number of 33.6, which he discovered to be the lifetimes of both Adam and Jesus.

So Denny, with his grand cycle of twelves, and Guinness, with his grand cycle of sevens, managed to come up with the same numbers for the six-millennium duration of man on earth prior to the final millennium: 5880 actual years plus 120 symbolic Jubilee years. Associated with these cycles is a wealth of information yet untapped.

Ten
The Good Seed

Matthew Chapter Thirteen begins with Jesus in a boat speaking the Parable of the Sower to a multitude of people. In that parable of seeds that represent people who hear the salvation-promising Word of God, only a portion of them are able to understand what they heard, bring it in fullness into their hearts, and maintain it through the tribulations and attractions of the material world. Jesus finishes this parable with an obscure reference to numbers, saying that these will bear fruit, some a hundredfold, others sixtyfold, and yet others thirtyfold. He places no difference in attributes or character among those who produce more fruit and those who produce less.

The only arithmetic relationship that I have found among these numbers that is both simple and meaningful is the partial sums of the arithmetic sequence

$$K\sum^{M}_{n=1} (n + (n+1) + (n+2) + (n+3) + \ldots)$$

For the values K = 10 and M = 2, 3 and 4, the corresponding sums are 30, 60 and 100. I presented this pictorially in Part 5, Chapter 2 my book *Family of God* as four columns of people, where each column consisted of the number of people associated with a particular value of M, and where the top person in the first row bore fruit by passing the Word of God to those behind them, and, if there was an adjacent column, to the top person in the next column. In that pattern, the top person in the column would feed 30 people if there were two columns, 60 if there were three columns, and 100 if there were four columns. In such an arrangement, the amount of fruit that the top person in the first column would bear would be entirely dependent on the number of adjacent columns, which would be beyond his control, and, in fact, something he might not even know if he was able to perceive only his column and the next. I saw in this parable and the associated numbers an intimate connection between it and the accounts of Jesus' feedings of the multitudes, as both processes resulted in manifold increases. In numerous places, especially in the Gospel of John, Jesus clearly equates bread and eating with Himself as the Word of God. When He was feeding the multitudes He also was delivering the Word of God. The expansion of bread in these acts may be seen as merely symbolic of how the word of God is multiplied through word-of-mouth distribution. In fact, the miraculous element of the feedings was simply the restoration of the broken pieces of bread to wholeness with their transfer from one hand to the next, which is symbolic of the indestructible nature of the Word of God as it is handed from mouth to ear.

If some reasonable assumptions are made beforehand, there is sufficient numerical information in Scripture to calculate the answers to the numbers missing in the feeding accounts and to establish patterns by which the multitudes would have been fed. A vital piece of information beyond the Gospel accounts of the feeding of the five thousand and the four thousand is the account in 2 Kings 4 of Elijah feeding a hundred people with twenty loaves of bread; another piece of information is the account, in Acts 2, of Peter feeding three thousand with the Word of God.

Picturing the feedings to be a process within an orderly array of people breaking bread, retaining a portion and passing the other to neighbors, I established the following restraints and relationships, particularly the ones that Jesus reminded His disciples about in Mark 8:

For the feeding of the five thousand: 5 thousand, 5 starting loaves given to His disciples to distribute per Matthew 6, 12 baskets of remainders.

For the feeding of the four thousand: 4 thousand, 7 starting loaves given to His disciples to distribute, 7 baskets of remainders.

All the twelve apostles, and only the twelve apostles, would participate in the initial distribution of loaves; thus five apostles would distribute for the five thousand and seven apostles would distribute for the four thousand.

The apostles would give one loaf each to a single company nearest them.

The basic organization of the men would be in companies of 50 and 100 per Mark 6, where the companies, per Elijah's feeding in 2 Kings 4, would be arranged in a pattern of 20 x 5 for a company of 100, and 10 x 5 for a company of 50.

The collection of leftover bread would be on the basis of individuals rather than companies; each person in the final position would hand his leftover to a collector with a basket.

Performing the required calculations, the relationships were used to solve first the number of remainders per basket from the menfolk. The resulting number of 5 supported the following details:

For the five thousand, there were 5 columns corresponding to the 5 loaves and 5 apostles participating in the initial distribution; the center column consisted of companies of 100; the four outside columns consisted of companies of 50, resulting in 60 columns of individuals and 12 baskets of remainders; there were 17 rows of companies, resulting in 85 rows of individuals and producing 5100 individuals; one company of 100 was subtracted from this array to produce an exact number of 5000 individuals. This deletion did nothing to alter the number of baskets of leftovers or any other number of interest associated with the feedings.

For the four thousand, a solution demanded that the orientation of this array be at right angles to that of the five thousand, requiring a substitution of rows for columns. With that orientation, there were 7 rows corresponding to the 7 loaves and 7 apostles participating in the initial distribution; all companies were of 50, resulting in 35 rows of individuals and 7 baskets of remainders; there were 11 columns of companies, resulting in 110 columns of individuals and producing 385 individuals, and leaving a much smaller array of 150 individuals in 3 companies of 50.

These patterns weren't perfect. Jesus' two feeding events seemed to generate three arrays rather than two, the largest array had a missing piece, and two of the arrays were at right angles to each other.

Yet the derived numbers matched perfectly with the numbers given in the Gospel accounts, and the patterns described above were the only ones that did so.

I found that once the calculations established the patterns for the feedings, the math was not necessary to verify the satisfaction of all the information in the Gospel accounts. A mere visual inspection of the patterns is all that is needed to confirm that they correctly represent that information. The calculations are presented as appendices in *Family of God.* A verbal description of the feedings with figures is included in my book *Marching to a Worthy Drummer* as Appendix Two. A strictly verbal description also is given in my novel *Cathy.*

If there is nothing else to say about the results, it is their proof of the amazing self-consistency of Scripture, even down to the smallest details. Scripture, as the Word of God, is pure truth.

But there is more to say about the results. It turns out that there is a message in the very characteristics that are thought of as imperfections. That will be the topic of the next chapter.

Eleven
Perfection in Imperfection

This chapter is a digression from the primary theme of this volume, but is included here because it is so closely related to the information regarding Jesus' feedings of the multitudes.

Having finished the analysis of the feedings as described in the previous chapter, I was left with a sense of disappointment in the little deviations from what I had pictured as what would be an ideal description of the details. Things just didn't come together as I would have wished. The missing company of eleven in the array of the five thousand, for example, gnawed at me. Why would God do that?

Then I remembered that Elijah had fed a hundred individuals with twenty loaves. Those hundred, in a 20 x 5 configuration, actually furnished the template for a company. If Elijah's company were to be inserted into the missing slot in the array of five thousand, it would make a perfect rectangle. Did God actually intend to imply that this should be done? What was His point?

The point, I finally realized, may have been that the arrays were intended to be integrated together. Applying that factor to the problem with the array of the four thousand being at right angles to the first array, I was astonished at the figure that was emerging from the integration: the array of the four thousand, placed atop that of the five thousand, began to look like a familiar figure, but yet imperfect in itself.

At this point, it will be useful to explore the Scriptural meaning of bread, and of Peter's role with respect to it. In John 21, the risen Jesus shares breakfast with His disciples, and then addresses Peter, asking him the same question three times:

Peter, do you love Me?

Peter responds each time by affirming his love for Him, to which Jesus follows with a command:

Feed my sheep.

Peter, not appreciating that Jesus was gifting him with a threefold pardon for his denying Jesus three times, responds to each question with increasing anxiety. With the coming of Pentecost ten days after Jesus has left the earth, Peter is filled with the indwelling Holy Spirit, enabling him to fulfill Jesus' commandment to feed His sheep. He does so, three significant times. The first time he preaches Jesus to the salvation of three thousand.

But Peter's feeding is with the word, not the bread. Perhaps, with the doing, he came to understand John's characterization of Jesus in Chapter One of his Gospel that Jesus is the Word in the flesh. Maybe he began, then, to appreciate Jesus' words, recorded in John 6:30-35 and 51-58, that the Word is the spiritual equivalent of material bread, and that the bread Jesus gave the multitudes was only incidental to the Word.

> **They said, therefore, to [Jesus], what sign do you show us, then, that we may see, and believe you? What do you work? Our fathers ate manna in the desert; as it is written, He gave them bread from heaven to eat.**
>
> **Then Jesus said to them, Verily, verily, I say to you, Moses gave you not that bread from heaven; but my Father gives you the true bread from heaven. For the bread of God is he who comes down from heaven, and gives life to the world. Then they said to him, Lord, evermore give us this bread. And Jesus said to them, I am the bread of life; he who comes to me shall never hunger, and he who believes on me shall never thirst.**
>
> **I am the living bread who came down from heaven; if any man eat of this bread, he shall live forever; and the bread that I will give is my flesh, which I will give for the life of the world.**

The Jews, therefore, strove among themselves, saying, How can this man give us his flesh to eat? Then Jesus said to them, Verily, verily, I say unto you, Except you eat the flesh of the Son of man, and drink his blood, you have no life in you. He who eats my flesh, and drinks my blood, has eternal life; and I will raise him up at the last day. For my flesh is food indeed, and my blood is drink indeed. He who eats my flesh, and drinks my blood, dwells in me, and I in him.

As the living Father has sent me, and I live by the Father, so he who eats me, even he shall live by me. This is that bread which came down from heaven, not as your fathers ate manna, and are dead; he who eats of this bread shall live forever.

Appreciating that the bread of significance in Scripture is the immortal Word of God, Peter's feeding of three thousand with the Word took on real importance, to the extent that it should be integrated into the figure that was being formed. Accordingly, the three thousand were encapsulated in an array of ten symbolic rows of companies of 100 by three columns.

When this was added atop the array for the four thousand, which itself was atop the array of five thousand, the resulting figure stood out as a cross.

But what about that extra little three-company array? The answer was found in Matthew 27:37, which declares that a sign was placed on the cross over his head that stated in three languages, Hebrew, Greek and Latin, "This is Jesus of Nazareth, the King of the Jews" The sign is called the titulus, and belongs with the cross.

In passing on this message of the sign of the cross in Jesus' feedings, I encountered a person who pointed out to me that my assumption that all the baskets had the same size was false. The basket for the feeding of the five thousand, I was told, was a small handbasket, whereas the basket for the feeding of the four thousand was larger. The smaller handbasket would be appropriate for 5 loaves per basket, but the larger basket could hold more.

Actually I didn't assume a common basket size; rather, I assumed that the leftovers from the feeding of the menfolk were of a common number of five per basket.

There were women and children in addition to the menfolk in both feeding events. According to Mark 7:31 the four thousand were fed near Decapolis on the south shore of the Sea of Galilee, while, according to Luke 9:10, the five thousand were fed near Bethsaida on the north shore, the implication being that the four thousand were mostly Gentile, while the five thousand were primarily Jewish. Further weight is given to this difference by the fact that the seven baskets of the four thousand correspond to the seven representative Churches that Jesus addressed in Revelation 1:20, while the twelve baskets of the five thousand match the twelve tribes of Israel.

Christianity is more inclusive of women than Judaism as suggested in Acts 2:16-18, and this difference supports the possibility that the larger baskets for the four thousand included the leftovers from the womenfolk as well as those for the men. Yet the contribution from the menfolk in each basket would have remained at five.

Twelve

Daniel's Abomination of Desolation

In His Olivet Discourse, recorded in Matthew 24, Jesus calls Daniel to mind in the following statement (24:15-22):

> **When you, therefore, shall see the abomination of desolation, spoken of by Daniel the prophet, stand in the holy place (whosoever reads, let him understand), then let them who are in Judea flee into the mountains; let him who is on the housetop not come down to take anything out of his house; neither let him who is in the field return back to take his clothes. And woe to those who are pregnant, and to those who are nursing their children in those days! But pray that your flight not be in the winter, neither on the sabbath day; for then shall be great tribulation, such as was not since the beginning of the world to this time, no, nor ever shall be. And except those days should be shortened, there should no flesh be saved; but for the elect's sake those days shall be shortened.**

Jesus went on from there to speak of signs of what is called the tribulation period and of the time directly following that. In this passage Jesus is considered by most theologians to be speaking of a dreadful seven-year time of terrible events detailed more thoroughly in the Book of Revelation that have a worldwide effect just before Jesus Christ comes either for (post-tribulation rapture) or with (pre-tribulation rapture) His Church.

Daniel 9:24-27 speaks of an abomination of desolation, and this passage is usually interpreted as being in lockstep with Matthew 24:15, in which Daniel describes the death of Jesus for our sakes, followed by the destruction of Jerusalem and the temple by the Antichrist in the middle of a seven-year tribulation period that is to be initiated by a peace treaty with Israel. In this midpoint of the tribulation period the Antichrist sets up the abomination of desolation after causing the normal sacrifice to stop.

> **Seventy weeks are determined for your people and for your holy city, to finish the transgression, and to make an end of sins, and to make reconciliation for iniquity, and to bring in everlasting righteousness, and to seal up the vision and prophecy, and to anoint the most Holy.**
>
> **Know, therefore, and understand, that from the going forth of the commandment to restore and to build Jerusalem until the Messiah, the Prince, shall be seven weeks, and sixty-two weeks; the street shall be built again, and the wall, even in troublous times.**
>
> **And after sixty two weeks shall Messiah be cut off, but not for himself; and the people of the prince to come shall destroy the city and the sanctuary, and the end of it will be with a flood, and to the end of the war desolations are determined.**
>
> **And he shall confirm the covenant with many for one week; and in the midst of the week he shall cause the sacrifice and the oblation to cease, and for the overspreading of abominations he shall make it desolate, even until the consummation, and that determined shall be poured upon the desolate.**

The portion of this passage that deals with the timing of Jesus' first advent was covered in an earlier chapter. Sixty nine weeks of years after the rebuilding of Jerusalem, Jesus appears in the flesh. Daniel tells us here that after Jesus' crucifixion at the end of the sixty-nine week period, there will be a prince to come. This prince is usually interpreted as the Antichrist, whose people, according to Daniel, will destroy Jerusalem and the Temple again. This destruction is usually perceived as coming much earlier than the coming of the Antichrist, being the destruction of Jerusalem and the burning of the temple that occurred in 70 A.D.

Because the General who commanded the soldiers who destroyed the temple in 70 A.D. was the Roman Titus, the people of the Antichrist to come are usually thought of as being Romans as well, or as Europeans. I question this association, noting that the soldiers under Titus were local Arabs who were conscripted by Rome. This, to me, opens the door to a Muslim Antichrist. After the destruction of the temple, this prince, the Antichrist, will finally appear at a time yet in the future to confirm a covenant, usually interpreted as a peace treaty between Israel and its antagonistic neighbors. This event, it is commonly said, will initiate the beginning of the final seven-year fulfillment of the seventy weeks of which Gabriel instructed Daniel, which is separated from the previous sixty nine weeks by the Church Age. It is this seventieth seven-year period spoken of in Daniel 9:24, along with comparable passages in Revelation that speak of periods of three and a half years that has led Bible scholars to think of the tribulation period as consisting of seven years, with the Great Tribulation occurring at the latter half of that period. Whether or not there is to be a third temple built during the time of tribulation, and a consequent third destruction, is an open issue. Paul speaks of our bodies being temples of flesh; perhaps the Church, being an aggregate of such temples, will be the one that is involved in the Tribulation.

In Daniel 11:31 is another passage that appears to match what Jesus spoke of in His Olivet discourse.

> **And forces shall stand on his part, and they shall pollute the sanctuary of strength, and shall take away the daily sacrifice, and they shall place the abomination that makes desolate.**

Because Jesus, being on earth five centuries after the birth of Daniel, spoke of Daniel's Abomination of Desolation as being yet in the future, Bible scholars commonly interpret the passage from Daniel quoted above as also being a future event. But others, thinking back on history, see that this passage and the surrounding verses match quite well with an event that occurred after Daniel but before Jesus, at around 165 B.C. The villain in this precursor event is Antiochus Epiphanes, a brutal persecutor of the Jews and a type of the Antichrist to come. Antiochus did indeed invade the Temple in Jerusalem, stopped the normal sacrifice, and he sacrificed instead a pig on the altar there. A pig is considered by the Jews to be an unclean animal.

Actually, Daniel may have been speaking of both the precursor event and the follow-on event, yet in the future, spoken of by Jesus. The future event is almost universally anticipated as happening at the beginning of the latter three and a half years of an upcoming seven-year tribulation period just before the return of Christ to Earth.

Thirteen
Rethinking Daniel

For those of us who dare to wonder about the timing of the upcoming Great Tribulation period despite the stern denunciation of that practice by some conservative pastors, the scenario established by virtually all of the popular eschatologists seems appropriate: the abomination of desolation spoken of by Daniel and referred to by Jesus comes prior to it and viciously confirms the identity of the antichrist; the three-and-a-half-year Great Tribulation follows immediately after that. This scenario, in fact, is so well-established within eschatological circles that it remains untouched by the various arguments about the sequence and timing of the Rapture and other associated end-time events.

It might be appropriate to first insert here a few words about that apparently abhorrent practice of date-setting. An effort to understand where we are in time with respect to Jesus' second advent is considered to be improper in some Christian circles. After all, Jesus Himself declared in His Olivet Discourse (Matthew 24) that "*But of that day and hour knows no man, no, not the angels of heaven, but my Father only.*" Pastors for centuries have used those words to justify their neglect of prophecy despite the fact that at least a fourth of the Bible is devoted to prophecy, and that in Matthew 24 and elsewhere, including Revelation, Jesus Himself provided us with some very detailed prophecies of end-time events. Moreover, Jesus also chastised the Pharisees regarding their indifference toward prophecies relating to their own times, saying in Matthew 16:

> **When it is evening, you say, It will be fair weather; for the sky is red. And in the morning, It will be foul weather today, for the sky is red and overcast. O you hypocrites, you**

can discern the face of the sky; but can you not discern the signs of the times?

The bottom line is that although we may not have access to the specific day or hour of the end of the age, we are encouraged – no – commanded – to understand that approximate time, perhaps even to the year and month. Paul seconds this perception in 1 Thessalonians 5:1-6:

But of the times and seasons, brethren, you have no need that I write to you. For you yourselves know perfectly that the day of the Lord so comes as a thief in the night. For when they shall say, Peace and safety, then sudden destruction will come upon them, as travails a woman with child, and they shall not escape.

But you, brethren, are not in darkness, that that day should overtake you as a thief. You are all children of light, and children of the day; we are not of the night, nor of darkness. Therefore, let us not sleep, as do others, but let us watch and be sober-minded.

Having made that commentary on the suitability of speculations about the end-time scenario, this article returns to the topic of speculating about it.

Thoughtful and courageous Christian scholars like Hal Lindsey have taken those words of Paul in 1 Thessalonians to be marching orders, developing a view of end-time events and timing that is now accepted throughout the Christian community as the established paradigm. In that view, derived chiefly from Daniel 7 and 9, Matthew 24 and Revelation, the world will endure a seven-year Tribulation Period, the latter three and a half years of which will be the terrible Great Tribulation of widespread suffering and enormous destruction. A prime cause of this pain will be a general descent into ungodliness and rejection of God which will support the rise of a one-world government, including an economic system in which anybody who wishes to conduct a normal life, or perhaps even to survive, will be required to worship the dark leader to come by accepting an electronic implant. In the light of the standard interpretation of Daniel 9:26, the world leader will have Roman roots. Christians will escape the brunt of this awful period through the pre-Tribulation Rapture, where they will meet Jesus Christ in the air.

More recently, Irvin Baxter has challenged some of these assumptions. Among these differences, Baxter views the Rapture as occurring at the end of the Tribulation, rather than at the beginning. Because the actual destruction of Jerusalem and the Jewish temple was carried out by local Arab conscripts under the Roman leadership, Baxter interprets Daniel 9:26 as allowing for an antichrist out of the Mideast. Baxter may well have the edge on Lindsey (and a great many others) on both of these points.

Nevertheless, Lindsey and Baxter agree on the basic scenario, including a seven-year Tribulation, in the midst of which the antichrist commits the Abomination of Desolation in the Jerusalem temple. For that reason, they hold to the expectation, as do virtually all other prophetic scholars, that a third temple will be built on the Temple Mount in Jerusalem in order that an abomination may be committed against it. The source of the generally-accepted view on how the Tribulation and its associated events fits into Bible eschatology is Daniel 9:27, in which the antichrist will confirm the covenant (interpreted as a peace treaty) with many for one week (of years); in the middle of the week he stops the temple sacrifice and initiates the Abomination of Desolation. Jesus Himself referred to this abomination in Matthew 24:15:

> **When you, therefore, shall see the abomination of desolation, spoken of by Daniel the prophet, stand in the holy place (whosoever reads, let him understand), . . .**

But there may be a problem here. Paul repeatedly tells us that there already is a third temple – one made without hands, the temple components of our own bodies, collectively the Temple of the Church, indwelt by the Holy Spirit just as the Shekinah Glory indwelt the Tabernacle of the Wilderness (Exodus 40) and Solomon's Temple (1 Kings 8) at their dedications. Moreover, something is missing in the generally-accepted scenario, and it is far from trivial: with respect to

Christianity, an abomination of desolation has already occurred, and it was an enormous event with repercussions all the way up to the present time, and nobody has addressed it as such. This abomination qualifies in all respects with descriptions by both Daniel and Jesus as an eminently appropriate abomination of desolation.

What if the actual abomination was just that event that had occurred long ago – the erection of the Al Aqsa Mosque and the Dome of the Rock on the Temple Mount way back in the seventh century A.D.? If indeed this is the case, how does it affect the end-time scenario? The rest of this chapter will explore that possibility and its ramifications.

The occupation of the Temple Mount by entities foreign to the Judeo-Christian God for a very long time has excluded the possibility of rebuilding the Jewish Temple on that site. The Islamic presence there, having taken place after Jesus spoke of Daniel in Matthew 24, is itself an abomination that attempts to glorify Islam over the God of Scripture, a situation as monstrous as imaginable to the followers of the Hebrew God. I find it difficult to understand why such an important event would have been overlooked by Bible scholars, who seem to have presumed that it was not spoken of in Scripture. After some reflection on this state of affairs, one almost inevitably arrives at the rather obvious conclusion that this event may indeed have been spoken of in Scripture, being the very abomination of desolation noted by both Daniel and Jesus. The relevant account is Daniel 9:27:

> **And he shall confirm the covenant with many for one week; and in the midst of the week he shall cause the sacrifice and the oblation to cease, and for the overspreading of abominations he shall make it desolate, even until the consummation, and that determined shall be poured upon the desolate.**

If the mosque and the dome are the abominations, history records the start of their construction as 687 A.D. and their completion as 705/6 A.D. If this construction represents the actual abomination of desolation, one of these dates would be an appropriate midpoint of the week spoken of in Daniel 9:27.

How so? At this point a discussion of what God means by "days", "weeks" and "months" is necessary. In Scripture, a week is a time period of seven units, where those units are often, particularly in Daniel, something other than days. In Daniel, the units within a "week" are often interpreted as years. In Ezekiel 4, God equates a day with a year. By the same application of the notion of varied designations of time units in Scripture, some of which we might perceive as unconventional, the units comprising "months" can just as well be years as days, the context determining the unit that applies. God also makes multiple associations of a day with a millennium, as He clearly stated in Psalm 90 and 2 Peter 3:8 which strongly suggests that He has taken the seven days of Creation and stretched them out into seven thousand years of human history. Beyond those direct equations of days to millennia is God's obvious equation of a day to a millennium in Genesis 2:17:

> **But of the tree of the knowledge of good and evil, thou shalt not eat of it; for in the day that thou eatest thereof thou shall surely die.**

As P.J. Hanley remarked in Chapter Five in his book *The Seven Lost Keys of End-Time Prophecy*, Adam died before the end of a millennium at the age of 930 years. In fact, no human has ever lived to be a thousand years old. Given that limitation of Adam's life to just under a thousand years, the "day" intended by God in Genesis 2:17 must have been a millennium. Hanley also asserts that the association of a day with a thousand years of human history was a common interpretation among the Jewish prophets and rabbis.

Further confirmation of this is abundant: the four days of keeping the Passover Lamb according to Exodus 12 in light of the four days Jesus waited to resurrect Lazarus. Jesus waited those four days to render exact in time this prophecy of His own resurrection, in which the fourth millennium that had passed before Jesus' first advent stood for the fourth day before the sacrifice of the Passover Lamb. Moreover, Jesus spoke in the Gospels of His return on the third day, which followed the fourth day from Creation of His first advent. He thus implied that his return would be on seventh day, the final millennium specified in Revelation. Again, a careful reading of John 1 and 2 reveals that Jesus came to the wedding at Cana in anticipation of His marriage to His Church on the third day after the fourth day, or on the seventh day. Yet further, Hosea's prophecy in Hosea 6:2 spoke of the restoration of Israel after two days, which indeed was fulfilled two millennia later.

It should also be noted that in prophetic statements, a year consists of 360 days and a month of 30 days, rather than our usual interpretation of a year as consisting of approximately 365.25 days and a month that varies from 28 to 31 days. This duration of a prophetic year is confirmed in the actual fulfillment, to the very day, of Daniel's forecast of Jesus' triumphal entry into Jerusalem.

Returning after that aside to the statement made above that if the mosque and the dome represent the abomination of desolation, the dates of 687 or 705/6 A.D. might be the midpoint of the "week" spoken of in Daniel 9:27, the time span involved in his "week" would necessarily be considerably longer than the present understanding of seven years. That the "week" of Daniel 9:27 differs substantially from the number of days in seven years may be confirmed in Daniel 12:11:

> **And from the time that the daily sacrifice shall be taken away, and the abomination that makes desolate set up, there shall be a thousand two hundred and ninety days.**

The temple was first destroyed by Babylon's Nebudchadnezzar, causing the daily sacrifice to be taken away. If a "day" is equated to a year as in Ezekiel 4, this terrible event that was foremost in Daniel's mind would precede another important event that would occur, according to Daniel 12:11, 1290 years later. It is a straightforward arithmetic procedure to assess whether such an event did indeed occur at that time.

The calculation in actual time of the 1290-year interval between the destruction of the temple in 586 B.C. and the assumed abomination of desolation involves the application to the number

1290 of a conversion of prophetic to actual years, resulting in 1272 actual years. Adding that to the time of the temple's destruction in 586 B.C., one arrives at a date of 687 A.D. As noted above, this is precisely the date that construction, or the "setting up" began on the mosque and the dome. Whether or not it represents the midpoint of the week will be ascertained below from additional information supplied in Daniel 9 and associated information in Revelation.

That particular week described in Daniel 9 begins with a different event, the confirmation of a covenant, commonly understood as the antichrist's signing of a peace treaty with Israel. Whatever the nature of the event actually is, at the midpoint of this week the use of the Temple Mount for Jewish worship is severely curtailed. Such an event is described in Revelation 11:1 and 2:

> **And there was given me a reed like a rod; and the angel stood, saying, Rise and measure the temple of God, and the altar, and them that worship in it. But the court, which is outside the temple, leave out, and measure it not, for it is given to the gentiles, and the holy city shall they tread under foot forty two months.**

If the gentiles associated with this prophecy are taken as the followers of Islam and the court outside the temple refers to that area occupied by the Al-Aqsa Mosque and the Dome of the Rock, a time duration of forty two months would apply from the time that these structures were completed rather than begun, as then the Islamic structures would be in use. The projects were completed in 705/6 A.D.

As noted above, a prophetic month has a duration of thirty days. Just as Daniel's "weeks" were intended to represent "sevens" of years, so also may the "months" in this passage represent "thirties" of years. In that interpretation, forty two months is equivalent to 1260 years, which would be the midpoint of a 2520-year duration. (As a side point, it is interesting to note that 2520 years is equivalent to 360 weeks of years, or a prophetic year of weeks.)

Looking backward 1260 prophetic years, or 1242 actual years

according to the ratio of 360 to 365.25, from this "midpoint" of 705 A.D., one arrives at the date of 537 B.C. Is this date significant with respect to the confirmation of a covenant with Israel?

Yes, emphatically so, if one recognizes that the common equation of this "covenant" with a peace treaty is just an interpretation, and that other interpretations are possible. As described in the Book of Ezra, the Persian King Cyrus, as specifically foretold by the prophet Isaiah (Is 44:28) long before Cyrus' birth, assumed control over Babylon seventy years after her captivity precisely as predicted by Jeremiah (Jer 25:12). Cyrus issued a decree permitting Israelites to return to Jerusalem to rebuild their temple. Wikipedia and other sources place the subsequent Israelites' return in confirmation of the decree, or covenant, at 537 B.C. Some Internet sources place the decree itself at that date. At any rate, this decree indeed represents a confirmation of the covenant that God made with Israel.

This date is consistent with setting of the midpoint of Daniel's "week" at 705/706 A.D., which differs slightly from 687 A.D. But the earlier date is also significant, being consistent with the 1290 days of Daniel 12 between the removal of the sacrifice in 586 B.C. and the setting up of the abomination. Both "weeks" are consistent with Daniel's prophecy, one referring to the beginning of the abomination, and the other referring to its completion.

Looking forward from this midpoint of 705/6 A.D., the corresponding interpretation of this passage in Revelation regarding the latter half of the "week" is that the Temple Mount is given to the gentiles for a duration of 1260 prophetic years, or 1242 actual years, from their completion in 705/6 A.D.

This leads to the year 1948 A.D., the year that Israel resumed as a nation. It would take another nineteen years for Israel to recapture the Temple Mount, but, like God's promise to Caleb regarding the possession of Hebron, when Israel became a nation again, she clearly possessed God's promise that the Temple Mount belonged to her as well.

Now that the speculation that the Al Aqsa Mosque and the Dome of the Rock represents the abomination of desolation spoken of by

Daniel and Jesus has been found to stand on the solid ground of fitting in quite well with Scripture, what is one to make of it? What are the ramifications of this interpretation?

In Daniel 12:12 another duration is listed, this one being considerably more optimistic:

> **Blessed is he who waits, and comes to the thousand three hundred and thirty five days.**

This duration is usually taken to include the 1290-day period noted in the previous verse. This interpretation is not necessary – it is just as likely that it refers to an entirely separate duration, consecutive rather than an extension. Assuming that to be the case, also assuming that the "days" represent prophetic years, a conversion from prophetic to actual results in the number 1316, which, when added to the completion date of the mosque and dome, results in the year 2021 A.D. Given the blessed nature of this date, it is possible that it represents the end of the Tribulation period, which would be the time of Jesus' second advent.

But there's other information to consider. Many prophecies have two fulfillments, one being of a long duration and the other being of a shorter time period. It is possible that this prophecy is one of them, wherein besides the long-term fulfillment noted above, the more common interpretation of a shorter, seven-year period at the very end will also come into play.

Suppose, in that context, the year 2021 A.D. does indeed represent the end of the seven-year Tribulation. The Great Tribulation, then, would begin three and a half years before that, or in the middle of 2017 to early-to-mid 2018. Interestingly, this would also be around the seventieth anniversary of Israel's nationhood in 1948, and around the fiftieth anniversary of the 1967 War in which Israel took back the Temple Mount. This anniversary could be immediately subsequent to a Jubilee Year for Israel, as there is a Jubilee after every forty-nine years, and the reclamation of the Temple Mount in 1967 would have been an excellent occasion for a Jubilee year.

It's quite possible that the speculation made here will, like its numerous predecessors, fail to be fulfilled. Other valid interpretations are possible, given the large number of moving parts and corresponding interpretations of the numbers given in Scripture. One alternate scenario places the year 2021 as the time that the Rapture occurs. Of course, that possibility introduces three more time variables, depending on whether one favors the Rapture as being a pre-tribulation, mid-tribulation, or post-tribulation event.

But we do know one thing: given the closeness of the relevant numbers to the anticipated events, it won't take long to find out whether the scenarios outlined above represent actuality or not. At the least, this exercise confirms the existence of numerous possible interpretations of Daniel's prophecy in his Chapter 9. We will really know which (or whether any) interpretation is correct only as the prophesied events come to pass.

Volume Three

Delightful Scriptural Appetizers

Contents

Preface 141

One: Naming the Animals 143

Two: Solomon's Wisdom 146

Three: Holy Cloud 150

Four: Ark of the Covenant in the Holy of Holies 155

Five: Ark of the Covenant in Flesh and Spirit 158

Six: Good Leaven 162

Seven: Sea Story 165

Eight: Jesus' Fulfillment of the Mosaic Feasts 168

Nine: The Road to Emmaus 173

Ten: Psalm 22 176

Eleven: The Migdal Edar Story 179

Preface

The integrating theme for the present volume, Volume Three, is not a specific topic. Instead, this volume is a compendium of Scriptural stories that have had a special appeal to me as providing insights into Scripture and the nature of God that have been both surprising and welcome. Included are some uplifting examples of God's benevolence toward man, some glimpses of God's expectations for us, and some amplifications of God's own nature.

The desire of God, as revealed in the Bible, to endow us with personal qualities of character that are particularly appealing to Him, speaks to His loving plan for His Church to become without flaw Jesus' worthy partner in her future role as the Bride of Christ. The Bible takes a pull-no-punches approach to describe to us what it means to follow Jesus without sugar-coating the message. That feature establishes the Bible above other books and venues as the true Word of God, as asserted by Paul in 2 Timothy 3:16 and 17, and Peter in 2 Peter 1:20 and 21:

> **All scripture is given by inspiration of God, and is profitable for doctrine, for reproof, for correction, for instruction in righteousness, that the man of God may be perfect, thoroughly furnished for all good works.**

> **Knowing this first, that no prophecy of the scripture is of any private interpretation. For the prophecy came not at any time by the will of man, but holy men of God spoke as they were moved by the Holy Spirit.**

As noted in the preface to Volume Two, there have been attempts in the past to deny the supernatural character of the Bible, one attempt being to date the source of time information within the Bible to after Jesus' advent. How wonderfully ironic it was that Ahmed the Wolf, a simple peasant, tossed a rock into a cave at Qumran and thus brought to nought the misguided pronouncements of the religious intellectuals.

One
Naming the Animals

In Genesis 2, God pronounces it *not good* that Adam should be without a mate. But before He proceeds to do something about it, He brings the animals of His Creation to Adam and asks him to name them. Then he forms Eve out of Adam's rib.

> **And the Lord God said, It is not good that the man should be alone; I will make him an help fit for him.**
>
> **And out of the ground the Lord God formed every beast of the field, and every fowl of the air; and brought them unto Adam to see what he would call them: and whatsoever Adam called every living creature, that was the name thereof. And Adam gave names to all cattle, and to the fowl of the air, and to every beast of the field; but for Adam there was not found an help fit for him.**
>
> **And the Lord God caused a deep sleep to fall upon Adam, and he slept: and he took one of his ribs, and closed up the flesh instead thereof. And the rib, which the lord God had taken from man, made he a woman, and brought her unto the man.**

This passage raises a number of questions, particularly in the sequence of events, but with other issues besides. Why did God insert the naming of the animals between His concern over Adam being alone and His forming of Eve? What was so important about Adam naming the animals? How could he possibly name all the animals, given the enormous diversity of life?

As to the first issue, the sequence of the Biblical narrative, I like best an answer picked off the Internet on the *Creation Moments* website: God was using the simple tool of names to teach Adam to communicate, a skill that he would then pass on to Eve, enabling them to bond through joint communication. That answer is appealing, as it would be a valid prerequisite to the event of bringing Adam and Eve together, much to be preferred to the two staring dumbly at each other and at a total loss for words.

This reason also answers in part the second issue, the importance of Adam naming the animals. But there are other important reasons other than helping Adam to communicate with Eve, one of which is that in having Adam name the animals, God was asserting that these creatures were fixed kinds, finished designs whose basic properties would remain intact throughout history. Thus, this episode in Adam's life is a slap in the face to Darwin's theory of evolution, which postulates that life is unceasingly undergoing change. In Darwin's view, all life is in constant transition from one form to another, so that the animals we see now are simply snapshots in time of what may be very different in the future.

Noted biochemist Douglas Axe captures the essence of this contrast between God's stability of form with Darwin's corresponding instability in Chapter 6 of his book *Undeniable: How Biology Confirms our Intuition that Life is Designed.* There, under the heading "Life ala Darwin" Axe speaks of the salmon and the Orca whale, each very different but "utterly committed to being what it is." Life, as Axe sees it, magnificently represents completion of form, creatures living precisely as God designed them to live.

This stability of form leads to the next issue, the question as to how Adam could have named all the animals, even within his very long lifetime. If all kinds of life are stable as was asserted above, the very diversity of life would not only indicate that this variety existed at the time of Adam, but also would make his task extremely difficult. At this point I'll make a statement that appears to directly contradict this supposed stability of life: there must have been a relatively few "kinds" of animals that Adam was asked to name; first they were limited to birds and the larger animals; second, these "kinds" were the much-fewer basic precursors whose offspring branched out after

Noah's Flood to the diversity we see today. But then one might say, "See? Animals aren't stable in form at all!" But the post-Flood diversity has much more to do with designed-in adaptability than actual change corresponding to the evolutionary model. The difference is that God's engine of change is His inclusion in DNA of pre-existing alternate design modifications, whereas Darwin's "engine" is dumb, random variation.

Take, for instance, the dog. There exists today an enormous variety of dogs of varying shapes, sizes and attributes. But they're all still dogs, having the wolf as a common ancestor. The DNA of the wolf is information-rich, capable of accommodating plans "B", "C", and so on according to environmental conditions or the human interference of breeding. Most common breeds today are the product of the intelligent operation of selective breeding, and some, but not all, of their features would quickly revert back to those of their common ancestor if they were to be divested of their human overseers and returned into the wild. It is true the Mexican hairless creature would be in serious trouble in another ice age because some features such as length of hair might be incapable of reversion. But that would be due to DNA information loss arising from forced breeding.

Two
Solomon's Wisdom

According to 1 Kings 3:5-28, Solomon asked for wisdom and received it – in abundance:

> **In Gibeon the Lord appeared to Solomon in a dream by night; and God said, Ask what I shall give you. And Solomon said, You have showed to your servant David, my father, great mercy, according as he walked before you in truth, and in righteousness, and in uprightness of heart with you; and you have kept for him this great kindness, that you have given him a son to sit on his throne, as it is this day. And now, O Lord my God, you have made your servant king instead of David, my father; and I am but a little child: I know not how to go out or to come in. And your servant is in the midst of your people whom you have chosen, a great people, who cannot be numbered or counted for multitude. Give, therefore, your servant an understanding heart to judge your people, that I may discern between good and bad. For who is able to judge this your great people?**
>
> **And the speech pleased the Lord, that Solomon had asked this thing. And God said to him, Because you have asked this thing, and have not asked for yourself long life; neither have asked riches for yourself, nor have asked the life of your enemies, but have asked for yourself understanding to discern justice, behold, I have done according to your words: lo, I have given you a wise and an understanding heart, so that there was none like you before you, neither after you shall any arise like unto you. And I have also**

given you that which you have not asked, both riches, and honor, so that there shall not be any among the kings like unto you all your days. And if you will walk in my ways, to keep my statutes and my commandments, as your father, David, did walk, then I will lengthen your days.

And Solomon awoke, and, behold, it was a dream. And he came to Jerusalem, and stood before the ark of the covenant of the Lord, and offered up burnt offerings, and offered peace offerings, and made a feast to all his servants. Then came there two women, who were harlots, to the king, and stood before him. And the one woman said, O my lord, I and this woman dwell in one house, and I was delivered of a child with her in the house. And it came to pass the third day after that I was delivered, that this woman was delivered also, and we were together. There was no stranger with us in the house, except we two were in the house. And this woman's child died in the night, because she lay on it. And she arose at midnight and took my son from beside me, while your handmaid slept, and laid it in her bosom, and laid her dead child in my bosom. And when I rose in the morning to nurse my child, behold, it was dead; but when I had looked at it in the morning, behold, it was not my son whom I did bear. And the other woman said, Nay; but the living child is my son, and the dead is your son. And this said, No; but the dead child is your son, and the living is my son. Thus they spoke before the king.

Then said the king, The one says, This is my son who lives, and your son is the dead; and the other says, Nay; but your son is the dead child, and my son is the living. And the king said, Bring me a sword. And they brought a sword before the king. And the king said, Divide the living child in two, and give half to the one, and half to the other. Then spoke the woman whose the living child was unto the king, for her heart yearned over her son, and she said, O my lord, give her the living child, and by no means slay

it. But the other said, Let it be neither mine nor yours, but divide it.

Then the king answered and said, Give her the living child, and by no means slay it; she is the mother of it. And all Israel heard of the judgment which the king had judged, and they feared the king; for they saw that the wisdom of God was in him, to do justice.

The wisdom of God indeed was in Solomon, far beyond imparting to him the ability as king to elevate the nation of Israel over all others in space and time. For his noble desire to place his service to God above self, God gave him an understanding of Wisdom as a Person, the Divine Member of the Godhead whom we know as the Holy Spirit and the Person of whom Solomon wrote in the Book of Proverbs.

In like manner God gave his father David an understanding of the Divine Will, the Holy Father. Subsequently, David wrote about Him in the Book of Psalms, of which David was the primary author.

The Psalms and Proverbs do more than inform us of the nature of God; they also informed the Jesus who came in the flesh about His own Divine Roots. To that end, the Book of Psalms was a loving letter of greeting and instruction from the Divine Father to His only begotten Son. In that circumstance, David was the surrogate Father who, in writing that letter, inserted that knowledge of the Father into Scripture for Jesus to read and study. Perhaps that is why Jesus called Himself the Son of David.

In the same way the Book of Proverbs also was a loving letter of greeting and instruction from Jesus' other Divine Parent, the Holy Spirit.

If that is the case, He would have understood Psalms and Proverbs to have been written especially for His intimate understanding of his Divine Parents. Proverbs 1:8 is a particularly appropriate remark in that context:

My son, hear the instruction of your father, and forsake not the law of your mother;

Perhaps also Jesus would have rejoiced in reading Proverbs 8:22-31:

> **The Lord possessed me in the beginning of his way, before his works of old. I was set up from everlasting, from the beginning, or ever the earth was. When there were no depths, I was brought forth – when there were no fountains abounding with water. Before the mountains were settled, before the hills, was I brought forth; while he as yet he had not made the earth, nor the fields, nor the highest part of the dust of the world. When he prepared the heavens, I was there; when he set a compass upon the face of the depth; when he established the clouds above; when he strengthened the fountains of the deep; when he gave to the sea its decree, that the waters should not pass his commandment; when he appointed the foundations of the earth, then I was by him, as one brought up with him; and I was daily his delight, rejoicing always before him, rejoicing in the habitable part of his earth; and my delight was with the sons of men.**

Perhaps a filial concern clouded Jesus' features when he came to Proverbs 8:36:

> **But he who sins against me wrongs his own soul; all who hate me love death.**

If so, it explains why Jesus spoke so protectively in Matthew 12:31 and 32 against blaspheming the Holy Spirit:

> **Wherefore, I say to you, All manner of sin and blasphemy shall be forgiven men; but the blasphemy against the Holy Spirit shall not be forgiven men. And whosoever speaks a word against the Son of man, it shall be forgiven him; but whosoever speaks against the Holy Spirit, it shall not be forgiven him, neither in this age, neither in the age to come.**

Three
Holy Cloud

If one looks up the word "cloud" in a Bible concordance, even a modest one, he will see well over forty entries. They don't all have the same meanings, of course, but there are several that do. And some that do have the same meanings don't seem to at first, because they are used in different contexts. The Biblical clouds that are mentioned here all have the same meaning, and that meaning is a holy one.

In Exodus 40 and 1 Kings 8, the Glory of the Lord, called by the Hebrews the Shekinah, indwelt as a Cloud both the tabernacle in the wilderness and Solomon's Temple at their dedications. This indwelling feminine Presence was a type – a representative precursor to – the Holy Spirit who indwelt Jesus' disciples at the Pentecost described in Acts 2 and now, as the Comforter promised by Jesus in John 14, indwells every constituent of Jesus' entire Church, described by Paul as living temples of God.

The Shekinah Glory of the Wilderness Tabernacle is described in Exodus 40:33-38:

> **And [Moses] reared up the court round about the tabernacle and the altar, and set up the hanging of the court gate. So Moses finished the work. Then a cloud covered the tent of the congregation, and the glory of the Lord filled the tabernacle. And Moses was not able to enter into the tent of the congregation, because the cloud abode thereon, and the glory of the Lord filled the tabernacle. And when the cloud was taken up from over the tabernacle, the children of Israel went onward in all their journeys; but if the cloud were not taken up, then they journeyed not till the day that**

it was taken up. For the cloud of the Lord was upon the tabernacle by day, and fire was on it by night, in the sight of all the house of Israel, throughout all their journeys.

The description "cloud of the Lord", "fire by night" and "taken up" leaves no doubt that this "cloud" is equivalent to the *Shekinah* of the Red Sea adventure and of Isaiah 4:5.

The Shekinah Glory of Solomon's Temple is described in 1 Kings 8:5-11:

And King Solomon, and all the congregation of Israel, who were assembled before him, were with him before the ark, sacrificing sheep and oxen, that could not be counted nor numbered for multitude. And the priests brought in the ark of the covenant of the Lord unto its place, into the inner sanctuary of the house, to the most holy place, even under the wings of the cherubim. For the cherubim spread forth their two wings over the place of the ark, and the cherubim covered the ark and its staves above. And they drew out the staves, that the ends of the staves were seen out in the holy place before the inner sanctuary, but they were not seen outside; and there they are unto this day. There was nothing in the ark except the two tables of stone, which Moses put there at Horeb, when the Lord made a covenant with the children of Israel, when they came out of the land of Egypt. And it came to pass, when the priests were come out of the holy place, that the cloud filled the house of the Lord, so that the priests could not stand to minister because of the cloud; for the glory of the Lord had filled the house of the Lord.

In Daniel 7:13 and 14, and Matthew 17:1-5, the Holy Spirit, still represented by a Cloud, accompanies Jesus in His spiritual appearance before men.

I saw in the night visions, and, behold, one like the Son of man came with the clouds of heaven, and came to the Ancient of days, and they brought him near before him.

> And there was given him dominion, and glory, and a kingdom, that all people, nations, and languages should serve him; his dominion is an everlasting dominion, which shall not pass away, and his kingdom that which shall not be destroyed.

> And after six days Jesus took Peter, James, and John, his brother, and brought them up into a high mountain, privately, and was transfigured before them; and his face did shine like the sun, and his raiment was as white as the light. And, behold, there appeared to them Moses and Elijah talking with him. Then answered Peter, and said to Jesus, Lord, it is good for us to be here; if you will, let us make here three booths; one for you, and one for Moses, and one for Elijah. While he yet spoke, behold, a bright cloud overshadowed them; and, behold, a voice out of the cloud, which said, This is my beloved Son, in whom I am well pleased; hear you him.

In Matthew 24:30, Acts 1:8-11, and Revelation 1:7 and 14:14 that same Cloud conveys Jesus between earth and heaven:

> And then shall appear the sign of the Son of man in heaven; and then shall all the tribes of the earth mourn, and they shall see the Son of man coming in the clouds of heaven with power and great glory.

> But you shall receive power, after the Holy Spirit is come upon you, and you shall be witnesses to me both in Jerusalem, and in all Judea, and in Samaria, and to the uttermost part of the earth. And, when [Jesus] had spoken these things, while they beheld, he was taken up, and a cloud received him out of their sight. And while they looked steadfastly toward heaven as he went up, behold, two men stood by them in while apparel, who also said, You men of Galilee, why stand you gazing up into heaven? This same Jesus, who is taken up from you into heaven, shall so come in like manner as you have seen him go into heaven.

Behold, [Jesus] comes with clouds, and every eye shall see him, and they also who pierced him; and all kindreds of the earth shall wail because of him. Even so, Amen.

And I looked, and behold, a white cloud, and upon the cloud one sat, like the Son of man, having on his head a golden crown, and in his hand a sharp sickle.

In 1 Thessalonians 4:16 and 17 and Revelation 11:11 and 12, the cloud also conveys from earth to heaven special humans, constituting the Church and the prophetic witnesses in Jerusalem at the last days of the age:

For the Lord himself shall descend from heaven with a shout, with the voice of the archangel, and with the trump of God; and the dead in Christ shall rise first; then we who are alive and remain shall be caught up together with them in the clouds, to meet the Lord in the air; and so shall we ever be with the Lord.

And after three days and a half the spirit of life from God entered into [the two witnesses], and they stood upon their feet, and great fear fell upon them who saw them. And they heard a great voice from heaven saying unto them, Come up here. And they ascended up to heaven in a cloud, and their enemies beheld them.

In each of the passages noted above, the settings, associations and contexts readily identify the Cloud as representing the Holy Spirit. But our appreciation of and involvement with the Holy Spirit is greater than mere recognition or even conveyance. As I noted in my book *Marching to a Worthy Drummer*, the connection between the precursor temple Presence and the indwelling of Christian believers is given in 1 Corinthians 3:16 and Ephesians 2:19-22, wherein Paul asserts that the Church herself, through her constituents, is a temple indwelt by the Holy Spirit:

Know you not that ye are the temple of God, and that the Spirit of God dwells in you?

Now, therefore, you are no more strangers and sojourners, but fellow citizens with the saints, and of the household of God; and are built upon the foundation of the apostles and prophets, Jesus Christ himself being the chief corner stone, in whom all the building fitly framed together grows unto a holy temple in the Lord; in whom you also are built together for a habitation of God through the Spirit.

Four
Ark of the Covenant in the Holy of Holies

The Ark of the Covenant has an interesting and rather enigmatic history. Its fabrication was commanded by God to Moses at the time that Moses went up to Mount Sinai to receive the Ten Commandments. God issued very specific instructions as to how it was to be constructed. It had an intimate connection to the tabernacle in the wilderness and to Solomon's Temple, where it occupied the Holy of Holies in both temples. It was above the ark that the Shekinah Glory indwelt both houses of the Lord.

Details of the Ark of the Covenant are presented in Exodus 24:15-18 and 25:1-22:

> **And Moses went up into the mount, and a cloud covered the mount. And the glory of the Lord abode upon Mount Sinai, and the cloud covered it six days; and the seventh day he called unto Moses out of the midst of the cloud. And the sight of the glory of the Lord was like devouring fire on the top of the mount in the eyes of the children of Israel. And Moses went into the midst of the cloud, and got up into the mount; and Moses was in the mount forty days and forty nights.**
>
> **And the Lord spoke to Moses, saying, Speak to the children of Israel, that they bring me an offering: of every man that gives it willingly with his heart you shall take my offering. And this is the offering which you shall take of them: gold, and silver, and bronze, and blue, and purple, and scarlet,**

and fine linen, and goats' hair, and rams' skins dyed red, and badgers' skins, and acacia wood, oil for the light, spices for anointing oil and for sweet incense, onyx stones, and stones to be set in the ephod and in the breastplate.

And let them make me a sanctuary, that I may dwell among them. According to all that I show you, after the pattern of the tabernacle, and the pattern of all the furnishings thereof, even so shall you make it.

And they shall make an ark of acacia wood: two cubits and a half shall be the length thereof, and a cubit and a half the breadth thereof, and a cubit and a half the height thereof. And you shall overlay it with pure gold, within and without shall you overlay it, and shall make upon it a rim of gold round about. And you shall cast four rings of gold for it, and put them in the four corners thereof; and two rings shall be in one side of it, and two rings in the other side of it. And you shall make staves of acacia wood, and overlay them with gold. And you shall put the staves into the rings by the sides of the ark, that the ark may be borne with them. The staves shall be in the rings of the ark; they shall not be taken from it. And you shall put into the ark the testimony which I shall give you. And you shall make a mercy seat of pure gold: two cubits and a half shall be the length thereof, and a cubit and a half the breadth thereof. And you shall make two cherubim of gold, of beaten work shall you make them, in the two ends of the mercy seat. And make one cherub on the one end, and the other cherub on the other end: even of the mercy seat shall you make the cherubim on the two ends thereof. And the cherubim shall stretch forth their wings on high, covering the mercy seat with their wings, and their faces shall look one to another; toward the mercy seat shall the faces of the cherubim be. And you shall put the mercy seat above upon the ark; and in the ark you shall put the testimony that I shall give you. And there I will meet with you, and I will commune with you from above the mercy

seat, from between the two cherubim which are upon the ark of the testimony, of all things which I will give you in commandment to the children of Israel.

The testimony referred to in this passage consisted of the stone tablets upon which God had written the Ten Commandments. According to Hebrews 9:4, the ark also contained the golden pot of manna and Aaron's rod. These artifacts spoke of the intimacy of God's relationship with mankind, and of His power in fulfilling His Word. According to 2 Chronicles 5:10, the pot of manna and Aaron's rod were later removed.

The ark was captured by the Philistines during one of Judah's frequent fallings away from God. During its return, it was touched with the result that the offender died. Some Christians speculate that the man died not because of the touching, but because he was filled with sin.

The ark's fate becomes murky after that; Isaiah was said to have buried it at the time that the ten northern nations of Israel were assaulted by Assyria and dispersed. Other legend has it that King Menelek of Ethiopia, who was the offspring of Solomon's romance with the Queen of Sheba, stole it after having replaced it with an imitation and took it with him back to Ethiopia. To this day either the real ark of the covenant or its duplicate is under heavy guard in the Ethiopian city of Axum. The ark is mentioned in the Bible a final time in Revelation 11, but this ark is probably a much different one, the nature of which will be explored in the next chapter.

Five

Ark of the Covenant in Flesh and Spirit

In the previous chapter, the Ark of the Covenant was described as the enclosure located in the area of the temple known as the Holy of Holies. It was noted that the Ark of the Covenant is mentioned again in Revelation, but that this ark is probably a very different one. In my novel *Jacob,* book three of the four-book *Buddy* series, Earl Cook connects this later ark with the earlier one in his talk to fellow Christians in a Bible study:

> **This one's about the Ark of the Covenant. This ark was a wooden box, overlaid with gold and topped with two cherubs. Inside the box were relics of past interactions between God and man, including the staff that Aaron used, the one that turned into a snake in front of pharaoh, and a sample of the life-sustaining bread that fell from heaven during the great exodus from Egypt and, most important, the tablets upon which God had written the Ten Commandments and which he gave to Moses on the mountain. These tablets encapsulated the Law of the Old Testament in covenant between God and man. The Ark of the Covenant was placed within the Holy of Holies of the Tabernacle in the wilderness, and later in Solomon's temple. At the dedication of both of these temples the glory of God, called the Shekinah, descended in a cloud and dwelt within the temples. There is a great significance to this indwelling of the Shekinah glory, and I'll probably go into it in another sermon. But for now I want to focus**

on the Ark, which has had a very colorful history. There's a question as to whether Menelek, the queen of Sheba's son with Solomon, went back to Ethiopia with a copy of it or actually had stolen the real thing. To this day, that version is jealously guarded by Ethiopians. The ark that remained in Israel was eventually lost. Apparently, the prophet Jeremiah buried it in a cave toward the end of the sixth century B.C. when Jerusalem was in danger of being overrun by enemy forces. There's another story in that too, but to forge ahead, the Ark of the Covenant is finally mentioned again toward the end of the Bible, in the Book of Revelation, where John sees it in heaven. But this may be a different Ark altogether.

Let me tell you why. In Revelation 12, immediately after John's sighting of the Ark in heaven at the end of Chapter 11, he goes on to describe another heavenly wonder: a woman clothed with the sun, who gives birth to a man-child who is to rule the world, obviously Jesus. This woman has variously been identified as several different personages by people of differing faiths, each one being the favorite of one faith or another. Many have thought of this woman as representing Israel. Catholics have picked up on this passage, claiming her to be Mary. For reasons that I won't go into now, I don't think that's quite accurate. But it's very close. Whether this woman actually is Mary or not, it does evoke an image that makes me want to say, "Of course! It can be no other way." That image, which I cherish now with all my heart, I know to be true, and I want to share it with you now. Mary herself, in containing the Word of God in her womb, was herself the flesh-and-blood Ark of the New Covenant in Jesus Christ. That may well have been the Ark that John saw in heaven.

But there may also be a yet greater Person to whom this later ark may be attributed, wherein the connection is spiritual rather than fleshly. The Biblical account of this ark is presented in Revelation 11:19 through 12:17:

And the temple of God was opened in heaven, and there was seen in his temple the ark of his covenant; and there were lightnings, and voices, and thunderclaps, and an earthquake, and great hail.

And there appeared a great wonder in heaven – a woman clothed with the sun, and the moon under her feet, and upon her head a crown of twelve stars. And she, being with child, cried, travailing in birth, and pained to be delivered.

And there appeared another wonder in heaven; and, behold, a great red dragon, having seven heads and ten horns, and seven crowns upon his heads. And his tail drew the third part of the stars of heaven and did cast them to the earth; and the dragon stood before the woman who was ready to be delivered, to devour her child as soon as it was born.

And she brought forth a male child, who was to rule all nations with a rod of iron; and her child was caught up unto God, and to his throne. And the woman fled into the wilderness, where she hath a place prepared by God, that they should feed her there a thousand two hundred and threescore days.

And there was war in heaven; Michael and his angels fought against the dragon, and the dragon fought and his angels, and prevailed not, neither was their place found any more in heaven. And the great dragon was cast out, that old serpent, called the Devil and Satan, who deceives the whole world; he was cast out into the earth, and his angels were cast out with him. And I heard a loud voice saying in heaven, Now is come salvation, and strength, and the kingdom of our God, and the power of his Christ; for the accuser of our brothers is cast down, who accused them before our God day and night. And they overcame him by the blood of the Lamb, and by the word of their testimony; and they loved not their lives unto the death. Therefore rejoice, you heavens, and you who dwell in them. Woe to

the inhabitants of the earth and of the sea! For the devil is come down unto you, having great wrath, because he knows that he has but a short time.

And when the dragon saw that he was cast unto the earth, he persecuted the woman who brought forth the male child. And to the woman were given two wings of a great eagle, that she might fly into the wilderness, into her place, where she is nourished for a time, and times, and half a time, from the face of the serpent. And the serpent cast out of his mouth water like a flood after the woman, that he might cause her to be carried away by the flood. And the earth helped the woman, and the earth opened her mouth and swallowed up the flood which the dragon cast out of his mouth. And the dragon was angry with the woman, and went to make war with the remnant of her seed, who keep the commandments of God, and have the testimony of Jesus Christ.

Could this spiritual Woman be the same Shekinah who indwells Christian believers, as described in an earlier chapter? Could She be the same Holy Spirit of whom Jesus spoke in John 3 as giving spiritual birth? Could She be the spiritual Mother of Jesus?

Just as Revelation 11 and 12 symbolize Mary as the ark of the covenant in flesh, so do those same passages symbolize God the Holy Spirit as the ark of the Word, God's covenant to mankind, in spirit.

Six
Good Leaven

I've heard in Church more than once that leaven is unconditionally bad. It supposedly represents evil. The pastor who makes this claim usually follows it up with a recital of the several passages in Scripture that describe leaven in a negative light.

But there's a problem with that blanket generalization. In Leviticus 23:15-17 the Lord spoke to Moses regarding the observance of the Feast of Pentecost,

> **And you shall count to you from the next day after the sabbath, from the day that you brought the sheaf of the wave offering; seven sabbaths shall be complete: even to the next day after the seventh sabbath shall you number fifty days; and you shall offer a new meal offering to the Lord.**
>
> **You shall bring out of your habitations two wave loaves of fine flour; they shall be baked with leaven; they are the first fruits to the Lord.**

Here is a case that includes leaven in an offering to God, and it represents an important exception to the generality that equates leaven with evil.

A relevant characteristic of the Feast of Pentecost is that it follows fairly quickly the Passover and the Feast of Unleavened Bread, where the old leaven is discarded. After this feast, the household resumes the use of leaven, but it is new. The discarding of the old leaven and its replacement with the new suggests that the old leaven had become contaminated over the course of the year. The use of the new leaven in the Feast of Pentecost adds weight to this suggestion.

With this understanding about leaven we come to realize that the term "bad" is a qualifying term to leaven, rather than representing an intrinsic characteristic of it. In other words, not all leaven is bad. Contaminated leaven is bad, but not all leaven is contaminated.

Jesus qualified leaven in another way. In His feeding of the multitudes, Jesus employed spiritual leaven to extend the meager number of original loaves to enough bread to satisfy the hunger of the masses. In doing so, he used bread to show how His Word would propagate like good leaven from the few disciples to the multitude throughout earth who would come to a saving knowledge of Him and His work in their behalf on the cross. In connection with these feeding events, in Mark 8:14-21, Jesus contrasts the good leaven of His Word with the bad:

> **Now the disciples had forgotten to take bread, neither had they in the boat with them more than one loaf. And he charged them, saying, Take heed, Beware of the leaven of the Pharisees, and of the leaven of Herod. And they reasoned among themselves, saying, It is because we have no bread. And when Jesus knew it, he said unto them, Why reason you, because you have no bread? Perceive you not yet, neither understand? Have you your heart yet hardened? Having eyes, see you not? And having ears, hear you not? And do you not remember? When I broke the five loaves among five thousand, how many baskets full of fragments took you up? They said to him, Twelve. And when the seven among four thousand, how many baskets full of fragments took you up? And they said, Seven. And he said unto them, How is it that you do not understand?**

Aside from the fact that this particular passage led me into a ten-year investigation into the details of the feedings, the results of which are presented in my books *Family of God, Cathy, Jacob,* and *Marching to a Worthy Drummer,* Jesus is seen here as making qualifying statements about leaven, and not about leaven itself. Keep in mind that Jesus, in feeding the multitudes, showed the use of good leaven. His qualification of leaven to His disciples was very specific, addressing the personages of the Pharisees and Herod. Herod himself was evil, and the understanding of God by the Pharisees represented the contamination of the Word of God over the centuries, just like old leaven becomes contaminated over the course of a year and must be replaced with the new. That is why all Christians would do well to return periodically to Scripture as the only reliable source of the Word of God, to refresh their understanding of God and of His interaction with mankind. It is also why Acts 17:10-12 shows favor towards the Bereans:

> **And the brethren immediately sent away Paul and Silas by night to Berea, who, coming there, went into the synagogue of the Jews. These were more noble than those in Thessalonica, in that they received the word with all readiness of mind, and searched the scriptures daily, whether those things were so. Therefore, many of them believed; also of honorable women who were Greeks, and of men, not a few.**

Seven
Sea Story

Going back in time from the revolutionary period of our history, those who look for them can find many examples of God's Hand, both positive and negative, in the affairs of the American political experiment in freedom.

Why negative? Because that's how God operates, as He has told us numerous times. In Deuteronomy 11:26-26-28, for example, Moses told the Israelites who had left Egypt with him:

> **Behold, I set before you this day a blessing and a curse; A blessing if you obey the commandments of the Lord your God, which I command you this day: And a curse, if you will not obey the commandments of the Lord your God, but turn aside out of the way which I command you this day, to go after other gods, which you have not known.**

This admonition applies to every Christian today just as much as to the Israelites whom Moses addressed back then. It applied as well throughout the American experience. According to the authors of *The Light and the Glory*, it took only one or two generations after they landed before the pilgrims, in experiencing an increasing ease of existence, began to fall away from their daily devotion to God. At first the chastising was mild, and quickly returned to blessing as the people heeded the correction:

> **Perhaps the most extraordinary chastisement in this vein was the rain of caterpillars which Winthrop reported in the summer of 1646. "Great harm was done in corn (especially wheat and barley) in this month by a caterpillar, like a black worm about an inch and a half long. They eat up first the blades of the stalk, then they eat up the tassels, whereupon**

> **the ear withered. It was believed by divers good observers that they fell in a great thunder shower, for divers yards and other bare places where not one of them was seen an hour before, were presently after the shower almost covered with them, besides grass places where they were not so easily discerned. They did the most harm in the southern parts, as in Rhode Island, etc., and in the eastern parts in their Indian corn. In divers places the churches kept a day of humiliation, and presently after, the caterpillars vanished away."**

God also is a champion of justice, particularly when mixed with compassion. There are several Old Testament references to how God prefers justice and mercy over lip service to Him. One example is found in Hosea 6:6; another in Isaiah 58:6 and 7:

> **For I desired mercy, and not sacrifice, and the knowledge of God more than burnt offerings.**

> **Is not this the fast that I have chosen- to loose the bands of wickedness, to undo the heavy burdens, and to let the oppressed go free, and that you break every yoke? Is it not to deal your bread to the hungry, and that you bring the poor that are cast out to your house? When you see the naked, that you cover him; and that you hide not yourself from your own flesh?**

Jesus repeated these sentiments in Matthew 12:7 while He explained to the

Pharisees how much more important it is to show mercy, even on the Sabbath, than to participate in spiritually empty adherence to the law:

> **But if you had known what this means, I will have mercy, and not sacrifice, you would not have condemned the guiltless.**

It is much more fun to describe blessings than curses, and justice served rather than justice denied. Here is a good sea story, also taken from *The Light and the Glory* regarding that time period in America's history:

> **Our favorite of these sea stories involves *two* ships in distress. The first, under the mastery of William Laiton, was out of Piscataqua and bound for Barbados, when, some thousand miles off the coast, she sprang a leak which could not be staunched. He crew was forced to take refuge in their longboat. It happened that they had a plentiful supply of bread, more than they could possibly eat, but so little water that after eighteen days of drifting, they were down to a teaspoon per man per day. Meanwhile, another ship, captained by one Samuel Scarlet, was having its own difficulties, being "destitute of provisions, only they had water enough, and to spare." The spied the drifting longboat, but as Scarlet made ready to take them aboard, his men ". . .desired that he would not go to take the men in, lest they should all die by famine. But the captain was a man of too generous a charity to follow the selfish proposals thus made unto him. He replied, 'It may be these distressed creatures are our own countrymen, and [anyway] they are distressed creatures. I am resolved I will take them in, and I'll trust in God, who is able to deliver us all.' Nor was he a loser by this charitable resolution, for Captain Scarlet had the water which Laiton wanted, and Mr. Laiton had the bread and fish which Scarlet wanted. So they refreshed one another, and in a few days arrived safe to New England. But it was remarked that the chief of the mariners who urged Captain Scarlet against his taking in these distressed people, did afterwards, in his distress at sea, perish without any to take him in."**

Eight
Jesus' Fulfillment of the Mosaic Feasts

At the time of Jesus' crucifixion, three events occurred in rapid succession: His crucifixion, His resurrection, and the Pentecost, where the Holy Spirit indwelt believers and empowered them to do exploits. All three of these events were imprinted in the minds of the Israelites over a millennium earlier by Moses in terms of feasts and observances.

The first event, Jesus' crucifixion, was initially foreshadowed in detail by God's call to Abraham to sacrifice his son Isaac, as related in Genesis 22. But the commemorative feast for this event is the Passover, as instituted by Moses just before the Israelites were to cast off their enslavement and depart for Egypt. The account of the institution of this feast is given in Exodus 12:1-3, 5-7, and 12 and 13:

> **And the Lord spoke to Moses and Aaron in the land of Egypt, saying, "This month shall be to you the beginning of months: it shall be the first month of the year to you. Speak you to all the congregation of Israel, saying, In the tenth day of this month they shall take to them every man a lamb, according to the house of their fathers, a lamb for a house . . . Your lamb shall be without blemish, a male of the first year: you shall take it out from the sheep, or from the goats. And you shall keep it until the fourteenth day of the same month; and the whole assembly of the congregation of Israel shall kill it in the evening. And they shall take of the blood, and strike it on the two side posts**

and on the upper door post of the houses, wherein they shall eat it. And they shall eat the flesh in that night, roast with fire and unleavened bread; and with bitter herbs they shall eat it . . . For I will pass through the land of Egypt this night, and will smite all the first-born in the land of Egypt, both man and beast; and against all the gods of Egypt I will execute judgment: I am the Lord. And the blood shall be to you for a token upon the houses where you are; and when I see the blood, I will pass over you, and the plague shall not be upon you to destroy you, when I smite the land of Egypt. And this day shall be to you for a memorial; and you shall keep it a feast to the Lord throughout your generations; you shall keep it a feast by an ordinance forever."

The lamb was kept in the house for four days, just long enough for it to become a household pet with the formation of a loving bond between the people and this innocent creature. Then it was slain and its blood spread on the doorposts and lintel as a sign to God to spare the occupants within as He went out to slay the firstborn of Egypt.

The Passover Lamb was, of course, a type of Jesus, who was crucified on the day of preparation for the Passover, the exact time when the lambs were traditionally slain. He was described as the Lamb of God by the Apostle John, first in John's Gospel and then in the Book of Revelation. Christians claim the remission of their sins and their spiritual salvation by the washing of Jesus' blood: He is our Passover Lamb.

The second event that was linked to a feast was Jesus' resurrection after three days and three nights in the grave following His crucifixion. The corresponding feast established by Moses is the wave offering of first fruits of the barley harvest, traditionally held during the week of the Feast of Unleavened Bread from the 15th to the 21st of Nisan. The exact day is given in Leviticus 23:11 as the day following the Sabbath. The Sabbath after Jesus' crucifixion was Saturday, Nisan 16, making the Feast of First Fruits the following day, or Sunday, Nisan 17. The account is given in Leviticus 23:9-14:

> **And the Lord spoke to Moses, saying, "Speak to the children of Israel, and say to them, When you are come into the land which I give unto you, and shall reap the harvest thereof, then you shall bring a sheaf of the first fruits of your harvest to the priest, and he shall wave the sheaf before the Lord, to be accepted for you: on the next day after the sabbath the priest shall wave it. And you shall offer that day when you wave the sheaf an he-lamb without blemish of the first year for a burnt offering to the Lord. And the meal offering thereof shall be two tenth parts of fine flour mixed with oil, an offering made by fire to the Lord for a sweet savor: and the drink offering thereof shall be of wine, a quart. And you shall eat neither bread, nor parched corn, nor green ears, until that same day that you have brought an offering to your God: it shall be a statute forever throughout your generations in all your dwellings."**

The wave offering was intended to commemorate Jesus' resurrection from the dead, as Jesus was the first fruit of resurrected mankind.

The third feast is related in Leviticus 23:15-21:

> **And you shall count to you from the next day after the Sabbath, from the day that you brought the sheaf of the wave offering; seven Sabbaths shall be complete: even to the next day after the seventh Sabbath shall you number fifty days; and you shall offer a new meal offering unto the Lord. You shall bring out of your habitations two wave loaves of two tenth parts; they shall be of fine flour; they shall be baked with leaven; they are the first fruits unto the Lord. And you shall offer with the bread seven lambs without blemish of the first year . . .**

The passage continues with additional offerings, ending with the command that the feast is a holy convocation, no work being permitted, and a statute forever.

As it traditionally occurred fifty days after the Feast of First Fruits, this event is called the Feast of Pentecost. It is named after the root word *pente*, which means fifty. Pentecost is known by Christians as the mighty presence of the indwelling Holy Spirit that took place fifty days after Jesus' resurrection and ten days after His return to heaven as related in Acts 1.

The event itself is described in Acts 2:1-18:

> **And when the day of Pentecost was fully come, they were all with one accord in one place. And suddenly there came a sound from heaven like a rushing mighty wind, and it filled all the house where they were sitting. And there appeared unto them cloven tongues as of fire, and it sat upon each of them. And they were all filled with the Holy Spirit, and began to speak with other tongues, as the Spirit gave them utterance. But Peter, standing up with the eleven, lifted up his voice, and said to them, "You men of Judaea, and all you who dwell at Jerusalem, be this known to you, and hearken to my words; for these are not drunk, as you suppose, seeing it is but [nine o'clock in the morning]. But this is that which was spoken through the prophet, Joel: 'And it shall come to pass in the last days, said God, I will pour out of my Spirit upon all flesh; and your sons and your daughters shall prophesy, and your young men shall see visions, and your old men shall dream dreams; and on my servants and on my handmaidens I will pour out in those days of my Spirit, and they shall prophesy.'"**

We can glean a number of facts from this correspondence between the Mosaic feasts of the spring and major events associated with Jesus' crucifixion.

First, Jesus' crucifixion was a *preplanned event.* Some false theologians are fond of asserting that Jesus was caught unawares by His arrest. That notion violates the clear teaching of the Old Testament.

Second, Scripture is not only truthful, it is *precise.* It is truthful in *every detail.* The days of Jesus' crucifixion, His resurrection, and the birth of the Church were set with precision over a thousand years before the events took place.

Third, the Church is an *integral part* of God's master plan. The mystery of Ephesians 5:25-31 wherein the Church is defined as the Bride of Christ is not trivial. It is *essential.*

Nine
The Road to Emmaus

This touching account in Luke 24:13-22 is notable on several levels. At its most poignant, it shows the loving intimacy with which the risen Jesus associates with the human race. He speaks to the two men as would a loving, compassionate Parent intent on comforting their grieving souls.

The story also shows how closely the Old Testament is associated with the New, and how highly Jesus regarded it. When He revealed to the two travelers how the Scriptures foretold Him, the only Scriptures that were available to them were those of the Old Testament.

> **And, behold, two of them went that same day to a village called Emmaus, which was from Jerusalem about seven and a half miles. And they talked together of all these things which had happened since Jesus' crucifixion.**
>
> **And it came to pass that, while they talked together and thought of these events, Jesus himself drew near, and went with them. But their eyes were prevented from recognizing Him. And He said to them, What manner of communications are these that you have one with another, as you walk, and are sad? And one of them, whose name was Cleopas, answered Him, saying, Are you only a stranger in Jerusalem, and have not known the things which are come to pass there in these days? And He said to them, What things? And they replied, Concerning Jesus of Nazareth, who was a prophet, mighty in deed and word before God and all the people; and how the chief priests and our rulers delivered Him to be condemned to death, and have crucified Him. But we hoped that it had been**

He who should have redeemed Israel; and, besides all this, today is the third day since these things were done. Yea, and certain women also of our company amazed us, who were early at the sepulcher; and when they did not find His body, they came, saying that they had also seen a vision of angels, who said that He was alive.

Then He said to them, O foolish ones, and slow of heart to believe all that the prophets have spoken! Ought not Christ to have suffered these things, and to enter into His glory? And beginning at Moses and all the prophets, He expounded to them, in all the scriptures, the things concerning Himself.

And they drew near to the village, to which they went; and He made as though He would have gone farther. But they constrained Him, saying, Abide with us; for it is toward evening, and the day is far spent. And He went in to linger with them. And it came to pass, as He sat eating with them, He took bread, and blessed it, and broke it, and gave it to them. And their eyes were opened, and they recognized Him, and He vanished out of their sight. And they said one to another, Did not our heart burn within us, while He talked with us along the way, and while He opened to us the scriptures?

Perhaps Jesus explained to the travelers how He had to die for their benefit, presenting that information in terms of Joseph in Genesis, and how Joseph suffered for the salvation of his brothers who hated him, and, in the end, how he did so willingly. He could have added the account of Abraham's attempted sacrifice of Isaac, and of how that story foretold the Father's suffering as He had to turn His head away in sorrow from the sin that Jesus had become on the cross. He also could have explained how Moses prophesied of Him in the institution of the Passover ceremony, and by becoming sin by holding up the bronze serpent on a pole to heal those in the wilderness who had been bitten by snakes. He could have topped that off with Psalm 22, which foretold in agonizing detail how it felt to be crucified.

Maybe Jesus also explained to them why He had to wait for four days before He resurrected Lazarus, and how in doing so he was prophesying of His own resurrection after the fourth millennium from Creation.

It could be that Jesus went on to speak of the love of God toward mankind, quoting from passages of the Song of Solomon to show the exquisitely romantic nature of that love. In looking forward to that day when the Church would become the Bride of Christ, Jesus could have noted His first miracle at the wedding in Cana, where He changed water into wine to make complete the joy of marriage.

Ten
Psalm 22

Psalm 22 was written by David about a thousand years before Christ and several hundred years before the punishment of crucifixion was known in Israel.

> **My God, my God, why have you forsaken me? Why are you so far from helping me, and from the words of my roaring?**
>
> **O my God, I cry in the daytime, but you hear not; and in the night season, and am not silent. But you are holy, O you who inhabits the praise of Israel. Our fathers trusted in you; they trusted, and you did deliver them. They cried to you, and were delivered; they trusted in you, and were not confounded. But I am a worm, and no man; a reproach of men, and despised by the people. All they who see me laugh me to scorn; they shoot out the lip, they shake the head, saying, He trusted on the Lord that he would deliver him; let him deliver him, seeing he delighted in him.**
>
> **But you are he who took me out of the womb; you made me hope upon my mother's breasts. I was cast upon you from the womb; you are my God from my mother's belly. Be not far from me; for trouble is near; for there is none to help. Many bulls have compassed me; strong bulls of Bashan have beset me round. They gaped upon me with their mouths, like a ravening and a roaring lion.**
>
> **I am poured out like water, and all my bones are out of joint: my heart is like wax; it is melted within me. My strength is dried up like a potsherd, and my tongue cleaves to my jaws; and you have brought me to the dust of death.**

For dogs have compassed me; the assembly of the wicked have enclosed me; they pierced my hands and my feet. I may count all my bones; they look and stare upon me. They part my garments among them, and cast lots for my vesture.

But be not far from me, O Lord. O my strength, hasten to help me. Deliver my soul from the sword; my darling from the power of the dog. Save me from the lion's mouth; for you have heard me from the horns of the wild unicorns. I will declare your name to my brothers; in the midst of the congregation will I praise you.

You who fear the Lord, praise him; all you, the seed of Jacob, glorify him; and fear him, all you, the seed of Israel. For he has not despised nor abhorred the affliction of the afflicted, neither has he hidden his face from him; but when he cried to him, he heard. My praise shall be of you in the great congregation; I will pay my vows before them who fear him. The meek shall be satisfied; they shall praise the Lord who seek him; your heart shall live forever. All the ends of the world shall remember and turn to the Lord; and all the kindreds of the nations shall worship before you. For the kingdom is the Lord's; and he is the governor among the nations. All they who are fat upon the earth shall eat and worship; all they who go down to the dust shall bow before him, and none can keep alive his own soul.

A seed shall serve him; it shall be accounted to the Lord for a generation. They shall come, and shall declare his righteousness to a people that shall be born, that he has done this.

Matthew 27:46 records Jesus, after suffering for at least three hours after He was nailed to the cross, as echoing the cry given by David at the start of his psalm:

And about three o'clock in the afternoon, Jesus cried with

a loud voice, saying, Eli, Eli, lama sabachthani? that is to say, My God, my God, why have you forsaken me?

It was noted in another volume of this series that God had to forsake Jesus, as He, in his moral perfection, could not look upon the sin that Jesus had personified. Jesus knew this beforehand, probably no later than while praying in the Garden of Gethsemane the evening before, and this knowledge may have contributed greatly to his agony there. He certainly agonized over it on the cross, but He also may have intended this utterance to point the future reader of Scripture to that Psalm.

Psalm 22 itself described in detail the physiological effects of crucifixion. The account has a supernatural element, as the Psalm preceded the punishment of crucifixion in Israel.

Eleven
The Migdal Edar Story

During one Christmas season our pastor gave his Church a special treat. He began reading the familiar Christmas story from Luke 2:7:

> **And she brought forth her first-born son, and wrapped him in swaddling clothes, and laid him in a manger, because there was no room for them in the inn.**

Pastor looked up at us and said, "How sad that man couldn't find a more appropriate place for the Son of God to be born. Plan B it was, then," which echoed our own thoughts. But then, smiling, he continued at Luke 2:8:

> **And there were in the same country shepherds abiding in the field, keeping watch over their flock by night. And, lo, the angel of the Lord came upon them, and the glory of the Lord shone round about them: and they were sore afraid. And the angel said to them, Fear not; for, behold, I bring you good tidings of great joy, which shall be to all people. For unto you is born this day in the city of David a Savior, which is Christ the Lord. And this shall be a sign to you: You shall find the babe wrapped in swaddling clothes, lying in a manger.**

As our pastor recited this oft-told story, I formed my own familiar mental imagery: a large grassy field with flocks of sheep mixed with cattle, and the barn where Mary, Joseph and Jesus dwelt surrounded by the usual barnyard animals: cows, donkeys and, yes, perhaps a sheep or two. My mind drifted into a contemplation of the poverty surrounding Jesus' birth. Of course the setting was appropriate, given the humble character of Jesus' sojourn in the flesh. But being born in a manger certainly couldn't have been plan A for Joseph's family.

But then our pastor embellished on the story. It wasn't well known, he said, that the region near Bethlehem where Jesus was born was a rather special place. He quoted another familiar passage, the prophecy in Micah 5:2 foretelling of Jesus' birth in Bethlehem:

> **But you, Bethlehem Ephrathah, though you be little among the thousands of Judah, yet out of you shall he come forth unto me that is to be ruler in Israel; whose goings forth have been from of old, from everlasting.**

Pastor didn't stop there. He went on to read another passage out of Micah, verse 4:8, which is much less well-known:

> **And you O watchtower of the flock [Migdal Edar], the strong hold of the daughter of Zion, unto you shall it come, even the first dominion; the kingdom shall come to the daughter of Jerusalem.**

Before commenting further on the function of Migdal Edar, pastor took us back to Genesis 35:19-21:

> **And Rachel died, and was buried in the way to Ephrath, which is Bethlehem. And Jacob set a pillar upon her grave: that is the pillar of Rachel's grave to this day. And Israel journeyed, and spread his tent beyond the tower of Edar.**

Pastor put his Bible aside and looked at his congregation as if he had something momentous to tell us. And well he did. Finding his voice, he said that the region where Jesus was born was under the watchtower of the flock, a special lookout of the shepherds there because of the importance of that particular place. It was, he said with emotion, the place where lambs were born and raised for the Passover sacrifice. The manger of Jesus' birth was, in fact, the birthing place for these special lambs, so maybe while it didn't represent plan A for Joseph, it certainly did for God.

Pastor topped off that shocking disclosure by saying that,

according to the Passover account in Exodus 12, the lambs had to be perfect in every way. When birthed, they tended to struggle some, putting themselves at risk to injury. There was a procedure in place to prevent this: upon their birth, these lambs were wrapped in swaddling clothes.

I was so enthusiastic about this revelation that I attempted to share it with other Christians, some of whom were rather cynical about it. It seemed that if this were to be true, they already would have known about it. Faced with that negativity, I pursued the topic on my own on the Internet, where I found a wealth of commentary regarding it, all of which was positive and some of which furnished excellent justification for accepting it as truth. I recommend the interested reader to do the same, simply by Googling "Migdal Edar", or, alternatively, "Migdal Eder".

Volume Four

God's Feminine Side

Contents

Preface: 187

One: In the Image of God 189

Two: Creation's Epic Love 193

Three: The "He" Issue 197

Four: Arguments Based on False Premises 200

Five: Scripture Exalts Femininity 204

Six: The Significance of a Feminine Holy Spirit 207

Seven: Creation's Ultimate Purpose 210

Eight: The Bride of Christ 214

Nine: The Nature of Our Marriage to Jesus Christ 218

Ten: The Early Moravian Church 222

Eleven: Ten Reasons for a Feminine Holy Spirit 225

Twelve: Why Should it Matter? 231

Preface

The integrating theme for the present volume, Volume Four, is the romance that supports and deepens the most vital attribute of God, love. The love that is intrinsic to God is intimately related to gender and the functional differentiation among the Members of the Trinitarian Godhead. This volume explores the nature of God's love and the relationship among love, function and gender.

God's enormous capacity for love points to the unity within the Godhead. It also puts gender at the forefront of His interaction with man, now and in the future, as hinted at in Matthew 19:4-6:

> **And [Jesus] answered and said to them, Have you not read that He who made them at the beginning, made them male and female; and said, For this cause shall a man leave father and mother, and shall cleave to his wife, and they two shall be one flesh: Wherefore, they are no more two, but one flesh. What, therefore, God has joined together, let not man put asunder.**

The gender-based unity within the Godhead is far deeper than the benign fellowship associated with an *agape* relationship as a non-gendered relationship would demand it to be. It represents instead the form of family with all the romance and mutual possession that this more intense form suggests.

One
In the Image of God

Man is typically treated as the primary subject of Genesis 1:26 and 27. This passage is routinely viewed as descriptive of the manner in which God created man to reflect certain attributes of His own. These attributes are generally considered to be related to character and intellect, chiefly man's personality, rationality, and morality.

> **And God said, Let us make man in our image, after our likeness; and let them have dominion over the fish of the sea, and over the fowl of the air, and over the cattle, and over all the earth, and over every creeping thing that creeps upon the earth. So God created man in his own image, in the image of God created he him; male and female created he them.**

Reference to man's gendered creation is usually omitted or, at best, treated as incidental. But there it is in Scripture, in black and white, in a context that discourages it from being disregarded with such appalling ease. This passage speaks as much about God as of man. The attribute of gender isn't trivial, but instead is presented as among the most profound of the attributes of which man was made in God's image.

And to what end have we denied this beautiful attribute to God? So that we may maintain a distance from Him in direct opposition to what He desires in His relationship with us? So that we can equate purity with chastity, when the two are manifestly different concepts? The key to this blatant falsehood is found in the end of the passage above: . . . *"And they were both naked, the man and his wife, and were not ashamed."*

As I had noted in *Marching to a Worthy Drummer*, it is the shame, not the act, that has driven us to think of gender as inappropriate to God. And the shame came not from God but from Adam's fall. It persists to this day, and prevents most of us from perceiving the Trinitarian Godhead in all Its beauty and glory.

In Genesis 2:18 and 21-24 is another passage that tends to be trivialized. As is commonly accepted, God the Father existed forever. Our minds, particularly in the material realm, are too limited to grasp any more of the nature of the Father, the Divine Will. But that same limitation doesn't apply to the Holy Spirit, as Scripture itself gives us a clue as to Her origin. In Genesis 2, Scripture brings out details for emphasis of Eve's creation out of Adam. This account of the creation of Eve out of Adam is commonly but quite mistakenly treated as a secondary or afterthought account of the creation of man, simply providing additional detail to the first account in Genesis 1:26 and 27.

> **And the Lord God said, It is not good that the man should be alone; I will make him a help fit for him. . . And the Lord God caused a deep sleep to fall upon Adam, and he slept: and he took one of his ribs, and closed up the flesh instead thereof; and the rib, which the Lord God had taken from man, made he a woman, and brought her unto the man. And Adam said, This is now bone of my bones, and flesh of my flesh; she shall be called Woman, because she was taken out of Man. Therefore shall a man leave his father and his mother, and shall cleave to his wife, and they shall be one flesh.**

But the repetition of the latter part of this passage by both Jesus, in Matthew 19, and Paul in Ephesians 5, places it far above the trivial in importance. This account of the creation of Eve out of Adam, rather than furnishing incidental details of man's creation, was far more likely to have been included in Scripture for emphasis as describing the romance of the loving formation of the Holy Spirit out of the essence of the Father.

The thought that this portion of the creation epic might be

descriptive of the Godhead Itself points back to the very beginning, Genesis 1:1-5:

> **In the beginning God created the heaven and the earth. And the earth was without form, and void; and darkness was upon the face of the deep. And the Spirit of God moved upon the face of the waters.**
>
> **And God said, Let there be light: and there was light. And God saw the light, that it was good: and God divided the light from the darkness. And God called the light Day, and the darkness he called Night. And the evening and the morning were the first day.**

In this first passage of Scripture, the Holy Spirit is seen responding to the Father in giving birth to the first spoken Word of God, the Light. But that is precisely what John said in verses 1:1-5 of the Prologue to his Gospel of Jesus Christ:

> **In the beginning was the Word, and the Word was with God, and the Word was God. The same was in the beginning with God. All things were made by him; and without him was not anything made that was made. In him was life, and the life was the light of men. And the light shone in darkness; and the darkness comprehended it not.**

We in the Church have been conditioned to believe, in opposition to the notion of Jesus being a created Being, that Jesus eternally co-existed with the Father. But that comes from the various Christian creeds, not from Scripture. Scripture itself, in Revelation 3:14 where Jesus describes Himself, stands in plain opposition to that notion:

> **And to the angel of the church of the Laodiceans write: These things say the Amen, the faithful and true witness, the beginning of the creation of God.**

Can it be that the Holy Spirit, in union with the Father, did indeed give birth to Jesus Christ? John, in Chapter Three of his Gospel, attributes spiritual birth to the Holy Spirit. The details of the Holy Spirit's participation in creation are provided in Proverbs 8:22-31:

> **The Lord possessed me in the beginning of his way, before His works of old. I was set up from everlasting, from the beginning, or ever the earth was. When there were no depths, I was brought forth – when there were no fountains abounding with water. Before the mountains were settled, before the hills, was I brought forth; while as yet He had not made the earth, nor the fields, nor the highest part of the dust of the world. When He prepared the heavens, I was there; when He set a compass upon the face of the depth; when He established the clouds above; when He strengthened the fountains of the deep; when He gave to the sea its decree, that the waters would not pass His commandment; when He appointed the foundations of the earth,**
>
> **Then I was by Him, as one brought up with Him; and I was daily His delight, rejoicing always before Him, rejoicing in the habitable part of His earth; and my delight was with the sons of men.**

Why did God emphasize the detail of Eve's formation out of Adam? And why, if it was not good for the man to be without a complementary woman, would it be good for God Himself to be so, as theologians commonly assume? Could it be that at one stage before the beginning of time all the attributes of the Godhead resided within the Father alone, and that in self-denial the Father parted an element of Himself to form the Holy Spirit as a separate but complementary Entity in order that love transcend all other attributes of God? Could it be that what He lost in the parting He regained in love according to the words of Adam that a man shall cleave unto his wife and they two shall be one?

Two
Creation's Epic Love

In re-reading the Creation epic of Genesis 1, I was rather surprised to see in it an intense and beautiful love story. I was more surprised that I hadn't picked up on that sooner, as my view of the Godhead and Creation dovetailed quite well into that understanding.

That same understanding is emphasized throughout Scripture itself. 1 John 4:8 defines God as the very essence of love:

He that does not love does not know God; for God is love.

Scripture virtually pleads with us to apply that understanding to the relationship between the Father and the Holy Spirit.

With respect to Creation, I understand Scripture in the original to be inerrant and inspired of God as both Paul, in 2 Timothy 3 and Peter, in 2 Peter 1, have claimed. That means that I accept the Creation epic as truth, and its competing worldview, (macro)evolution, to be false. That clash with secular wisdom led me into a rather lengthy research of modern molecular biology which, in the end, more than justified my rejection of evolution on purely scientific grounds as itself being mythical in nature and not to be trusted.

With evolution out of the way, the Creation epic stood boldly as an account that deserved much reflection. From the many hours spent in consideration of Genesis 1, I eventually reached an understanding that not only reconciled a large number of ill-fitting odds and ends regarding the nature of the Godhead, but also managed to blow my mind with its simple, majestic elegance. I couldn't have come up with the ideas myself, so I give credit where credit is due: to the Holy Spirit and the Wisdom She embodies. I have written of my vision of the Godhead before in numerous places, so here I will limit myself to a brief review of what was touched on in a previous chapter: the Godhead as I perceive it consists of three Divine Members, Father, Holy Spirit and Son, tightly united as a Divine Family, and each with different but complementary roles: the Father as the Divine Will, the Holy Spirit as the Divine Means, and the Son as the Divine Reality.

That view of the Godhead implies much about the relationship between gender and love as well as about the origin and function of the Trinity. There are many forms of love, as reflected in the several names for love in the Greek language: *fileo, agape, eros.* Of these differing forms, *eros* or gendered love is unique in its possessive nature. That quality of mutual ownership grants gendered love an intensity and passion of an altogether higher level than the other forms. Love of that nature is fervent.

The functional relationship involving Will, Means and Reality, where the functionally male Father, in marital union with the complementary functionally feminine Means, gave birth to the Reality, is an intrinsically gendered one. The intimacy involved in this functional relationship identifies gendered love as the driving force behind all of creation.

At its core, the nature of this functional relationship evokes the notion of complementary otherhood, where the other responds to initiation and operates in complementary harmony with it. The joyful execution of this teaming activity elevates love to beauty of the highest order. When it is performed in selflessness, it becomes noble as well.

If complementary otherhood is considered to be the essence of gender, virtually all of creation exhibits that characteristic. Even at the cellular level, as biologists have recently discovered, cell division involves the search for a complementary other. Below that level as well, a complete atom has matching numbers of protons and electrons; a mismatch of these causes the atom to search for balance.

The ubiquitous display of love in Creation verifies Paul's words in Romans 1:19 and 20:

Because that which may be known of God is manifest in them; for God has shown it to them. For the invisible things of Him from the creation of the world are clearly seen, being understood by the things that are made, even His eternal power and Godhead, so that they are without excuse;

It was with Adam and Eve that God brought gender and love together in the form that most closely matched that which exists within the Godhead. Had not the Fall of man occurred, man would have been free of the numerous perversions that produce debauchery in the place of love. Because of Jesus, man can look forward to a restoration of love to its original meaning.

It is fervor of this order that lies at the center of Moses' *Shema* in Deuteronomy 6:4 and 5, connecting the oneness of God with love of a passionate nature:

Hear, O Israel: The Lord our God is one Lord: and you shall love the Lord your God with all your heart, and with all your soul, and with all your might.

Gendered love and its associated fervor is why Scripture describes the spiritual union between Jesus and His Church in terms of marriage, and why Jesus, in Matthew 22, repeats the commandment of Moses to love God with passion and labels it the greatest of commandments.

If we look beyond the level of the individual to the composite Church, we see that there is nothing in Scripture to suggest, as do many pastors both now and in the distant past, that this marriage is no more than a figure of speech connoting a relationship that in actuality lacks gender and its corresponding intensity. A profound joy of gendered love is implied by Jesus' turning water into wine through His first miracle at the wedding in Cana. Jesus obviously is anticipating in His marriage a far more intimate bond with His Church than a genderless relationship would produce.

The desire of God, as revealed in the Bible, to endow us with appealing personal qualities of character, speaks to His loving plan for His Church as Jesus' worthy partner in her future role as the Bride of Christ.

Three
The "He" Issue

Something's definitely wrong about the Church's current understanding of the Holy Spirit. A recent poll of evangelicals revealed that 68% of us consider the Holy Spirit to be an impersonal force, contradicting Scripture and indicating the shallowness of a large group of Christians that would permit the movie *Star Wars* to influence their perception of God to such an extent. But shallowness isn't the only culprit. Theologians with advanced degrees in Divinity admit to being stumped by the nature of the Holy Spirit.

The problem is at once both simpler and more profound than confusion or shallowness of thought. The primary source of our misapprehension of the Holy Spirit has been with us for a very long time as is our presupposition, inculcated by the Church herself, that the Holy Spirit is either genderless or weakly masculine.

With regard to the common perception of the Holy Spirit's masculinity, the enormous hostile animal in the room is the use, in virtually all translations and versions of the Bible, of masculine pronouns in reference to the Holy Spirit.

Examples of this include John 14:16, 14:26, 15:26, 16:7 and 8 and 13-15, and Hebrews 3:7 and 10:15, although some verses reference the Holy Spirit as neuter. These masculine references constitute the most common argument against a feminine Holy Spirit.

The most likely reason for all those "he"s in the Bible is the certainty that the Bible we use today does not represent the original. While I believe that the original autographs of Scripture are inspired and inerrant, I don't extend that trust to the various translations and versions that are available to us today. There is ample reason to suspect that a gender switch took place around the time of Constantine under the misguided motive of purifying the heavenly domain from all connotations of sexuality. Many well-known Church Fathers at that time have conveyed, through their writings, their repulsion of matters involving gender and their equation of purity with chastity.

We know that the Hebrew name of Spirit, *ruah,* is feminine, while the Greek equivalent is neuter and the Latin equivalent is masculine. These language-based gender differences may partially account for the gender switch in the translations. The more likely scenario, unpleasant as it may be to consider, is that the switch was deliberate. The Jewish religion had, for the most part, viewed the Holy Spirit as feminine, as did a large group of early Christians, as demonstrated by the femininity of the Holy Spirit in the Syriac Scriptures. In addition, the Sinaitic Palimpsest, the original writing of which is thought to be close or identical to the Gospel that Paul taught from, depicts Jesus in John 14:26 as describing the Holy Spirit as feminine.

There are multiple reasons why it is thought that the switch was deliberate: first, the neuter description of the Arm of the Lord in Isaiah 51:9 and 10 is known to be a deliberate switch from the feminine; second is the motive: the prevailing sexual debauchery of the secular society surrounding the Christian community led the Christian leaders to set the Church apart in perfect purity, even to the extent that motivated some early Christian males to attempt to castrate themselves. Sometimes, as was possibly the case with Origen (according to Eusebius), the attempt was successful. Many of the early Church Fathers, including Justin Martyr, Clement of Alexandria, Tertullian, Origen, Ambrose of Milan, and, most famously, Augustine, vehemently equated purity with chastity. Some of them were misogynistic as well. Supporting that urge to switch genders was the pressure of numerous heresies that confronted the early Church. One important threat to the Church was Gnosticism, which favored a femininity of the Holy Spirit. The heresies embraced by the Gnostics placed their belief in a feminine Holy Spirit, which was common to Jewish faith and early Christian expressions in general, in disrepute. The rejection of gender in God seems to have been a classic case of throwing the baby out with the bathwater.

The switch to the masculinity of the Holy Spirit was probably complete around the time of Constantine or not much later.

It's a matter of concern how reluctant the Church leadership has been throughout the past several centuries to see God in the light of His Word rather than blindly adhering to Church doctrine in the face of Scriptural passages that are inconsistent with dogma. There are plenty of indications in Scripture, even in the versions we use today, to support the femininity of the Holy Spirit in opposition to the use of male pronouns in reference to Her. All it takes to see this is scripturally-compatible eyes.

We revere Christians of the past who had the insight and courage to reform the Church in the face of the corruption that accompanied her political power. But these Church Greats were human just like the rest of us. None of them was perfect, nor were their insights complete. Martin Luther, for example, was a rabid anti-Semite; he also thought that Jesus had an affair with Mary Magdalene despite obvious Scriptural reasons to the contrary. Those who are inclined to avoid any questioning of the Bible as it stands now should apply that same inclination to Luther, who lashed out against the Book of James and supported the removal of the Book of Wisdom and others from the Protestant canon of Scripture.

Four
Arguments Based on False Premises

If we've managed to shove the 800-pound "He"-issue gorilla out the door, there's still a few 200-pound animals lurking in the corners of the room. They supposedly refute the notion of a feminine Holy Spirit. But do they? Are they even relevant to the issue?

Scriptural references to gender neutrality: Two such references stand out in particular: Galatians 3:28, which declares that in the spiritual realm humans are neither male nor female, and Matthew 22:30, in which Jesus asserts that in the resurrection, men and women neither marry nor are given in marriage. These passages are frequently interpreted as declaring that the realm of God in heaven is genderless.

The obvious alternative interpretation, which also is a more logical one, is that while individual humans aren't gendered in the spiritual realm, their aggregate, as the Church, is indeed gendered, that gender being female. Paul himself, in describing spiritual gifts in 1 Corinthians 12, depicts spiritual humans as components of the church, likening them to body parts such as ears. Body parts of themselves are not gendered. In the material realm, the exercise of gender requires a multitude of body parts, including the mind, interacting in close cooperation. Scripture indicates that this is precisely how gender works in the spiritual realm. That being the likely case, the Scriptural references noted above make no statement whatsoever about a supposed lack of gender in the spiritual realm.

Wisdom associated with the Holy Father as a personal attribute:

To those who consider the Godhead to be either masculine or genderless, the intra-Godhead bond is seen in somewhat similar terms to that which may be found in a corporate boardroom. In that context, in Jeremiah 10:12, where God describes His creation as being made by His power and wisdom, those descriptors are naturally interpreted as His personal attributes.

But there is an alternate interpretation that not only makes more logical sense, but is beautifully descriptive. In that alternate interpretation which again is obvious, the Father and Holy Spirit are considered to be a tightly-bonded couple, each possessing the other in a romantic relationship. Under that alternate understanding, the Holy Spirit, along with Her attributes of Wisdom and Power, are naturally seen as an intimately-loved possession of the Father, and therefore belong to Him as part of Him in the same context as Adam's understanding of Eve and his description of two joining to become one.

The personification of Wisdom in Proverbs is often interpreted as simply a literary device: Those who would deny the femininity of the Holy Spirit correspondingly deny the Personhood of Wisdom. Instead, they view the feminine voice of Wisdom in Proverbs as a literary embellishment of the wisdom of God.

An alternate and more reasonable interpretation exists here as well. It is supported by Jesus Himself who in Luke 7:35, in opposition to the interpretation of wisdom as a mere literary device, confers motherhood on Wisdom. Motherhood is an eminently personal attribute, was well as being a hallmark of femininity. Jesus more emphatically personifies wisdom in Luke 11:49 and 50, having Her speak and perform actions.

Femininity is viewed as inappropriate to Godhood: This slanderous, misogynistic rebuke of womanhood is surprisingly common among theologians. Paul's commentary in 1 Corinthians 14 on the role of women in Church ("it is a shame for women to speak in the church") is often taken as justification for this view.

Given Paul's beautiful description of the future spiritual woman, the Church, in Ephesians 5, and his friendship with many women and use of them in Church activities, his probable intent with regard to womanhood is much more benign than the usual interpretation of this passage would suggest.

My view in opposition to that stance attributed to Paul, as I had noted in *Marching to a Worthy Drummer*, sees that Scriptural passage as supportive of a feminine Holy Spirit rather than the other way around. Eve's error in the Garden was a transgression of her proper role as a type of the feminine Holy Spirit by failing to limit her responsive role to that of the will of either her husband Adam or of the Holy Father.

God is above the passion that a gendered Godhead would suggest: This view arose from the attempt to purify the Church of all sexuality. It was supported by Augustine and other Church Fathers and, centuries later, was formalized by medieval cleric Jerome Zanchius in his tome on Absolute Predestination. This work consulted very little, if any, Scripture.

Scripture itself provides a rich source of alternate viewpoints, all of which endow God with passion, including love, possession, anger and sorrow. Examples include Exodus 32:10, Hosea 1, Matthew 19, 21, 23 and 26, and Luke 24. Jesus' response to the Pharisees in Matthew 19 indicated a familiarity beyond His human form with love and its implications regarding inter-gender relationships. He was fully aware of the passionate nature of the marital bond and went so far as to claim (Matthew 19:6) that the source of the bond was God Himself.

The grammatical "she" in the Hebrew language does not necessarily indicate femininity: There has been much ado made by deniers of femininity in the Godhead about the fact that some objects are given feminine designators when no actual femininity is involved. The situation here is similar to the standard practice in English of calling a genderless object such as a ship "she".

This argument would typically apply to objects, but not to sentient beings such as humans or Members of our Trinitarian God. If indeed the personification of Wisdom in Proverbs did not refer to an actual Person but was simply a literary device, then this argument might apply. But, as already noted, the Holy Spirit is indeed a Person within the Godhead.

Moreover, the gender distinction in Hebrew (the original versions of the manuscripts) is more rigidly applied in the modifiers, which very often define the Holy Spirit as feminine. This important point is often overlooked by those who would claim that a noun in Hebrew doesn't necessarily depict gender.

The bottom line is that for every argument of which I am aware that calls into question the femininity of the Holy Spirit there is at least one alternate explanation, often considerably more reasonable than the original argument, that negates the argument itself and supports the notion of a feminine Holy Spirit. Furthermore, where the argument references Scripture, the rebuttal also appeals to Scripture.

As I review these arguments I find myself thinking of those responsible for establishing and maintaining Church doctrine in terms of the Pharisees of Jesus' day. Did the Jews get it wrong in refusing to see Jesus as God? So did we in refusing to see the Holy Spirit as the feminine complement of the Father. Perhaps God wishes us to be a little less holier-than-thou regarding the transgressions of the Jews.

These irritating red-herring claims advanced against a feminine Holy Spirit also bring to mind "Pauli's Sneer" as recalled by William Dembsky in his book "Intelligent Design," wherein Wolfgang Pauli, in commenting on an intellectual exercise performed by a peer, claimed that "It isn't even false!"

Five
Scripture Exalts Femininity

Having dispensed with the alleged animals in the room, we'll turn next to a review of some elements of Scripture that support our view of the femininity of the Holy Spirit.

Spiritual birth: In John 3, Jesus describes the Holy Spirit as giving spiritual birth. Birth is an eminently feminine function.

Original Scriptural references to femininity: As several qualified scholars have noted, the feminine gender is applied to the Holy Spirit in the original Hebrew Old Testament Scripture and in the original Aramaic and Syriac New Testament Scriptures. These references include Genesis 1:2, numerous instances in Job and Judges, Isaiah 51:9 and 10, John 14:26 (Sinaitic Palimpsest) and Romans 9:25. In the instances cited, the application of feminine descriptors went beyond mere grammatical convention. Among these scholars are experts in the languages appropriate to the original Scriptural passages, including Drs. R.P. Nettelhorst and JohannesVan Oort, whose commentaries regarding the femininity of the Holy Spirit are available on the Internet.

The Shekinah Glory: The Shekinah Glory, seen as fire and smoke from God, indwelt the Tabernacle in the Wilderness (Exodus 40) and Solomon's Temple (1 Kings 8) at their dedications. This indwelling was a type of the Holy Spirit's indwelling of the human temples of believers, beginning at the first Pentecost following Jesus' resurrection (1 Corinthians 3:16, 2 Corinthians 6:16 and Ephesians 2:19-22). The Shekinah Glory is grammatically feminine and was seen as feminine in Jewish tradition as well.

The marriage of Christ with His Church: In Ephesians 5:31 and

32, Paul plainly writes that in the spiritual realm, Jesus will marry His Church. His manner of description identifies that marriage as more than a trivial play on words. There and elsewhere, the Church is identified as feminine. In Romans 7:4, Paul reveals that this marital union will bear fruit. If Jesus, a Member of the Trinitarian Godhead, marries the gendered Church, it is likely that the other Members are married as well. This would require that the Holy Spirit be feminine. Jesus' commitment to this future marriage also explains His celibacy during His sojourn on Earth.

The femininity of Wisdom in Proverbs: The gender of Wisdom in Proverbs is consistently feminine throughout. The linkage of Wisdom with creation, particularly in Proverbs 3 and 8, suggests that Wisdom represents the Holy Spirit.

The linkage of Wisdom with the Holy Spirit in the Book of Wisdom: The Book of Wisdom, which remains canonical in the Catholic Scriptures, depicts Wisdom as the Holy Spirit and feminine.

The executive function of the Holy Spirit: The Holy Spirit is described in Scripture in the role of executive to the Father. The executive function of the Holy Spirit is acknowledged by multiple mainstream theologians. This responsive role to the Father's will is feminine in nature.

The creation of Adam and the formation of Eve are suggestive of the femininity of the Holy Spirit: The creation of mankind as gender-differentiated in the image of God (Genesis 1:26 and 27) is suggestive of the gendered nature of the Godhead and consequent femininity of the Holy Spirit; the follow-on description of the formation of Eve out of Adam (Genesis 2:18-25) probably is a repetition for the sake of emphasis instead of its usual awkward and confusing interpretation as a redundant secondary creation account. The account may well be a type of events within the Godhead Itself. Genesis 1:26 and 27 are even more overtly suggestive of the gendered nature of the Godhead.

The romantic nature of the Song of Solomon: The Song of Solomon, considered by many Bible commentators to be representative of the romantic and passionate nature of the marriage between Christ and His Church, depicts the Church as feminine. The romance in Songs must typify either the relationship between Christ and His Church, or between the Father and the Holy Spirit, or both; otherwise it wouldn't belong in the Bible. The same comment made with regard to the marriage between Christ and His Church in Ephesians 5 applies here: if one Member of the Godhead marries, it is suggestive that marriage applies to all within the Godhead.

Monotheism vs. the Trinitarian Godhead: Christianity is a firmly monotheistic religion. In the face of this, it also acknowledges a Trinitarian Godhead. Only in the context of marriage and family can the declared oneness of God (Deuteronomy 6:4) be intuitively reconciled with a Trinitarian Godhead. I personally have been exposed to admissions of confusion by multiple theologians who, while not accepting the family nature of the Godhead, remain oblivious to the importance of the unnecessary paradox that results from their view.

Biblical proscriptions against the gay lifestyle and other violations of a single male/single female marital bond: In the context of a genderless or all-male Godhead, the proscriptions against the gay lifestyle in Leviticus 18 and 20 and Romans 1 appear to be arbitrary, as does the Seventh Commandment regarding adultery; in the context of a gendered masculine and feminine Godhead, on the other hand, the gay lifestyle would represent a violation of the type of the Godhead Itself.

Six
The Significance of a Feminine Holy Spirit

A major and rather immediate result of perceiving the Holy Spirit's femininity is the replacement of confusion with understanding. Once that connection is made, the Godhead's attribute of Unity in the face of Trinity is no longer a logical inconsistency. The understanding itself quickly emerges with the depth of full intuition, so boldly as to evoke not only a sense of functional differentiation among the Members of the Godhead, but also to resolve the former paradox of unity in Trinity and to encourage the assignment of specific functions to each of them.

The Trinity, given the inclusion of femininity, at once is seen in a Family context. Viewing the Godhead in context of Family, the Family Entity is seen to reside above the three Members of the Trinity, representing the oneness of God in loving relationship, to which the individual Members are subordinate. In that setting, the Trinitarian Godhead represents the unity of Family, whereas the individual Members of the Godhead represent the three familiar functional roles of Father, Mother and Son.

In the context of function, the Father naturally represents the Divine Will in accordance with that assignment as given in Scripture, whereas the Holy Spirit responds to that Will by furnishing the Means by which it may be actualized. Pursuing that context, the Son represents the result of the union between Will and Means, being the Will's actuality in Creation.

Key to understanding the Divine Family is the notion of

complementary otherness implicit in the relationship. The importance of complementary otherness is its very partiality, which in the incompleteness of one partner without the other removes the exaltation of the individual. Even, or perhaps especially in the Godhead, ego is deliberately minimized by design.

It is my conviction that the Father Himself, in his own selfless nobility, willed the implementation of His subordination to Family, with love as His motive for doing so. Parting Himself in two, He voluntarily limited His unrivaled personal sovereignty over the universe to a shared arrangement with that element of His former essence that we call the Holy Spirit. This parting created gender differentiation within the Godhead Itself. As the Complementary Other to the masculine initiative essence of the Divine Father, the Holy Spirit necessarily possesses the responsive gender attribute of femininity.

This Family-based gendered view of the Godhead elevates several verses of Genesis 1 and 2 beyond mere descriptive images of mankind, as we are used to understanding them, to very elemental depictions of the Godhead Itself.

Note in Genesis 2 that God described the state of Adam being without a companion as not good. Being without a feminine companion would render Adam, for all practical purposes, genderless. The attribute of gender was important to God, which suggests that God considers gender and its exercise as intrinsically good, rather than bad. The passage goes out of its way to make that plain. In an interpretation more in line with what the Scripture suggests, the formation of Eve from Adam echoes rather distinctly the Father's extraction of the Holy Spirit from His own essence.

Scripture tells us that before man's fall from grace the primal couple was not ashamed of their nakedness. It was only after the Fall that sexual shame came into the picture.

In Matthew 19 Jesus repeats Adam's statement in Genesis 2 regarding Adam and Eve's gender-based relationship in which the man cleaves to his wife, but attributes the act to God Himself, concluding that what God had put together, no man should separate.

In the like passage in Ephesians 5, Paul repeats the event of God having made man in male and female versions for the purpose of the man's leaving father and mother and cleaving to his wife to become one flesh. Then he makes the starkly momentous statement that he's really talking about the relationship between Jesus and His Church.

Adam's quote about leaving father and mother and cleaving to his wife is obviously important to God, not only because it was echoed by Jesus and Paul, but makes the claim that Jesus, as a Member of the Godhead, will marry the Church. The implication in this is that if gender union applies to one of its Members, it places the attribute of gender squarely in the Godhead, suggesting that gender is an attribute shared by the Father and Holy Spirit as well. Moreover, gender appeals to our intuition, making sense of the relationships within the Godhead. It is easy to picture the fruit of the union between Father and Holy Spirit being the Son Jesus, the glorious actualization of the Will as given birth by the Divine Means.

Here's the great beauty of what the Father did in his selfless parting of Himself to form the Holy Spirit: what He gave up in doing that He regained in love in union with Her. *That* is the true significance of Adams words: "a Man shall cleave unto to his Wife, and they two shall be one Spirit."

Just as Adam's side was rent to form Eve, and as the Church was formed out of Jesus' pierced side on the cross, so did the Father part Himself to form the Holy Spirit, with Whom He united in love to form Jesus Christ.

God intended our relationship with Him to be intimate and romantic. Only through our perception of the Godhead in Family terms can we begin to appreciate and love God as Jesus calls us to do in Matthew 22:37 and 38:

> **. . .You shall love the Lord, your God, with all your heart, and with all your soul, and with all your mind. This is the first and great commandment.**

Seven

Creation's Ultimate Purpose

God's act of Creation was an epic of love that started with the begetting of Jesus Christ, the Light and the first Word of God, who was glorified thereafter with the colorful clothing of Creation itself.

There is a deeper purpose behind creation than material beauty. That purpose is to clothe Jesus Christ not only with the apparel of Creation, but to propagate Love, the essence of God, by endowing Jesus Christ with a Bride of His own, the Church, with whom He can continue the epic of Creation as did the original Will and Spirit.

Scripture captures this notion in Matthew 9:14 and 15, Romans 7:4, and Ephesians 5:28-32, leaving no room for a lesser understanding:

> **Then came to [Jesus] the disciples of John, saying, Why do we and the Pharisees fast often, but thy disciples fast not? And Jesus said unto them, Can the children of the bridechamber mourn, as long as the bridegroom is with them? But the days will come, when the bridegroom shall be taken from them, and then shall they fast.**
>
> **Wherefore, my brethren, you also are become dead to the law by the body of Christ, that you should be married to another, even to him who is raised from the dead, that we should bring forth fruit to God.**
>
> **So ought men to love their wives as their own bodies. He that loves his wife loves himself. For no man ever yet hated his own flesh, but nourishes and cherishes it, even as the Lord the church; for we are members of his body, of his flesh, and of his bones.**

> **For this cause shall a man leave his father and mother, and shall be joined unto his wife, and they two shall be one flesh. This is a great mystery, but I speak concerning Christ and the church.**

Note from Romans 7:4 above that the marriage will be consummated, being far more than symbolic or a mere figure of speech. Further Scriptural confirmation of this future promise to the Church may be found in the preview of it in Jesus' parable of the marriage in Matthew 22, the wedding at Cana, as described in John 2, and the Lamb's wife in Revelation 21.

Just as Scripture suggests that the Holy Spirit was brought forth out of the essence of the Father as He parted Himself to form Her, and as Scripture describes Eve as having been formed from Adam's pierced side, so did Jesus bring forth the Church from His pierced side as he suffered on the cross on Her behalf.

In his book *Destined for the Throne*, reviewed and recommended by Billy Graham, Paul Billheimer expands with eloquence on the theme of Jesus' marriage to the Church. Excerpts from Billheimer's Introduction and Chapter 1, as extracted from my book *Marching to a Worthy Drummer,* are given below:

> **The following chapters present what some consider a totally new and unique cosmology. The author's primary thesis is that the *one* purpose of the universe from all eternity is the production and preparation of an Eternal Companion for the Son, called the Bride, the Lamb's Wife. Since she is to share the throne of the universe with her Divine Lover and Lord as a judicial equal, she must be trained, educated, and prepared for her queenly role.**
>
> **From this it is implicit that romance is at the heart of the universe and is key to all existence. From all eternity God purposed that at some time in the future His Son should have an Eternal Companion, described by John the Revelator as "the bride, the Lamb's wife" (Rev. 21:9) John further revealed that this Eternal Companion in**

God's eternal purpose is to share the Bridegroom's throne following the Marriage Supper of the Lamb (Rev. 3:21). Here we see the ultimate purpose, the climactic goal of history.

As in the case of Adam, God saw that it was not good for His Son to be alone. From the very beginning it was God's plan and purpose that out of the riven side of His Son should come an Eternal Companion to sit by His side upon the throne of the universe as a bona fide partner, a judicial equal, to share with Him His sovereign power and authority over His eternal kingdom. "Fear not, little flock, for it is your Father's good pleasure to give you the kingdom." (Luke 12:32) "To him that overcometh will I grant to sit with me in my throne, even as I also overcame and am set down with my Father in his throne."(Rev. 3:21)

To be given a kingdom is more than to internalize kingdom principles and ethics. That is only one phase of it. To be given a kingdom is to be made a king, to be invested with authority over a kingdom. That this is God's glorious purpose for the Church is authenticated and confirmed by Paul in 1 Corinthians 6:2-3: "Do ye not know that the saints shall judge the world? . . . Know ye not that we shall judge angels?" This is an *earnest* of what Jesus meant when He said, "The glory that thou gavest me I have given them." (John 17:22)

This royalty and rulership is no hollow, empty, figurative, symbolical, or emblematic thing. It is not a figment of the imagination. The Church, the Bride, the Eternal Companion is to sit *with* Him on His throne. If His throne represents reality, then here is no fantasy. Neither joint heir can do anything alone (Rom. 8:17).

We may not know why it pleases the Father to give the kingdom to the little flock. We may not know why Christ chooses to share His throne and His glory with the

> **redeemed. We only know that He *has chosen* to do so and that it gives Him pleasure.**

Billheimer stopped short of asserting that the Church, in her spiritual form, may be integrated into the Godhead, nor did he directly imply that a feminine element exists within the Trinity. For example in his Chapter 2, page 37, he commented: "As sons of God [speaking of the individuals within the Church], begotten by Him, incorporating into their fundamental being and nature the very 'genes' of God, they rank above all other created beings and are elevated to the most sublime height possible short of becoming members of the Trinity itself."

But Billheimer came very close to those two intimately related associations. Two pages earlier, on page 35, he stated "Thus, through the new birth – and I speak reverently – we become 'next of kin' to the Trinity, a kind of 'extension' of the Godhead." Even more telling, in a footnote at the end of that chapter, he claimed "There is a clear and convincing implication in Genesis 1:27 that sex, in its spiritual dimension, constitutes an element of the image of God."

Regarding Billheimer's comment on not knowing "why it pleases the Father to give the kingdom to the little flock," I do believe that Scripture supplies the answer to that question as to why Christ chooses to share: because, in harmony with the selflessness intrinsic to the Him, the Father Himself chose to share, elevating love over majesty.

Eight
The Bride of Christ

The beautiful mystery explained by Paul in Ephesians 5:25-32 has instilled in me the wonderful and emotionally moving view of the Church as the Bride of Christ:

> **Husbands, love your wives, even as Christ loved the Church, and gave Himself for it, that He might sanctify and cleanse it with the washing of the water by the Word; that He might present it to himself a glorious Church, not having spot, or wrinkle, or any such thing; but that it should be holy and without blemish. So ought men to love their wives as their own bodies. He that loves his wife loves himself. For no man ever yet hated his own flesh, but nourishes and cherishes it, even as the Lord the Church; for we are members of His body, of His flesh, and of his bones.**
>
> **For this cause shall a man leave his father and mother, and shall be joined unto his wife, and they two shall be one flesh. This is a great mystery, but I speak concerning Christ and the Church.**

In repeating the words of Adam in the Garden and of Jesus in Matthew 19, both in the setting of marriage and in the physical union between a man and his wife, Paul, by placing this marital union in the context of Jesus and His Church, plainly stated that the Church will be the spiritual Bride of Christ in an intimate relationship with a meaning that extends far beyond that of a mere figure of speech, as is the prevailing custom within the Church.

Unfortunately, the Church for a very long time has attempted to minimize the nature of this spiritual relationship, to the extent of denying that gender and the romance associated with it exists in heaven. There are two particular passages in Scripture that are used to foster that thought. One is in Matthew 22, and the other is in Galatians 3.

In Matthew 22: 28-30, Jesus responds to the Sadducees' attempts to trick Him by telling them that in heaven people don't marry:

> **Jesus answered and said unto the, Ye do err, not knowing the Scriptures, nor the power of God. For in the resurrection they neither marry, nor are given in marriage, but are like the angels in heaven.**

Notice that in this context Jesus mentioned the power of God. This doesn't square with the common interpretation of the passage as describing a feature that is absent. Those who would deny the existence of gender in heaven overlook that point. Why the deniers miss this is that they're thinking too small. Jesus didn't deny the existence of marriage; He denied the existence of marriage among individuals. But the Church, as a composite of a multitude of individuals, is perfectly capable of marriage, and that's where the power of God comes into play.

Paul addresses the same issue in Galatians 3:28 regarding individuals in the spiritual realm:

> **There is neither Jew nor Greek, there is neither bond nor free, there is neither male nor female; for you are all one in Christ Jesus.**

Again, the subject is the individual. But in 1 Corinthians 12: 4-11 and elsewhere in Scripture, Paul very plainly develops the idea that the individual is not the Church, but rather just a component of her, and a rather small element at that:

> **Now there are diversities of gifts, but the same Spirit. And there are differences of administrations, but the same Lord. And there are diversities of operations, but it is the same God who works all in all. But the manifestation of**

the Spirit is given to every man to profit.

For to one is given, by the Spirit, the word of wisdom; to another, the word of knowledge by the same Spirit; to another, faith by the same Spirit; to another, the gifts of healing by the same Spirit; to another, the working of miracles; to another, prophecy; to another, discerning of spirits; to another, various kinds of tongues; to another, the interpretation of tongues. But all these work that one and the very same Spirit, dividing to every man severally as he will.

In verses 12-17, Paul develops the role of the individual within the Church as similar to the roles of parts within our bodies:

For as the body is one, and has many members, and all the members of that one body, being many, are one body, so also is Christ. For by one Spirit we were all baptized into one body, where we are Jews or Greeks, whether we are bond or free; and we have all been made to drink into one Spirit. For the body is not one member, but many.

If the foot shall say, Because I am not the hand, I am not of the body; is it therefore, not of the body? If the whole body were an eye, where would be the hearing? If the whole were hearing, where would be the smelling?

Paul continues to develop the point that individuals are only components of an integrated whole, and concludes by listing some specific individual roles of individuals within the Church: apostles; prophets; teachers; workers of miracles; healers; administrators; and speakers in tongues. His point is clear: there is a vast difference in the spiritual Church between the individual components and the whole, just as in our own bodies between our individual organs, which of themselves are genderless, even those that implement gender, and our composite selves, which are indeed gendered.

There are Old Testament prophecies of Jesus' marriage to His Church. The elaborate and moving description of it found in Genesis 24 certainly doesn't portray that relationship as trivial. Nor does the description in Ruth, nor in the Song of Solomon.

Genesis 24, for example, describes the betrothal and marriage of Rebekah to Isaac. In Genesis 22 God commands Abraham to sacrifice Isaac, which identifies Isaac as a type of Jesus Christ. In line with that identification, Isaac's marriage to Rebekah identifies her as a type of Christ's bride. According to Galatians 3:28, in which spiritual individuals do not possess gender, this bridehood cannot be fulfilled in individuals: the fulfillment must come for a collection or aggregate of individuals, which would suggest the Church. This identification of the Church as the Bride of Christ is strengthened by Paul's characterization of the Church in 1 Corinthians 12 as a collection of individuals, each possessing specific gifts of the Holy Spirit.

In the Book of Ruth, Ruth's husband Boaz is routinely identified by the Church as the Kinsman-redeemer, a type of Christ. It follows that Ruth, a female, represents His spiritual Wife, the Church.

Relating again to the Old Testament, it would be extremely difficult, if the Church was not a feminine entity, to justify the inclusion of the Song of Solomon in the canon of Scripture. Why, if the spiritual domain is genderless, would this overtly sexual document be a part of the Bible?

Jesus certainly didn't dismiss His future spiritual marriage to His Church as amounting to "a figure of speech". Jesus made numerous allusions to His own future marriage, including the parable of the marriage feast in Matthew 22, the parable of the ten virgins in Matthew 25, and, of course, his first miracle at Cana recorded in John 2, wherein He changed water into wine in anticipation of the joy of His own future wedding.

Nor, according to Paul in Romans 7:4, is this marriage to be empty of birth.

> **Wherefore, my brethren, you also are become dead to the law by the body of Christ, that you should be married to another, even to Him who is raised from the dead, that we should bring forth fruit to God.**

Nine
The Nature of Our Marriage to Jesus Christ

Having denied the existence of gender in heaven, some scholars of theology have taken this absence to the extreme of insisting that Jesus will wed a building, beautiful as it might be. Individuals of this persuasion have pointed to Revelation 21:1-3 in support of that notion, interpreting it to align with their particular vision of God:

> **And I saw a new heaven and a new earth; for the first heaven and the first earth were passed away, and there was no more sea. And I, John, saw the holy city, New Jerusalem, coming down from God out of heaven, prepared as a bride adorned for her husband. And I heard a great voice out of heaven saying, Behold, the tabernacle of Go is with men, and he will dwell with them, and they shall be his people, and God himself shall be with them, and be their God.**

But if that is the case, one might ask such an individual, what about the Church? Indeed, in John 3:29, where Jesus refers to Himself as the bridegroom of the bride, the object of His affection is usually interpreted as the Church.

But no, he who pictures the bride as a building would respond. The Church is the body of Christ, he would assert, pointing to 1 Corinthians 12:27;

> **Now you are the body of Christ, and members in particular.**

But Paul, in Ephesians 5:28, made a more possessive association of the Church with the body of Christ than one in which the Church actually takes over Christ's body. In developing in more detail the interpretation of the Church as being "the Body of Christ", Paul commented there that *"So ought men to love their wives as their own bodies."* In that phrase Paul emphasizes the image in which the wife is considered to belong to the man's body. The inclusion in marriage of the notion of ownership was developed at the very beginning of the Bible in the restatement of Adam's commentary regarding Eve of two becoming one flesh such that in the marital union the wife is considered to belong to the man's body.

In short, the Body of Christ represented by the Church is a possessive extension of Christ's own body, the Man and wife being considered as one flesh.

Scripture itself asserts that Jesus will marry a living entity rather than an inanimate object. In Matthew 22:31 and 32, Jesus declares that He is the God of the living:

> **But as touching the resurrection of the dead, have you not read that which was spoken to you by God, saying, I am the God of Abraham, and the God of Isaac, and the God of Jacob? God is not the God of the dead, but of the living.**

My own interpretation of the New Jerusalem in Revelation 20 is that this holy city is the mansion that Jesus spoke of in John 14:1-3:

> **Let not your heart be troubled; you believe in God, believe also in me. In my Father's house are many mansions; if it were not so, I would have told you. I go to prepare a place for you. And if I go and prepare a place for you, I will come again, and receive you to myself, that where I am, there you may be also.**

But if the New Jerusalem is itself Jesus' bride, it is a living building. There is some allusion to that in Scripture. In His message to the Church at Philadelphia in Revelation 3:12, Jesus graphically describes a member of the Church as a component of a building:

> **Him that overcomes will I make a pillar in the temple of**

my God, and he shall go no more out; and I will write upon him the name of My God, and the name of the city of My God, the new Jerusalem, which cometh down out of heaven from My God; and I will write upon him My new name.

Paul, in 1 Corinthians 3:9, 10 and 16, describes the members of the Church as living temples:

For we are laborers together with God; you are God's cultivated field, you are God's building. According to the grace of God which is given unto me, as a wise master builder, I have laid the foundation, and another builds on it. But let every man take heed how he builds upon it. . . Know you not that you are the temple of God, and that the Spirit of God dwells in you?

Paul makes this same association of Christians to living temples in Ephesians 2:19-22:

Now, therefore you are no more strangers and sojourners, but fellow citizens with the saints, and of the household of God; and are built upon the foundation of the apostles and prophets, Jesus Christ Himself being the chief corner stone, in whom all the building fitly framed together growth unto an holy temple in the Lord; in whom you also are built together for a habitation of God through the Spirit.

Note from these examples that while the imagery is one of a building or components thereof, the components themselves are living human souls, all redeemed by Jesus Christ and therefore identical to the components of the Church. Given that identity, the imagery in Revelation 21 of the New Jerusalem is not mutually exclusive with the imagery of the Church. Indeed, if one considers the mansion of John 14 to be supplied by God and the Church its living furnishings, the two images are entirely compatible with each other and mutually supportive, each adding color to the understanding of the Church as the spiritual Bride of Christ. This understanding brings this commentary full circle through Revelation 19: 7-9 back to the character of the Church as *not having spot, or wrinkle, or any such thing:*

> **Let us be glad and rejoice, and give honor to Him; for the marriage of the Lamb is come, and His wife has made herself ready. And to her was granted that she should be arrayed in fine linen, clean and white; for the fine linen is the righteousness of saints. And he said to me, Write, Blessed are they who are called unto the marriage supper of the Lamb. And he said to me, These are the true sayings of God.**

Not only is Jesus' bride alive, but His relationship with her will be romantic. If that was not the case, Jesus would not have joyfully worked His first miracle at Cana as recorded in John 2, nor would the Song of Solomon or the book of Ruth, both commonly recognized as prophetic of Jesus' marriage to His Church, have belonged in the Bible.

Ten
The Early Moravian Church

As I was browsing the Internet recently I came across a fascinating article written by Dr. Craig D. Atwood entitled *Motherhood of Holy Spirit in the 18th Century.*

According to Dr. Atwood's biography, his current title is the rather lengthy "Charles D. Couch Associate professor of Moravian Theology and Ministry Director of the Center for Moravian Studies." He is a faculty member of the Moravian College and Theological Seminary located in Bethlehem, Pennsylvania, where he teaches Moravian theology and history, Christian history, religion in America, and history of Christian thought.

His current interests include a desire to help the Christian community in general to "rediscover the riches of the Moravian theological heritage." There is a hint in this aspiration, supported in the article noted above, that he sees that something quite valuable was lost in the transition of the Moravian Church away from its unique early dogma toward a more mainstream perception of our Trinitarian Godhead.

The perception that ultimately was abandoned by the Moravian Church is identified in the nature of the article: the femininity of the Holy Spirit.

The article itself, which was delivered in a presentation to the faculty of the Moravian College in 2011, traces the history of the Moravian Church in America during its most controversial (and possibly its most fruitful) period, the two decades of the 1740s through the 1750s. From the establishment of the Moravian community of Bethlehem in 1741 on a 500-acre plot purchased from the estate of George Whitefield, the Church initially adhered to the theology of Moravian (now Czechoslovakian) Count Nicholas Ludwig von Zinzendorf.

Zinzendorf's theology is rooted in the Czech reform movement of the fourteenth century, in which John Hus' protests against the Catholic Church a full sixty years before Luther landed him astride a stake, where he was burned as a heretic in 1415. Followers of Hus organized the Moravian Church in 1457 in the village of Kunvald, about a hundred miles east of Prague. The Church spread into Poland through heavy persecution in the sixteenth century. Continuing persecution in the seventeenth century contributed to a relative stasis in the Church. It enjoyed a revival in the eighteenth century as the Church planted roots in Bethlehem, Pennsylvania under the leadership of Count Zinzendorf. Bethlehem lies on the outskirts of Allentown in southeastern Pennsylvania, just north of Philadelphia and west of the New Jersey border. It recently was recognized as being one of the one hundred best places to live in America.

According to Dr. Atwood, Bethlehem enjoyed particular favor from God, as the community was one of the most successful in pre-revolution America. Atwood implies that this favor resulted from the theology of the Moravian Church, unique at that time, in which the Holy Spirit was considered to be the Spouse of the Holy Father and the Mother of Jesus and His Church.

The Moravian Church was recognized for its emphasis on the love of God. God blessed it by endowing the Church with a very active missionary outreach, where it attained a position of leadership in sending emissaries of Jesus Christ to other lands as well as the local Algonquin-based Lenape Indian Tribe, many members of which were converted to Christianity. Bethlehem itself was blessed with stability and commercial prosperity, becoming a center for the production of steel and shipbuilding.

The Church's perception of the Holy Trinity continued at least for the twenty years following the establishment of Bethlehem. Following the death of Count Zinzendorf and his wife and son, the far weaker post-Zinzendorf Church leadership fell away into a desire to conform more closely to the more popular "mainstream" dogmas of the Protestant Churches in the surrounding communities. They completed their abandonment of their original dogma by burning Zinzendorf's writings.

The Church leadership now appears to lament this transition toward "normalcy" implying that Bethlehem and the Moravian Church did not continue in the favor of God thereafter. They have expressed disappointment in the manner in which this transition was handled, implying that in continuing embarrassment Church historians label the two initial decades of the Moravian presence in America as "a time of sifting', wherein the theological "experimentation" of the time eventually led to the more stable dogma of mainstream Christianity. In opposition to this false and rude dismissal, some Church members claim that a substantial segment of the Moravian Church continues in the initial dogma even to this day.

Some Church leaders appear to be seeking a re-establishment of that early doctrine of the Holy Spirit, not only for its intrinsic truth but for the good of the Church and perhaps even America.

Here's my take on this account of accommodation to popular thought: as the reader of my blog postings on *friendofthefamily.wordpress.com* is well-aware, I consider the perception of the femininity of the Holy Spirit not only to represent truth, but to be the only viable way to worship our Judeo-Christian God with the love that He demands of us. Beyond that, the transition of the Moravian Church to "normal" is just another sad tale in a very long litany of similar ungodly, cowardly acts of appeasement to majority thought, begun in the New Testament by Peter's threefold denial of Jesus and continuing on to this very day, where we see, among other examples of falling-away, the Church's attempt to accommodate herself to the false and thoroughly secular notion of evolution.

Eleven

Recap: Ten Reasons for a Feminine Holy Spirit

The following reasons are taken from Scripture, and are consistent with a view of the Bible as inspired and inerrant in the original.

ONE: The original Old Testament Scripture in the Hebrew language described the Holy Spirit in feminine terms. Evidence of this has been furnished by several language-expert Bible scholars, among whom is R. P. Nettelhorst of the Quartz Hill School of Theology. Dr. Nettelhorst's specific examples include Genesis 1:2 that pointed to the role of the Holy Spirit in Creation and Judges 3:10, which represented a turning point in his understanding of God. He claims that there are 75 instances of either a feminine or indeterminable reference to the Holy Spirit, and no instances, other than descriptors of the Father, where in the original Hebrew the word "Spirit" is described in masculine terms. Other investigators have listed a multitude of specific Old Testament Bible passages that describe the Holy Spirit in feminine terms. Other passages, including Isaiah 51:9 and 10, furnish evidence of a deliberate switch of the Holy Spirit (Arm of the Lord) from feminine to masculine, as both feminine and masculine translations still exist, the feminine version being the earliest.

TWO: The original New Testament Scripture in the Greek/ Aramaic language described the Holy Spirit in feminine terms, exposing a deliberate switch in descriptors from feminine to masculine. Evidence of this has been furnished by several Bible scholars, among whom is Johannes van Oort of Radboud University, Nijmegen, the Netherlands, and the University of Pretoria, South

Africa. Dr. van Oort, another language expert, claims that the primitive Christian Church, until at least through the second century A.D., and in some places through the fourth century A.D. spoke of the Holy Spirit as feminine. His sources include the Gospel of the Hebrews, which, while now lost, was quoted widely by early Christians, who noted that the Holy Spirit in that Gospel was described as feminine. He observed from the extensive quotations from that Gospel that it apparently was quite popular among the early Christians. Dr. van Oort notes that more modern Christian leaders, including John Wesley and Count von Zinzendorf of the Moravian Church, were influenced by quotes from that Gospel. Other investigators, including S. Santini and R. Nettelhorst, point to the Sinaitic Palimpsest, the earliest currently known of Gospel passages still extant, as quoting Jesus in John 14:26 as referencing the Holy Spirit in feminine terms. It is the originals that are to be respected for inspiration and accuracy, not the various translations. Next in line for respect, the earliest available versions are generally considered to be the most faithful to the original. Other passages, including Romans 9:25, retain an understanding of the Holy Spirit as feminine. It is important to note also that some of the interlinear translations of the Bible in Hebrew, Greek and Aramaic have also adjusted the language to conform to the Church tradition of replacing the feminine with the masculine.

THREE: The first Chapter of Genesis in commonly available translations and versions (including the King James) unequivocally depicts the Holy Spirit as feminine, regardless of the attempts to suppress that aspect of the Holy Spirit's nature. The passage most strongly indicative of a feminine Holy Spirit is Genesis 1:26 and 27, which identifies the gendered nature of mankind as conforming to God's own nature. While modern commentators on this passage refuse to address this gender issue, they have no basis to do so other than participating in a slavish conformance to Church tradition, and are dishonest in their attempts to remove this characteristic from the image of God. Direct support of the depiction in Genesis 1 of the Holy Spirit's feminine nature is found in Psalm 94:9, wherein God describes attributes of man, specifically ears and eyes, asking why man can't understand that God possesses the same attributes. In that context, it would be appropriate for God to ask why, if man was made a gendered being, why God Himself wouldn't possess as well that same profoundly important attribute.

FOUR: The account of the creation of Eve in Genesis 2 is a statement of the importance to God of gender. In opposition to the generally-accepted notion that the account of God's creation of Eve in Genesis 2 took place well after the creation of Adam as an incidental afterthought, the Genesis 2 account is so central to the intention of God that it is more detailed than the original description and is presented again for the purpose of emphasis. Back in Genesis 1:26-31, God already had created both Adam and Eve as gendered and capable of reproduction. Furthermore, it is in Genesis 1:31 that God describes His creation, including gendered humanity, as very good. In Genesis 2:18, God describes Adam without Eve as being not good, which would be a contradiction to the earlier account in Genesis 1 if Genesis 2 represented anything other than an emphatic revisit of Eve's creation. Yet more, in Matthew 19:4 and Mark 10:6-8, Jesus strongly defended the gendered nature of mankind as being the express intent of God from the beginning of Creation, pointing to its importance within the Godhead itself. This emphasis suggests the importance of Eve's creation from Adam to the extent that it says something about the gendered nature of the Godhead, which could easily be interpreted as a continuation of the information presented in Genesis 1:27 that the creation of Eve amounts to a reprise in mankind of God's own family nature.

FIVE: Only a union of a romantic, possessive nature between a male and a female is capable of fulfilling the passion intrinsic to God. Despite Church tradition that, influenced by the odd, cold theology of Zanchius and others of his cloth, the attributes of God include passion, and that passion includes romance. Scripture often attributes passion to Jesus and the other Members of the Godhead, most notably so in the Song of Solomon. The Song of Solomon is an overt description of gender-driven passion. Many respected Bible commentators see in this book a connection between Jesus and His Church in the spiritual domain, which places the attribute of gender firmly within the Godhead. Given the romantic, passionate nature of that Book, if romantic, possessive passion was not an attribute of God, the Song wouldn't belong in the canon of Scripture. Moreover, according to Jesus' greatest commandment to us in Matthew 22 (echoing Deuteronomy 6) God demands that same passion of us with respect to our relationship with Him. If God was incapable of experiencing that same passion, the commandment would be meaningless.

SIX: The selfless nobility intrinsic to God suggests a union within the Godhead of a harmony built upon complementary otherhood, which can only be fulfilled through gender differentiation. The Bible in its entirety, most emphatically presented in the work of Jesus on the cross, depicts God as selflessly noble. The alternatives to gender differentiation of an all-male or genderless Godhead would encourage narcissistic selfishness. The demand to love God with fervor requires us to view God in a family context as well. Any alternative to that view leaves us with confusion and a profound inability to obey the commandment of love that Jesus expressed in Matthew 22. The confusion is quite real: the confusion and lack of understanding has been confessed to me multiple times by theologians who possess impressive credentials, but who remain committed to a genderless or all-male Godhead. It is difficult to understand how a person who is confused about such an intimate detail regarding the nature of God would be able to worship Him with fervor.

SEVEN: In Ephesians 5, Paul claims that Jesus and His Church will be married, attributing functional gender to attributes within the Godhead. In Genesis 2, Adam states that Eve is bone of his bones and flesh of his flesh, and that therefore shall a man leave his father and his mother, and shall cleave unto his wife, and they shall be one flesh. The latter phrase represents the very words that Jesus repeated in Matthew 19:5 and 6, and in Mark 10:7 and 8. The importance of this phrase is confirmed in Ephesians 5:31 and 32, where Paul repeats it yet again, and then goes on to claim that it applies to the union of Jesus and His Church. Here, the Bible explicitly states that Jesus and the Church are fully gendered and will, in the spiritual domain, unite in marriage. That this union will be productive is asserted in Romans 7:4. The fact that Jesus is a Member of the Godhead and is slated to be married plainly suggests that the other two members of the Godhead are also gendered, and, in fact, are united with each other.

EIGHT: The Old Testament Shekinah Glory, generally acknowledged to be feminine, is revealed in the New Testament as the Holy Spirit. Paul goes to great lengths to describe the Church as a spiritual composite of individual Christians, in which the individuals are contributing elements of a whole, each individual being somewhat akin to the various organs that comprise a human body. In that context, gender is not important with regard to the individual (how would a gendered heart work?), but is a vital necessity, as in the complete human body, to the complete Church. An important aspect of the integrated spiritual Church is the indwelling Holy Spirit. As Paul declares in 1 Corinthians 3:16 and Ephesians 2:19-22, we Christians comprise a temple of God, wherein the Holy Spirit dwells. This temple described by Paul is a fulfillment of the type described in the Old Testament, where the Shekinah Glory indwelt the Tabernacle of the Wilderness and Solomon's Temple at their dedications (Exodus 40 and 1 Kings 8). The Shekinah Glory is generally acknowledged to be feminine in nature; the indwelling fulfillment in Christians identifies the Shekinah as the Holy Spirit.

NINE: The Book of Proverbs describes as feminine the Holy Spirit in Her role as complementary other to the Father. Proverbs 8:22-36, in particular, describes the Holy Spirit working alongside the Father in the Creation. That the feminine *Persona* of the Holy Spirit in Proverbs is far more than simply a figure of speech, is confirmed by Jesus Christ, who in Luke 7:35 described the Holy Spirit in terms of a sentient Mother. The connection between Wisdom and the Holy Spirit is also made in the Book of Wisdom, which, while having been removed from the canon of Protestant Scripture during the Reformation, remains canonical in the Catholic Church. In that book, Wisdom as a feminine Being is directly linked to the Holy Spirit.

TEN: In multiple passages, Jesus describes the Holy Spirit in feminine terms. In the Gospel of John, Jesus frequently links the Holy Spirit with feminine descriptors, such as "Comforter" and "Helper". This association is most direct in John 3, where Jesus connects the Holy Spirit with spiritual birth. Birth, of course, is an eminently feminine function. Moreover, many theologians see in Scripture the role of the Holy Spirit as an executive one. An executive function is feminine in nature, representing the essence of complementary otherhood in the carrying out of the will of the Father. More generally, even in translations that corrupt the original description of the Holy Spirit in feminine terms, the Holy Spirit in Genesis 1:2 is described as creatively responsive to the Father's will. A responsive role is a feminine one.

Twelve
Why Should it Matter?

The usual response to my multi-year heartfelt presentations of the Holy Spirit's femininity is glassy eyes and a shrug of the shoulders. *So what?* The body language says with eloquence. *Why should I care? Whoever or whatever God is or isn't, I'm a believer, so my faith is the only thing that really matters.*

But is it all that matters? More to the point, is faith without love really faith? In Matthew 22:37, Jesus echoes Moses' words in Deuteronomy 6:5 by claiming that the greatest commandment of God is that *Thou shalt love the Lord, thy God, with all thy heart, and with all thy soul, and with all thy mind.* Jesus stated that not as a suggestion, but as a commandment. Jesus also said in John 14:15 *If ye love me, keep my commandments.* These two passages can be paraphrased to say that your love must be fervent to truly be love.

Our faith itself must involve fervent love; otherwise, it isn't really faith at all, just some meaningless mind-exercise performed for the sake of acquiring peace of mind over the issue of where one goes after the game's up here on earth. But the faith of most of us is exactly that – fire insurance. Our worship of God seems to be based on a self-centered desire not to be left out of the joys of heaven (if heaven actually does exist, as we wonder within ourselves, and if it actually is joyful).

Fervent love toward God is far more than an exercise of the mind, because fervor doesn't come from the mind. It is an imprinting upon the soul akin to the passionate, possessive love between a man and a woman. It must be of such a magnitude that the thought of its removal invokes the same sense of desperate grief as the loss of a lifelong mate. It is the way that God made us to love Him.

Anything less is not love, nor is it faith. Less than fervent love has the potential of crumbling at the first threat to well-being. We see it happening now in the mass exodus from Church following the recent marginalization of Christians.

Here is where the issue of loving faith collides with our understanding of the nature of God. How can we possibly love that which we so imperfectly know? The Church for centuries has treated the Trinitarian Godhead as either void of gender or somewhat masculine, all three Members having essentially the same nature. The problem with that misrepresentation is that the Godhead and the functional roles within it are both alien and confusing. Some theologians, in recognizing that problem, have put forth the idea that each Member of the Godhead is endowed with traits belonging to both genders. But such theologians failed to use their heads: on a moral basis alone God's nobility resides far beyond such a narcissism-promoting arrangement as that would encourage. Beyond that issue, gender duality within each Member leaves unsolved the confusion of roles. Yet further, the gender ambiguity would attribute to God Himself gender traits which Scripture discourages in us. Because of the multiplicity of issues associated with it, most Churches recognize the problems inherent in that assignment, leaving us with the basic genderless or all-male model of the Godhead, returning us to confusion and alienation regarding the matter, which has led most Churches to ignore the issue completely.

But the issue is so important that it demands to be heard, for it involves faith. How can we worship God with the fervor He demands of us without even a basic understanding of who He is, and what little that we do know of Him is alien to us? That is exactly why the majority of self-styled Christians, lacking the love that God asks of us, are in blatant disobedience to God, holding to nothing more than a shallow semblance of faith. Most of us think more highly of ourselves than that, visualizing how we will hold fast to our faith in the face of persecution. But that kind of self-aggrandizing attitude is nothing but self-centered chest-pounding that will vaporize under any real threat.

The importance that I attach to this issue of the Holy Spirit's gender raises another issue of grave importance to all the millions of Christians who have lived and died over the many centuries that the Church has mischaracterized the Holy Spirit: has their failure to obey their God with the ardent love that He commanded denied them the eternal fellowship with God that He promised to His believers? Personally, I don't think that to be the case, particularly since the misleading came from the Church, not them. My belief that God is far more compassionate and merciful than that is reinforced by the numerous descriptions in Scripture of godly people who, at one time or another, failed to the extent of disobeying God's commandments. I certainly hope that He is that merciful, because I, for one, have been disobedient to God with distressing frequency.

Yet, if disobedience in loving God the way we should doesn't forever prohibit us from attaining favor with God, the issue of the Holy Spirit's feminine gender remains important to us regarding the depth of our commitment to God and to the advantages that are conferred upon us in the here and now for that understanding. For it is a great blessing to fellowship with God, and the closer we come to Him, the nearer that He comes and displays His love toward us. Then, of course, there is the matter of a shallow faith being subject to abandonment in the face of trouble, which is an issue that is not a threat to those closer to God.

In an enormous contrast to the prevailing state of affairs with the Church's misconception of God, an appreciation of a feminine Holy Spirit introduces the archetype of family into an understanding of the Godhead, instantly clarifying the respective roles of the individual Members and immediately removing all sense of confusion regarding the nature of God.

Most importantly, God is no longer alien to us, but One with whom we can identify through the personal experience of life itself. We can know this God intimately, and this intimacy grants us access to the kind of love that produces real faith in obedience to Jesus' command, a faith that is capable of withstanding all the negatives that life as Christians can bring us.

Principally because of the issue of holding fast to our faith under the pressure of worldly pleasures and the threat of persecution, the understanding of the Holy Spirit as of the feminine gender does indeed matter – under certain situations, it can be as important as the destination of our eternal souls.

There's still another reason for appreciating the Holy Spirit's feminine gender. Equipped with that understanding, a reading of Genesis 1 and 2 becomes a breathtakingly beautiful endeavor. For in the reading the prospect becomes convincing that these passages speak not only of the creation of mankind, but of the arrangement and roles within the Godhead itself of the Members comprising it. Is it not possible, then, that the Holy Spirit Herself was formed out of the Father's side in His effort to place Love above all other attributes of God, irretrievably far beyond self?

Volume Five

God's Confections of Love

Contents

Preface 239

One: Worshiping God 241

Two: The Romantic Bond 244

Three: The Romance of Jesus and His Church 248

Four: Discovering Hidden Beauty 251

Five: The Queen Mother 256

Six: Spiritual Eucharist 259

Seven: Ruth 263

Eight: Naomi 266

Nine: The Shekinah Glory 269

Ten: God's Mercy Toward Peter 272

Preface

The integrating theme for the present volume, Volume Five, is the love intrinsic to God, His most important attribute, and of the intimate manner in which God relates to us as we approach Him in faith and obedience. In this volume uplifting examples of God's love are presented, both within the Godhead and between God and man, the primary object of His affection.

The desire of God, as revealed in the Bible, to endow us with appealing personal qualities of character, speaks to His loving plan for His Church as Jesus' worthy partner in her future role as the Bride of Christ. As the Bible openly proclaims in 1 John 4:8:

> **He that loves not knows not God, for God is love.**

The Bible has often been described as a love letter from God to mankind. That is true. It is also true that the Bible quite richly describes the love that so strongly binds the Members of the Trinity together as One God.

One

Worshiping God

How does one go about worshiping God? In America today, there probably are as many styles and motives of worship as Jelly-Belly flavors – maybe even as much as Jelly-Bellys themselves.

We're pretty sure that God isn't dwarfish – most of us perceive Him as rather larger than we are. That size difference evokes a sense of God's magnificent power, and many Churches affirm that majesty in their communal worship. Others see in that difference in size and power that God possesses considerably more "things" than we do, and consequently adjust their style of worship toward pleas to share the wealth.

Still others, knowing of the promise of the Holy Spirit indwelling believers, seek to tap into that power, just like Simon attempted to do as described in Acts 8:9-24:

> **But there was a certain man, called Simon, who previously in the same city used sorcery, and bewitched the people of Samaria, giving out that himself was some great one, to whom they all gave heed, from the least to the greatest, saying, This man is the great power of God. And to him they had regard, because that for a long time he had bewitched them with sorceries. But when they believed Philip preaching the things concerning the kingdom of God, and the name of Jesus Christ, they were baptized, both men and women. Then Simon himself believed also; and when he was baptized, he continued with Philip, and was amazed, beholding the miracles and signs which were done.**

Now when the apostles who were at Jerusalem heard that Samaria had received the word of God, they sent unto them Peter and John, who, when they were come down, prayed for them, that they might receive the Holy Spirit; for as yet he was fallen upon none of them; only they were baptized in the name of the Lord Jesus. Then laid their hands on them, and they received the Holy Spirit.

And when Simon saw that through laying on of the apostles' hands the Holy Spirit was given, he offered them money, saying, Give me also this power, that on whomsoever I lay hands, he may receive the Holy Spirit. But Peter said unto him, Thy money perish with thee, because thou hast thought that the gift of God may be purchased with money. Thou hast neither part nor lot in this matter; for thy heart is not right in the sight of God. Repent, therefore, of this thy wickedness, and pray God, if perhaps the thought of thine heart may be forgiven thee; for I perceive that thou art in the gall of bitterness, and in the bond of iniquity. Then answered Simon, and said, Pray ye to the Lord for me, that none of these things which ye have spoken come upon me.

This incident has left us with the word *simony*, which has come to mean, according to one dictionary, "The act of buying or selling places of honor in the church", a practice that was particularly rampant in the medieval Church and contributed to Martin Luther's choler against it. People never learn.

Simony is practiced today in a more subtle form among the Church laity, wherein tithing is related to expectations regarding personal finances and workplace successes. But all of the worship practices noted above, including the obsequious slobbering, tail-wagging groveling associated with the worship of God's majesty, have one glaring characteristic in common: they all are, at their core, dreadfully self-serving. They all constitute nothing but lobbying God for favors. Of such practices, Scripture says in John 9:31:

Now we know that God hears not sinners; but if any man be a worshiper of God, and does His will, him He hears.

Self-service is not what God intended worship to be. According to the Bible, what God wants out of us is a restoration of communion with Him, as He initially enjoyed with Adam and Eve in the Garden. He even went so far as to sacrifice Jesus on the cross to provide the way for that to happen.

How, then, should we worship God in a manner pleasing to Him? Above all, we must know the God whom we worship. The only reliable way to know God is to read Scripture, His Self-revelation to us. That, of course, is a process, one which can be supported by the fellowship offered by the Church. Rather quickly, the reader of Scripture comes to understand the true majesty of God, which is pure love, always taking the form of noble selflessness and evoking the same from us. As we come to understand His greatness in love, our worship always should include the spirit of thanksgiving for what we do possess, most of all being His loving, gracious inclusion of us in His extended family.

As suggested in the passage in John quoted above, our worship also should involve active obedience to His will, as it is thoroughly described in Scripture. As Paul plainly notes, our salvation has nothing to do with works; nevertheless, as James also plainly notes, godly works come naturally through the Holy Spirit who indwells believers who have accepted the offer of salvation through Jesus' vicarious work on the cross in our behalf. The indwelling Spirit moves them toward service to God and gifts them with the wherewithal to do so. This means that it isn't necessary for the new Christian to immediately seek out the nearest soup kitchen, but rather that he or she should be available for service as moved by the Holy Spirit. Christians who do serve the Lord in that way quickly learn that such service brings them ever closer to God in a wonderfully loving, productive relationship.

Two
The Romantic Bond

Of all the possible relationships people may have among each other, the romantic bond uniquely involves three features harmoniously and synergistically combined: functional unity, mutual possession, and shared intimacy.

Of itself, the feature of functional unity is common among relationships. It is the essence of teamwork, wherein individuals, each having specialized tasks, operate together in coordinated fashion to achieve higher-level objectives. Functional unity serves as the most sought-after expectation of armies, factories, sports teams and virtually every human endeavor that requires multiple persons working toward a common goal. Most relationships, however, require instruction and training to achieve that feature of human interaction, and firm supervision to maintain it.

In a good romance, however, teamwork is achieved far more naturally than in other relationships, requiring neither instruction, training, nor coercion. Gender-based specialization automatically delineates the normal roles of the participants, enabling them to interact together in complementary fashion without giving much thought to the process. Moreover, this functional synergism within the romantic bond uniquely complements the other two distinctive features, mutual possession and shared intimacy.

Outside of romance, possession is essentially off the table for normal human relationships. As in slavery or prison, possession of one human being by another is always, with but one exception, unhappy and forced. That exception is a passionate romance, which involves mutual possession as not only a voluntary act by the partners, but a comfort as well, and an expectation that each places on the other. Any situation that threatens that possessive bond, such as a potential romantic interest outside that relationship, is seen in a vehemently negative light. Two of God's Ten Commandments address that very issue.

Scripture itself sometimes conveys that same sense of possession regarding relationships within the Godhead, between God and humanity, and between individuals. Unfortunately, instances in which possession is the topic is very often misinterpreted by Christians as meaning something entirely different than what the text plainly states. An example of that is found in Jeremiah 10:12:

> **[God] has made the earth by his power; he has established the world by his wisdom, and has stretched out the heavens by his discretion.**

This passage is frequently interpreted to mean the opposite of what it is intended to convey. In the common misinterpretation, the words "power," "wisdom" and "discretion" are taken as attributes of the Father. As this interpretation applies these claims to the Father alone, it effectively denies their potential application to the other Members of the Godhead. In other contexts within Scripture, and particularly throughout the Book of Proverbs, all three of these so-called "attributes" are associated with the Holy Spirit rather than the Father. In an alternate interpretation these "attributes" can be taken to be possessive in nature toward the Holy Spirit. In that context the "attributes" belong to the Father's Holy Spirit and it is the Holy Spirit who belongs to the Father. Under that very natural alternate interpretation a completely different understanding of that passage results, one with romantic implications.

Another example tends to corroborate the possessive interpretation of the passage noted above, wherein the object of the possession is an Entity rather than a mere thing or attribute. The Scriptural passage for this example is Ephesians 5:25-28:

> **Husbands, love your wives, even as Christ also loved the church, and gave himself for it, that he might sanctify and cleanse it with the washing of water by the word; that he**

> **might present it to himself a glorious church, not having spot, or wrinkle, or any such thing; but that it should be holy and without blemish.**
>
> **So ought men to love their wives as their own bodies. He that loves his wife loves himself.**

In verse 28 of this passage, the body of the wife is possessively related to the man. The man owns his wife's body, just as she owns his. Paul was very explicit in this connection in 1 Corinthians 7:2-5:

> **Nevertheless, to avoid fornication, let every man have his own wife, and let every woman have her own husband. Let the husband render to the wife due benevolence; and likewise also, the wife to the husband. The wife has not power of her own body, but the husband; and likewise also the husband has not power of his own body, but the wife. Defraud you not one the other, except it be with consent for a time, that you may give yourselves to fasting and prayer; and come together again, that Satan tempt you not for your incontinency.**

The possessive ownership of each others' bodies, while taken for granted in romantic relationships within humanity, is often avoided in the context of the relationship between Jesus and His Church. Yet Paul was quite explicit in his establishment of that as well, as Ephesians 5 continues in verses 29 through 32:

> **For no man ever yet hated his own flesh, but nourishes and cherishes it, even as the Lord the church; for we are members of his body, of his flesh, and of his bones.**
>
> **For this cause shall a man leave his father and mother, and shall be joined unto his wife, and they two shall be one flesh. This is a great mystery, but I speak concerning Christ and the church.**

But why, if the Church's marriage to Jesus is to be a meaningful one in the context of our marriages to each other, did Paul in Ephesians 3:28 declare us to be neither male nor female in the spiritual realm? The obvious answer is that we as individuals are simply components of the composite Church, which herself is gendered. Paul alludes to this differentiation between individuals and the composite Church in 1 Corinthians 12:12-17:

> **For as the body is one, and hath many members, and all the members of that one body, being many, are one body, so also is Christ. For by one Spirit were we all baptized into one body, whether we be Jews or Greeks, whether we be bond or free; and have been all made to drink into one Spirit. For the body is not one member, but many.**
>
> **If the foot shall say, Because I am not the hand, I am not of the body; is it, therefore, not of the body? And if the ear shall say, Because I am not the eye, I am not of the body; is it, therefore, not of the body? If the whole body were an eye, where were the hearing? If the whole were hearing, where were the smelling?**

Given the common misunderstanding of Ephesians 3:28, Ephesians 5:28 is often misinterpreted as supporting the common claim that the Church is the one and only spiritual body of Christ, inferring that the Church is the exclusive repository of that body. In the more natural context of possession, however, the Church belongs to Jesus as a body integral with His own, in the same sense that a wife's body belongs to her husband as an integral component of his own body, just as Adam in Genesis 2:24, Jesus in Matthew 19:5 and Paul in Ephesians 5:31 directly stated.

Of the three features of romantic love, the third, shared intimacy, is the strongest bonding agent to unite the couple. Other human relationships can involve intimacy, but never to the extent of the sexual union between a man and a woman in their romantic partnership. God designed it that way to impart to the gender-based relationship its unique fullness, to set the couple apart from others as a special inviolate unity. It is the intimacy of their shared sexuality, or the promise of it, in synergy with their shared possession of each other, that gives their romance its very strength of passion. Nothing other than that intimacy provides individuals with a bonding force of that strength or beauty.

Three
The Romance Between Jesus and His Church

While He resided on earth, Jesus, despite some unjustified speculations to the contrary, remained celibate. That refusal to marry has been a cause of consternation to some, who see in that a lack of fulfillment, an incompleteness in Jesus.

While indeed rendering Him incomplete, Jesus' celibacy also rendered Him faithful, for Jesus was betrothed to His Church.

That eloquent passage in Hebrews 11 of godly people who endure suffering for their faith, ends with the following phrase that tells us that these heroes of the faith did not receive the fullness of God's blessings themselves, because of us and our own contributions:

> **God having provided some better thing for us that they without us should not be made perfect.**

This statement implies that it must be equally true that "neither they nor us, without Jesus, should be made perfect."

In quoting Adam in Genesis 2:24, Paul explained to us in Ephesians 5:31 and 32 a mystery of enormous significance, that Adam's declaration in Genesis 2:23 and 24 applied not only to mankind, but to Jesus as well:

> **For this cause shall a man leave his father and mother, and shall be joined unto his wife, and they two shall be one flesh. This is a great mystery, but I speak concerning Christ and the church.**

Given this statement of Paul's in the light of Jesus' celibacy during His time on earth, a second and greatly significant restatement of that ending passage of Hebrews 11 could be made: ". . . even Jesus, God having provided some better thing for us, without us should not be made perfect."

Scripture actually gives us a sound reason to perceive that the union between Jesus and His Church will be a romantic one. The Song of Solomon is rather explicit in that regard, verses 12 through 17 of Chapter 1 being representative:

> **While the king sits at his table, my spikenard sends forth the smell thereof. A bundle of myrrh is my well-beloved unto me; he shall lie all night between my breasts. My beloved is unto me as a cluster of camphire in the vineyards of Engedi. Behold, thou art fair, my love; behold, thou art fair; thou hast doves' eyes. Behold, thou art fair, my beloved, yea, pleasant; also our bed is green. The beams of our house are cedar, and our rafters of fir.**

Perhaps the most appropriate commentary to the Song of Solomon is the one given in the Schofield Bible in its prelude to the Song:

> **Nowhere in Scripture does the unspiritual mind tread upon ground so mysterious and incomprehensible as in this book, whereas saintly men and women throughout the ages have found it a source of pure and exquisite delight. That the love of the divine Bridegroom, symbolized here by Solomon's love for the Shulamite maiden, should follow the analogy of the marriage relationship seems evil only to minds that are so ascetic that marital desire itself appears to them to be unholy.**
>
> **The book is the expression of pure marital love as ordained by God in creation, and the vindication of that love as against both asceticism and lust – the two profanations of the holiness of marriage. Its interpretation is threefold: . . .(3) as an allegory of Christ's love for His heavenly bride, the Church. . .**

Jesus himself hints at His future joy with the Church as His Bride in the wedding at Cana, John 2:1-11:

> **And the third day there was a marriage in Cana, of Galilee; and the mother of Jesus was there. And both Jesus was called, and his disciples, to the marriage. And when they lacked wine, the mother of Jesus said to him, They have not wine. Jesus said to her, Woman, what have I to do with you? My hour is not yet come. His mother said to the servants, Whatever he says to you, do it. And there were set there six waterpots of stone, after the manner of the purifying of the Jews, containing twenty or thirty gallons apiece. Jesus said to them, Fill the waterpots with water. And they filled them up to the brim. And he said to them, Draw some out now, and bear it to the governor of the feast. And they bore it. When the ruler of the feast had tasted the water that was made wine, and knew not from where it was (but the servants who drew the water knew) the governor of the feast called the bridegroom, and said to him, Every man at the beginning does set forth good wine and, when men have well drunk, then that which is worse; but you have kept the good wine until now. This beginning of miracles did Jesus in Cana, of Galilee, and manifested forth his glory; and his disciples believed on him.**

With an understanding of Jesus' romantic relationship with His Church in mind, a careful reading of Isaac's marriage to Rebekah in Genesis 24, the Song of Solomon, Isaiah 54, and Jesus' first miracle in John 2 of changing water to wine at the wedding in Cana, plainly reveals beforehand the mystery that Paul revealed in Ephesians 5.

Four
Discovering Hidden Beauty

For a long time now, modern Churchgoers have questioned the motive and, even more seriously, the guiding Hand of the Holy Spirit behind Paul's descriptions in 1 Corinthians 14 and 1Timothy 2 regarding the proper role of women in Church. Was Paul a misogynist, as some have claimed? Was he really listening to the voice of God when he wrote those passages?

> **Let your women keep silence in the churches; for it is not permitted to them to speak, but they are commanded to be under obedience, as also says the law. And if they will learn anything, let them ask their husbands at home; for it is a shame for women to speak in the church.**

> **Let the woman learn in silence with all subjection. But I permit not a woman to teach, nor to usurp authority over the man, but to be in silence. For Adam was first formed, then Eve.**

Given Paul's beautiful description of the marriage between Christ and His Church in Ephesians 5:22-33, it is highly doubtful that Paul was a misogynist.

> **Wives, submit yourselves unto your own husbands, as to the Lord. For the husband is the head of the wife, even as Christ is the head of the church; and he is the savior of the body. Therefore, as the church is subject to Christ, so let the wives be to their own husbands in everything. Husbands, love your wives, even as Christ also loved the church, and gave himself for it, that he might sanctify and cleanse it with the washing of water by the word; that he**

might present it to himself a glorious church, not having spot, or wrinkle, or any such thing; but that it should be holy and without blemish. So ought men to love their wives as their own bodies. He that loves his wife loves himself. For no man ever yet hated his own flesh, but nourishes and cherishes it, even as the Lord the church; for we are members of his body, of his flesh, and of his bones.

For this cause shall a man leave his father and mother, and shall be joined unto his wife, and they two shall be one flesh. This is a great mystery, but I speak concerning Christ and the church.

Nevertheless, let every one of you in particular so love his wife even as himself; and the wife, see that she reverence her husband.

It is inconceivable to me that Paul could have written the above passage under an attitude of disdain toward women, or worse, a rebellious streak of independence from God. It is far more likely that here, as well as in the two passages cited earlier, that Paul wrote under the guidance of the Holy Spirit, who had something more profound to impart to the reader of Scripture than we have so far been able to grasp.

The problem with attempting to attribute Paul's discussions of the woman's role in Church to going off the reservation is that he was not the only one in Scripture to say what he did. Isaiah 3:12 and 1 Peter 3:1-5 have much the same to say:

As for my people, children are their oppressors, and women rule over them. O my people, they who lead you cause you to err, and destroy the way of your paths.

In the same manner, you wives, be in subjection to your own husbands that, if any obey not the word, they also may without the word be won by the behavior of the wives, while they behold your chaste conduct coupled with fear; whose adorning, let it not be that outward adorning of braiding the hair, and of the wearing of gold, or of putting

on of apparel, but let it be the hidden person of the heart in that which is not corruptible, even the ornament of a meek and quite spirit, which is in the sight of God of great price. For after this manner in the old time the holy women also, who trusted in God, adorned themselves, being in subjection to their own husbands.

Knowing from 2 Peter 1:20 and 21 and from Paul himself in 2 Timothy 3:16 and 17 that all Scripture is inspired of the Holy Spirit and applies to all generations, I sense that something much more profound and supportive of the dignity of womanhood is in play here than what is commonly understood. Perhaps a major clue to our understanding of Paul's words is encapsulated in Ephesians 5:33: *". . .let every one of you. . .so love his wife even as himself; and the wife, see that she reverence her husband."* Notice in this sentence the different roles played by the man and his wife: the man loves, even sacrificially, while the woman reverences him. This difference harmonizes with the difference in roles spelled out for male and female from the very beginning in Genesis 2:

And the Lord God said, It is not good that the man should be alone; I will make him a help fit for him. . . And the Lord God caused a deep sleep to fall upon Adam, and he slept: and he took one of his ribs, and closed up the flesh instead thereof; and the rib, which the Lord God had taken from man, made he a woman, and brought her to the man. And Adam said, This is now bone of my bones, and flesh of my flesh; she shall be called Woman, because she was taken out of Man. Therefore shall a man leave his father and his mother, and shall cleave to his wife, and they shall be one flesh.

Out of this passage one can quickly discern a significant difference in roles: the man is to be the initiator, and the woman the responder. We can directly understand this difference today in a more practical and earthly setting, merely by observing the two genders in their actions and interactions among others. This difference is more basic than cultural: it is the way that we were designed by God. It has nothing to do with equality; male and female have exactly the same standing before God, as Paul noted in Galatians 3:28:

> **There is neither Jew nor Greek, here is neither bond nor free, there is neither male nor female; for ye are all one in Christ Jesus.**

Scripture also is quick to point out that the man's role involves the burden of responsibility, to the point of sacrifice, and that should a man fail to assume his proper role, it is perfectly acceptable for a woman to take his place. To back that statement up, I refer the reader to the example of Deborah in Judges 4.

God made male and female different for the purpose of harmony: the woman serves as a *complementary other* to the man. A responsive woman performs that purpose as a complementary other to the initiator man.

In my opinion the issue extends beyond the complementary way that God designed men and women. According to Genesis 1:26 and 27,

> **And God said, Let us make man in our image, after our likeness; and let them have dominion over the fish of the sea, and over the fowl of the air, and over the cattle, and over all the earth, and over every creeping thing that creeps upon the earth. So God created man in his own image, in the image of God created he him; male and female created he them.**

This passage, along with the story of Eve's creation out of Adam in Genesis 2, appears to point back to the very form in which the Godhead itself exists, with the Holy Spirit interacting with the Divine Will that we know as the Father as His responsive Other, the Divine Means. If in fact there is truth to this perceived connection, and if indeed the Holy Spirit is functionally feminine as I strongly suspect, Paul's demand of women that they remain silent during Church services represents nothing less than the call for women to behave as proper types of the Holy Spirit.

What an honor it would be for Christian women to represent the Holy Spirit! If such is the case, as I believe with my heart, the passages in Paul cited above, rather than maligning womanhood, exalts this gender with an awesome connection to God.

Five
The Queen Mother

In Chapter 2 of Scott Hahn's book *Hail, Holy Queen* (one of my favorites), he comments on Jesus' response during the wedding at Cana (John 2) to His mother's words that "They have no wine." At these words, Jesus tells her "O woman, what have you to do with me? My hour has not yet come."

Many Bible commentators, Scott asserts, take Jesus' words here as a rather harsh put-down to His mother, Mary. Scott defends Jesus' response, noting that the phrase "what have you to do with me" actually can convey respect.

Without attempting to put words into Scott's mouth or ideas into his head that he would take strong objection to, I see in this book numerous instances of what many readers readily could interpret as quite brilliant defenses of the vision of a feminine Holy Spirit. In doing so, Scott often seems to camouflage attributes rightly belonging to the Holy Spirit in the person of the Virgin Mary, just as the Catholic Church seems to do in a more general setting. Whether this tendency is intentional on Scott's part, only he can say. I seem to remember that he has denied such an intent.

While not intentionally disagreeing with Scott's attempt to defend the benign intent of Jesus' words to Mary in John 2, these words evoke in my own mind the thought that perhaps Jesus, while responding to Mary, was thinking of how the wedding at Cana was but a foreshadow of His future marriage to His Church in the spiritual realm. Perhaps He was anticipating with great joy the time when His hour would finally come, when His spiritual Mother, the Holy Spirit, would participate in His future wedding to His Church. In fact, Dr. Hahn himself appears to come to that same conclusion in his Chapter 2. If such were indeed the case, this exchange between Jesus and Mary can be viewed as providing a beautiful Scriptural reference in support of the Holy Spirit's femininity.

Farther along in the book, in Chapter 3, Dr. Hahn addresses the woman of Revelation 11:19 through 12, of which I extract parts below:

> **And the temple of God was opened in heaven, and there was seen in his temple the ark of his covenant; and there were lightnings, and voices, and thunderings, and an earthquake, and great hail.**
>
> **And there appeared a great wonder in heaven – a woman clothed with the sun, and the moon under her feet, and upon her head a crown of twelve stars. And she, being with child, cried, travailing in birth, and pained to be delivered.**
>
> **And there appeared another wonder in heaven; and, behold, a great red dragon, having seven heads and ten horns, and seven crowns upon his heads. And his tail drew the third part of the stars of heaven and did cast them to the earth; and the dragon stood before the woman who was ready to be delivered, to devour her child as soon as it was born.**
>
> **And she brought forth a male child, who was to rule all nations with a rod of iron; and her child was caught up onto God, and to his throne. And the woman fled into the wilderness, where she hath a place prepared by God, that they should feed her there a thousand two hundred and threescore days."**

Many evangelical Christians associate the woman of Revelation 12 with the nation of Israel. Scott Hahn notes that some theologians identify her as the Church, and proceeds to discuss why this identification doesn't quite fit the Scriptural description. He then applies a more fitting identification of her as Mary, adding a beautifully profound association of her with the ark of Revelation 11:19: "If the first ark contained the Word of God in stone, Mary's body contained the Word of God enfleshed."

The passage in Revelation 11:19, which immediately precedes Revelation 12's description of the woman clothed with the sun, actually seems to belong to that later chapter.

While Scott's association of the Ark with Mary may be quite true, here again I perceive a yet higher association, one that, while not taking away from Mary's role here, adds yet another layer to it. Noting that the location of the drama in Revelation 11 and 12 is in the spiritual domain, I would rephrase Scott's assertion as "If the first ark contained the Word of God in stone, and Mary's body contained the Word of God enfleshed, the Holy Spirit contained the Word of God in Spirit." I see the ultimate Woman of Revelation 12 as the Holy Spirit. To me, that image is quite beautiful.

Lately, I've taken to re-reading in the evenings the historical books of Scripture; Samuel, Kings and Chronicles. At the present time, in going through 2 Kings, I've noticed that as the kings and their deeds were recounted, mention was given of their mothers. In Chapter 4 of *Hail, Holy Queen*, Dr. Hahn addresses the importance of the Queen Mother to the King's regime. His explanation of her status is most interesting: the practice of the kings of that era of taking multiple wives led to the awkward situation of selecting to whom would be bestowed the honor of serving in the primary position of queen. This situation was wisely avoided by placing the mother of the king in that exalted position. Scott Hahn revisits Revelation 12 in this chapter, enthroning Mary, as mother of Jesus, as the woman of such queenly stature as described in Revelation 12:1 and 2, as co-Regent of Jesus in His ultimate role of kingship over the earth.

While there may be some truth to Scott's assignment here, I see a far more profound truth, and one more harmonious to the Scriptural text, in assigning to the Holy Spirit this same function.

Six
Spiritual Eucharist

When we think of feeding, we automatically relate to the stomach and material food, even when the topic is connected with God. Our material focus on food limits our understanding of what Jesus really meant when He spoke of food, even in the context of His Word. What does the Word have to do with feeding? There's nothing material about the Word, and it can't do anything for our stomachs.

But according to God, man possesses a soul, an attribute more precious and important by far than a stomach, or, in fact, anything material about our body. Jesus spoke of the relative importance of the soul. In Matthew 10:28, for example, He defined the soul as essential while the body is expendable:

> **And fear not them who kill the body, but are not able to kill the soul; but rather fear him who is able to destroy both soul and body in hell.**

The salvation of God, that enormous thing that Jesus died on the cross for, applies to the soul rather than to the body. In the spiritual realm, the material part of man is of little or no importance next to the soul. The Word of God, then, insofar as it leads to salvation, and, following that, an ongoing relationship with God, is an input, a nourishment, of the soul. It is spiritual food, without which the soul would wither and die. In that sense, the Word is the most important food that we can obtain. Despite the demanding nature of our stomachs, material food is of far less consequence to our well-being than the Word of God.

Jesus Himself made a direct association of His Word with food.

Further, John notes in His Prologue (verses 1-18 of John 1) that Jesus *is* the Word of God, the very embodiment of it.

In John 6:30-35, Jesus equates Himself with the Bread of Life:

> **They said, therefore, to him, What sign show you, then, that we may see, and believe you? What do you work? Our fathers did eat manna in the desert; as it is written, He gave them bread from heaven to eat. Then Jesus said to them, Verily, verily, I say to you, Moses gave you not that bread from heaven; but my Father gives you the true bread from heaven. For the bread of God is he who comes down from heaven, and gives life to the world. Then said they to him, Lord, evermore give us this bread. And Jesus said to them, I am the bread of life; he that comes to me shall never hunger, and he that believes on me shall never thirst.**

Again, in John 6:48 Jesus equates Himself with the bread of life, embellishing on its spiritual importance in verse 51:

> **I am the living bread that came down from heaven; if any man eat of this bread, he shall live forever; and the bread that I will give is my flesh, which I shall give for the life of the world.**

In response to this declaration, there were people that just couldn't lift themselves out of the material world sufficiently to comprehend the spiritual nature of Jesus' claim:

> **The Jews, therefore, strove among themselves, saying, How can this man give us his flesh to eat?**

A good many Christians, including pastors and theologians from the time that Jesus spoke until and including the present day, undoubtedly have voiced the same question with respect to this passage in John 6:52.

Significantly, in John's Gospel, Jesus equated Himself, and thus His Word, with bread just after performing two miracles, both of which were intimately related to the connection among Peter, Jesus and God's sharing of His glory with man. The first of these miracles was Jesus' feeding of the five thousand. The second was Jesus' walking on water and Peter's short-lived accomplishment of the same.

In Luke 22:15-20, Jesus again associates Himself, the living Word of God, with food and wine:

> **And he said to them, With desire I have desired to eat this Passover with you before I suffer; for I say to you, I will not any more eat of it, until it be fulfilled in the kingdom of God. And he took the cup, and gave thanks, and said, Take this, and divide it among yourselves; for I say to you, I will not drink of the fruit of the vine, until the kingdom of God shall come. And he took bread, and gave thanks, and broke it, and gave to them, saying, This is my body which is given for you; this do in remembrance of me. Likewise also the cup after supper, saying, This cup is the new testament in my blood, which is shed for you.**

The communion ritual of the Eucharist has been passed down in the Church to this day in honor of these words of Jesus. But for both Catholics and Protestants alike it is seen as an act unrelated to the understanding of Jesus as the Word of God. The deeper meaning of the Eucharist, however, is spiritual, as demonstrated by Jesus in linking His blood with the New Testament. We partake of this Eucharist as we partake of our daily bread: by digesting Jesus' Word in our hearts and living it.

There is another passage in Scripture, this time in Revelation 10:9-11, that treats the Word of God as spiritual food:

> **And I went to the angel, and said to him, Give me the little scroll. And he said to me, Take it, and eat it up; and it shall make your belly bitter, but it shall be in your mouth sweet as honey. And I took the little scroll out of the angel's hand, and ate it up; and it was in my mouth sweet as honey, and as soon as I had eaten it my belly was bitter. And he said unto me, You must prophesy again about many peoples, and nations, and tongues, and kings.**

That Jesus considered the spiritual food of the Word to be of like nature but far more significant and real than physical food is demonstrated in Matthew 4:2-4, when, after Jesus fasted in the wilderness, satan approached Him, tempting Him:

> **And when he had fasted forty days and forty nights, he was afterward hungry. And when the tempter came to him, he said, If you are the Son of God, command that these stones be made bread. But he answered and said, It is written, Man shall not live by bread alone, but by every word that proceeds out of the mouth of God.**

Seven
Ruth

The little book of Ruth gives us one of the loveliest stories in the Bible. In it, one may find strong representations of Jesus, the Church, and the Holy Spirit all interacting harmoniously and lovingly, as we ourselves can anticipate in our future spiritual relationship with God. At a higher level than the tale itself, Ruth plays the role of the Christian Church, while Boaz represents Jesus Christ. Ruth's mother-in-law Naomi is sometimes mistakenly misrepresented here as Israel or an individual, but in truth the story carefully and deliberately places her in the role of the beautiful and noble Holy Spirit.

This narrative that begins with such desolation of spirit finds Naomi returning from Moab back to her homeland in Judah, having lost her husband and two sons. The loss, emotionally wrenching as it is, also places her in jeopardy of starvation. As she begins her sad trek back, she releases her daughters-in-law Orpah and Ruth, having lost their husbands, to return to their families in Moab. Amid much tearful keening over this parting, Orpah sets off back to her family. Ruth, on the other hand, refuses to part. In her adamant insistence on staying with Naomi, she delivers the following immortal words of devoted love as she clings to her beloved mother-in-law:

> **Entreat me not to leave you, or to return from following after you; for wherever you go, I will go, and where you lodge I will lodge. Your people shall be my people, and your God, my God. Where you die, will I die, and there will I be buried; the Lord do so to me, and also more, if ought but death part you and me."**

Naomi must have imparted to her daughter-in-law Ruth much

wisdom and understanding, particularly of the loving nature of God. She also demonstrated this love through her own interaction with her daughters-in-law. Ruth was able to internalize this profound heart knowledge, returning this love with the fervor that Jesus commanded in Matthew 22:37 and 38 as He echoed the words of Moses in Deuteronomy 6:4 and 5:

> **Jesus said to [the Pharisee], You shall love the Lord your God with all your heart, with all your soul, and with all your mind. This is the first and great commandment.**

Upon her arrival at Naomi's homeland, Ruth's circumstances rapidly began to change as God Himself returned Ruth's love for Naomi with unforeseen blessings. Ruth's departed husband had a close relative in the wealthy Boaz, who showed an interest in her from the first time he laid eyes on her. Appreciating that interest, Naomi gave Ruth an understanding of Jewish law, under which a close relative of a widow's late husband could claim her as his own wife; moreover, Naomi also gave Ruth advice on how she might win his affection. In a few short but stirring paragraphs the tale becomes a love story between Boaz and Ruth, with the romance culminating in their marriage. The union produces a child, placing Ruth firmly into the Jewish fold as grandmother to the great King David. In the first chapter of Matthew, Ruth is further honored with her inclusion as a Gentile into the bloodline of Jesus Christ.

Much later in time, the Apostle Paul echoes this union between Boaz and Ruth in Ephesians 5:31 and 32:

> **For this reason shall a Man leave his Father and Mother and cleave unto his wife, and the two shall become one flesh. This is a great mystery, but I speak concerning Christ and the Church.**

We of the Church have a beautiful and noble Mother-in-law as well. In fact, She is the same Person who Naomi represented to Ruth: our wonderful, loving Holy Spirit. With Her guidance, the Church shall marry Jesus and will participate, as the beautiful story of Ruth suggests, in a fully-gendered relationship with Him, and that also will bear fruit, as plainly described by Paul in Romans 7:4:

> **Therefore, my brethren, you also have become dead to the law through the body of Christ, that you may be married to another – to Him who was raised from the dead, that we should bear fruit to God.**

This romantic relationship is beautifully captured in the Song of Solomon, which describes anything but the brittle sterility of a non-gendered union.

The marriage between Boaz and Ruth reprises an earlier marriage that also foretold the union of Jesus Christ with His Church. This was the marriage told in Genesis Chapter 24 between Isaac and Rebekah, wherein Isaac was a figure of Jesus and Rebekah represented the Church. This union also bore fruit in the twelve Patriarchs who formed the beginning of the twelve tribes of Israel and in Judah carried the bloodline to Jesus.

Appropriately, during the Jewish Feast of Pentecost, called in Hebrew *Shavuot,* it is traditional to read the Book of Ruth. This tradition links the Pentecost with the Holy Spirit through Naomi and her representation. Since the Holy Spirit rushed in to indwell believers at the first Pentecost after Jesus' resurrection, the Feast of Pentecost has even more directly honored the Holy Spirit among Christians. Yet further, this indwelling of the Holy Spirit was foretold in the coming upon the Tabernacle and Solomon's Temple of the feminine Shekinah Glory, as described in Exodus 40 and 1 Kings 8. I note this connection in the Introduction to my novel *Buddy*, and expand on it in my book *Marching to a Worthy Drummer.*

Eight
Naomi

In the Scriptural story of Ruth, read and recited every *Shavuot* (Pentecost) in the Jewish community, Naomi returns in sadness and poverty to her homeland in Israel following the deaths of her husband and two sons. She brings with her Ruth, her daughter-in-law who refused to leave her. Another daughter-in-law, Orpah, remains behind in Moab. A love story awaits Ruth in Israel, where she and the wealthy Boaz meet, are attracted to each other and marry. A son, Obed, is born through the union. Obed himself eventually gives birth to Jesse, who, in turn, is the father of David. The genealogy continues from there to the Gospels of Matthew and Luke, which list the forbears of Joseph and Mary, respectively, earthly parents of Jesus Christ.

The story of Ruth is a love story on multiple levels. At the most direct level, it involves Boaz and Ruth, Jewish and Gentile ancestors of Jesus Christ. At a higher level, Ruth represents the Church while kinsman-redeemer Boaz represents Jesus Christ, demonstrating the love involved in that spiritual union. Naomi is far more than a mere extra in this beautiful passion play, representing none other than the Holy Spirit. In my novel *Buddy*, I was moved by these representations of Ruth and Naomi to point to their relationship with each other as an answer to a theological question that I had posed:

"In Deuteronomy Chapter 6 is found one of the most beautifully hope-filled passages in the entire Bible. Moses, being guided by the Holy Spirit, addresses the nation of Israel, saying,

> **Hear, O Israel: The Lord our God is one Lord: And thou shalt love the Lord thy God with all thine heart, and with all thy soul, and with all thy might.**

"The practical implications of this one sentence are immense. Jesus in Matthew 22 called it the great commandment, to be observed above all else, and by repeating it during His incarnation He extended its application beyond Israel to the Church as well. It tells us that we *can* love our God with all our hearts, which means that we were created to do just that. It also implies that God can love us back, for love is not unidirectional.

"The theological implications of that commandment are no less profound. It means that Jesus' work on the cross was a demonstration of his love. Yet further, it says that our God is one, forming the basis of our monotheism, despite later passages that amply demonstrate His Trinitarian nature.

"Therein lies a question of exceeding import to every person who wishes, in obedience to Jesus' words in Matthew 22, to love God: how can God be one while being several?

"In the book of Ruth is found another beautiful passage that has tugged at the strings of countless hearts over the centuries since it was written. It has evoked tears and inspired poems and love stories and been held up as a golden example of devotion and loyalty.

> **And [Naomi] said, Behold, thy sister in law is gone back unto her people, and unto her gods: return thou after thy sister in law.**
>
> **And Ruth said, Entreat me not to leave thee, or to return from following after thee: for whither thou goest, I will go; and where thou lodgest, I will lodge: thy people shall be my people, and thy God my God: Where thou diest, will I die, and there will I be buried: the Lord do so to me, and more also, if ought but death part thee and me.**

"These words of Ruth were originally directed to her mother-in-law Naomi, but, as in all Scripture, they were written under the direction of the Holy Spirit, who had in mind a much greater application, one in which both Ruth and Naomi were but types. Embedded in this song of Ruth, as a matter of fact, is an answer to the question of our monotheism toward a Trinitarian God. The answer itself is quite beautiful as well as being a wonderful promise to mankind.

"Ruth, I would say, is a type of the Church; and Naomi of the Holy Spirit. Therein is the answer: the link between God as One and God as a Multiplicity is love within a perfect Family setting, as Paul declared in his letter to the Ephesians:

> **For this cause shall a man leave his father and his mother, and shall be joined unto his wife, and they two shall be one flesh. This is a great mystery, but I speak concerning Christ and his church.**

"The connection between Naomi and the Holy Spirit suggests a love of God that is so beautifully magnificent as to dwarf His other attributes. It is a story that begs to be told, and I attempt to tell a part of it here. The medium that I use for this treasured task is a novel that chronicles the extraordinary love that God shows toward four severely handicapped individuals, two having an affliction of the body and the other two of the heart. Many of the events described in the novel are based on fact."

There may be yet another level to this story, a prophetic one. Ruth and Orpah, both of Moab, were married to Naomi's Jewish sons, who may be thought of as representing the marriage between Church and Jesus in the material domain. Naomi continues to represent the Holy Spirit, at this point indwelling the members of the Church. As the crisis unfolds with the death of the sons representing Jesus and the subsequent persecution of the Church, that part associated with Orpah falls away back to the Gentile-secular world, while that part associated with Ruth follows the Holy Spirit into fellowship with a revived Israel and union with the resurrected, spiritual Jesus, represented by Boaz.

Nine
The Shekinah Glory

In 1 Corinthians 3:16 and Ephesians 2:19-22 Paul asserts that the Church is a temple indwelt by the Holy Spirit:

> **Know you not that ye are the temple of God, and that the Spirit of God dwells in you?**
>
> **Now, therefore, you are no more strangers and sojourners, but fellow citizens with the saints, and of the household of God; and are built upon the foundation of the apostles and prophets, Jesus Christ himself being the chief corner stone, in whom all the building fitly framed together grows into a holy temple in the Lord; in whom you also are built together for a habitation of God through the Spirit.**

The facts embedded in these passages are no surprise to Christians, who generally accept without question that believers are indwelt with the Holy Spirit and comprise, as the Church, a holy temple. What some of us may not be aware of is that this temple and its indwelling by the Holy Spirit was represented numerous times as the Glory of God in the Old Testament. An example taken from 1 Kings 8:6-11 is given below:

> **And the priests brought in the ark of the covenant of the Lord to its place, into the inner sanctuary of the house, into the most holy place, even under the wings of the cherubim. For the cherubim spread forth their two wings of the place of the ark, and the cherubim covered the ark and its staves above. And they drew out the staves, that the ends of the staves were seen out in the holy place before the inner sanctuary, but they were not seen outside; and**

> **there they are to this day. There was nothing in the ark except the two tables of stone, which Moses put there at Horeb, when the lord made a covenant with the children of Israel, when they came out of the land of Egypt. And it came to pass, when the priests were come out of the holy place, that the cloud filled the house of the lord, so that the priests could not stand to minister because of the cloud; for the glory of the Lord had filled the house of the Lord.**

A passage of the same flavor can be found in Exodus 40 regarding the Tabernacle in the wilderness.

Interesting as this passage and others like it may be in their apparent correlation with Paul's understanding of the Church as constituting a temple and of its being indwelt by the Holy Spirit, they're still not all that surprising. It's not a difficult reach, in this context, to view Solomon's temple as a type representing the Church and the Glory of God descending upon it as representing the indwelling Holy Spirit. Nor does it conflict in any way with our conventional understanding of Scripture.

This situation changes rapidly when we investigate the meaning of the phrase "Glory of God". In the original Hebrew this Glory that Paul understands to be the Holy Spirit is named "Shekinah".

There still is no problem so far, because in the English language nouns lack gender attributes. Not so, however, for the Hebrew language. The noun "Shekinah" does possess a gender attribute, which is female. Turning to the Internet, the Wikipedia entry for "Shekinah" begins as follows:

"Hebrew [Shekinah] is the English spelling of a grammatically feminine Hebrew ancient blessing. The original word means the *dwelling* or *settling,* and denotes the dwelling or settling of the divine presence of God, especially in the temple in Jerusalem." An accompanying figure shows the Shekinah, or the Glory of God, indwelling the temple as described in 1 Kings 8.

Noting the female gender of this indwelling Shekinah, we find here by comparing the indwelling presence of the Glory in Solomon's temple with the description in Ephesians 2 of the Holy Spirit indwelling the human temple that Scripture itself, by furnishing this direct comparison, supports an interpretation of the Holy Spirit as a female Entity. This does appear to conflict with conventional Christian thought, as driven by the use in Scripture of the male pronoun in reference to the Holy Spirit. I fully explain in the novel "Buddy" why that viewpoint of conflict is actually a misperception.

Those who are opposed to any attempt to place a feminine label on the Holy Spirit would insist that in the original Hebrew, any gender can arbitrarily be placed on an inanimate object. They miss an obvious point: the Holy Spirit is not inanimate.

This gender attribute in 1 Kings 8 was simply lost in the translation from Hebrew to English, which could have been a result of the lack of gender precision in the English language. But there is an associated gender misrepresentation in Isaiah 51:9, 10 that appears to be more deliberate. What the translators did in that passage was to substitute the grammatically incorrect 'it' for the gender-correct 'she' in reference to the Shekinah. In their desire to maintain a fully masculine Godhead, they neutered the female.

The inclusion of femininity into the Godhead endows our vision of God with a greatly enhanced attribute of love. The pervasive notion of an all-masculine or genderless God denies that beauty to Him and the other Members of the Godhead and renders Him alien to us.

Ten
God's Mercy Toward Peter

I'm grateful to God for Jesus' having selected Peter to be a disciple. I can't speak for anyone else, but before the Holy Spirit got hold of him, Peter was a lot like me – willful, impetuous and slow on the uptake. With some spectacular exceptions, he never quite seemed to get the point of what Jesus was saying. Worse, he denied Jesus to save his own neck. Not just once, but three times. It's there in the Gospels in all the sordid details. In Matthew 26:33-35, for example, Peter, as usual, thinks that he's good enough to follow Jesus on his own merit. He can do it all himself without help from God. Jesus rebukes him for that, saying that Peter would deny him three times before the rooster crowed. Sure enough, as Jesus was being abused by the religious "authorities", Peter three times denied any association with Him. At the sound of the rooster, Peter realized what he had done and was devastated by his own lack of faith.

The lesson, of course, is that without God we can't do anything, even come to Him. Peter's failure of faith was made all the worse by Jesus statement in Matthew 10:33,

> **But whosoever shall deny me before men, him will I also deny before my Father, who is in heaven.**

After Peter's denial Jesus was crucified and died, leaving Peter to fret, and continue to do so, as he thought, for the rest of his life over what he had done. But Jesus didn't leave Peter in that state. Instead, the resurrected Jesus came back to Peter, as recorded in John 21. Three times He asked Peter if he loved Him, each time following Peter's affirmation of love with the command to feed His sheep. In those three exchanges, Jesus forgave Peter three times for his denials, thus canceling out the terrible consequences of what Peter had done. But it didn't end there.

Beyond the forgiveness, Jesus also was sharing with Peter something of immense importance. He was including Peter in His own acts of speaking His Word to mankind, in that act increasing the Church. The first account of Peter's fulfillment of Jesus' command to feed His sheep, after he has been filled with the Holy Spirit, is given in Acts 2:22-41. In that account, Peter's bold exhortation resulted in the salvation of three thousand souls. It may be seen in that first fulfillment of Jesus' command that when Jesus talked about feeding His sheep, He wasn't talking about material food. Instead, the food of importance was the spiritual one, speaking the words of the Gospel to the salvation of souls. Having followed the prophet Jonah in ducking away from God, Peter was now following that same prophet in voicing God's displeasure with sin and exhorting the people to righteousness.

In the second instance of fulfilling Jesus' command to feed His sheep, Peter again spoke before a crowded audience, this time bringing five thousand souls to salvation through the Word of God.

In the third instance, Peter became involved in dialogue with the Italian Cornelius. This act, of course, involved the mighty, loving Arm of God, the Holy Spirit, who had to overcome Peter's Jewish attitude of repulsion by Gentiles to accomplish that task.

In fulfilling Jesus' commandment to feed His sheep, the first time Peter speaks the Word of God to the salvation of three thousand souls. The second time Peter feeds Jesus' sheep with the Word of God, five thousand souls are saved. Until this time, the Church was pretty much limited to Jews. (Even the Ethiopian eunuch who was baptized by Philip was probably a Jew, Ethiopia having enjoyed a long Jewish history extending back to Solomon and the queen of Sheba.) Now comes the third time that Peter, empowered by the Holy Spirit, obeys Jesus' command to feed His sheep, as described in Acts 10, and this time, after healing another lame man and raising Tabitha back to life in the name of Jesus Christ, Peter through the Word of God extends the Church, and salvation with her, to the entire Gentile world.

The immediate importance of this fulfillment by Peter of Jesus' threefold commandments to feed His sheep, beside its obvious demonstration of God's merciful love, is the support it gives to the assertion that God not only welcomes but desires the active participation of Peter, and consequently of mankind itself, in the sharing of His grand plan of salvation. Man is thus a participant, albeit with the necessary input of the Holy Spirit in the process, of his own salvation. Can anything demonstrate more fully than this the loving intimacy of sharing with which God relates to mankind?

Volume Six

God's Character

Contents

Preface 279

One: Showered With Blessings 281

Two: In the Beginning 284

Three: Faith 288

Four: Courage 291

Five: Selflessness 294

Six: Compassion 298

Seven: Otherness 301

Eight: The First Light of Creation 304

Nine: Family 309

Ten: Paul 313

Eleven: Perpetua 316

Preface

The integrating theme for the present volume, Volume Six, is the character of God, and of how His nature influenced the manner of man's creation and purpose within God's economy.

The nature of God and His character is reflected in the creation of man and subsequent events in our history, even our fall from grace that followed our disobedience in the Garden. The desire of God, as revealed in the Bible, for intimate companionship with us has driven His interaction with us in ways that we perceive as both positive and negative, but always in ways that bring us closer to His own noble nature. In John 15:13, Jesus speaks of the strength of selfless love, foretelling what He and His followers shall do to demonstrate that:

> **Greater love has no man than this, that a man lay down his life for his friends.**

Even when God takes us to the woodshed, it is for the sake of our future relationship with Him. As described in Hebrews 13:8-13, even our painful experiences bring us closer to commonality with Jesus:

> **But if you be without chastisement, of which all are partakers, then are you bastards, and not sons. Furthermore, we have had fathers of our flesh who corrected us, and we gave them reverence. Shall we not much rather be in subjection to the Father of spirits, and live? For they truly for a few days chastened us after their own pleasure, but He for our profit, that we might be partakers of his holiness.**
>
> **Now no chastening for the present seems to be joyous, but grievous; nevertheless, afterward it yields the peaceable fruit of righteousness to them who are exercised by it. Wherefore, lift up the hands which hang down, and the**

feeble knees; and make straight paths for your feet, lest that which is lame be turned out of the way; but let it rather be healed.

One

Showered With Blessings

Christian news outlets seem to have a common theme these days – a lamentation over the decline in Church attendance. This same theme can be seen in the frantic way that some Churches are trying to keep their flocks: daycare, latte machines, happy messages. Given the manner in which the Church seems to be falling away despite the almost hysterical attempts of pastors to stop the outward flow, it's natural to wonder whether the exiting masses really ever understood what they had signed up for. Maybe those who evangelized them didn't give them the big picture. Maybe the neophytes expected to get some blessings out of the deal, of the material kind.

Jesus' parable of the sower comes to mind. In Matthew 13:18-23, Jesus explains this parable to His disciples:

> **Hear, therefore, the parable of the sower. When any one hears the word of the kingdom, and understands it not, then comes the wicked one, and catches away that which was sown in his heart. This is he who received seed by the wayside. But he that received the seed in stony places, the same is he that hears the word, and immediately with joy receives it; yet has he not root in himself, but endures it for a while; for when tribulation or persecution arises because of the word, immediately he is offended. He also who received seed among the thorns is he that hears the word; and the care of this age, and the deceitfulness of riches, choke the word, and he becomes unfruitful. But he who received the seed in the good ground is he who hears the word, and understands it, who also bears fruit, and brings forth, some a hundredfold, some sixty, some thirty.**

I see this falling away as a good thing for the health of the Church. Those who had accepted a materialistic Jesus, expecting Him to come promptly down the chimney bearing goodies or handing them a check from Publishers' Clearing House, were worshiping a different god than Jesus anyway. I've seen Church spokespersons leading such people astray with blatant misrepresentations of who Jesus actually is, and what He actually represents. You can still see them on television hawking their wares. I once attended a Church where a young couple participated with fervent prayers for the removal of a cancer that was afflicting the wife; when she eventually died, the husband refused to come back to Church.

Jesus never promised such things; rather, He treated the material world with disdain, focusing instead on the spiritual world to come. In John 18:36 and Matthew 6:24, Jesus made this clear:

> **Jesus answered, My kingdom is not of this world; if my kingdom were of this world, then would my servants fight, that I should not be delivered to the Jews; but now is my kingdom not from here."**
>
> **No man can serve two masters; for either he will hate the one, and love the other; or else he will hold to the one, and despise the other. You cannot serve God and money.**

Those who received the Word of God in good soil are of a different sort. After the pseudo-Christians have left the fold, these others will remain, whatever the circumstances that try to draw them back into secular society. They see a more noble Jesus, and in their staying the course God in return is developing them into a people having a common trait, the possession of *valor.*

God will indeed shower them with blessings, but of a more spiritual nature. God will clothe them in riches of character, endowing them with an abundance of faith, courage, selflessness and compassion, those qualities that Jesus will treasure in His Bride, the Church. Just like Jonah, they will enjoy the spiritual companionship of souls that they have rescued with a true knowledge of God.

> **And the word of the Lord came to Jonah the second time,**

saying, Arise, go to Nineveh, that great city, and preach to it the preaching that I bid you. So Jonah arose, and went to the city a day's journey, and he cried, and said, Yet forty days, and Nineveh shall be overthrown. So the people of Nineveh believed God, and proclaimed a fast, and put on sackcloth, from the greatest of them even to the least of them. For word came to the king of Nineveh, and he arose from his throne, and he laid his robe from him, and covered himself with sackcloth, and sat in ashes . . . And God said to Jonah . . . And should not I spare Nineveh, that great city, in which are more that one hundred twenty thousand persons who cannot discern between their right hand and their left hand; and also much cattle?

Two
In the Beginning

Near the very beginning of Scripture, in Genesis 1:26 and 27, God asserts that man was created in His image:

> **And God said, Let us make man in our image, after our likeness; and let them have dominion over the fish of the sea, and over the fowl of the air, and over all the earth, and over every creeping thing that creeps upon the earth. So God created man in his own image, in the image of God created he him; male and female created he them.**

Commentaries on this passage commonly interpret the likeness of man to God to involve qualities of character. That they do not include gender and gender-based love in their descriptions, despite the obvious intent of Scripture to include this feature, is a deliberate and unjustified attempt to equate purity with chastity, as I've noted elsewhere. They simply don't address the most important underlying issue, which is that man's character at his creation reflects the character of God.

The Reformation Study Bible, for example, describes the similarities between God and man at his creation as possessing intelligence and creativity, the ability to communicate and relate to others, and moral uprightness. Regarding man's morality, the commentary does not go into details, other than to acknowledge that this faculty was diminished in man's fall from grace. Other commentaries are similarly vague.

The details are important. The regenerate man, he who has been born again upon his acceptance of the selfless act of Jesus Christ on the cross, and has received the indwelling Holy Spirit as Jesus promised to His followers, is capable of much more than the moral uprightness commonly thought of as being peaceful, avoiding "sinful" behavior, and not indulging in troublemaking. The more important qualities of his regenerated character as aided by the Holy Spirit include faith, courage, selflessness and compassion for others.

These four qualities sometimes occur together in events so profound as to define the person. When they do, they display nobility of the high order associated in wartime with recipients of the Congressional Medal of Honor. The reading of the recipient's deeds that led to the receipt of that medal often causes weeping in the audience due to the extraordinary greatness of the heroic action that is being cited.

That is the greatness of God's character, and the character in His image with which He endowed us at creation.

Psalm 22 describes the agony of crucifixion; Isaiah 53 describes the humility and suffering imposed on Jesus for our sins; and the Gospels affirm these forecasts.

The Gospels and the various letters of the New Testament place the same expectations on the followers of Jesus. In John 14:12, Jesus claims that some will do even greater works than Him:

> **Verily, verily, I say to you, He who believes on me, the works that I do shall he do also; and greater works than these shall he do, because I go to my Father.**

Jesus was able to make that assertion because after His resurrection and the subsequent Pentecost, the Holy Spirit was given by the Father in great measure to Jesus' followers in the Upper Room of Acts 2. The Acts of the Apostles bears witness of the amazing healings, resurrections and transmission of the Gospel message performed by Peter, Paul and others. That they managed to do so under severe persecution is even more remarkable.

Or is it? Are the acts of the Apostles remarkable despite the persecution they were forced to endure, or are they remarkable because of that persecution? There has been talk in some Churches that many of those first gifts of the Holy Spirit no longer apply, for one very flimsy reason or another, the excuse most often put forward being that the gifts ceased at the final canonization of Scripture, and the establishment of Churches throughout the known world, rendering that Power from God no longer necessary. This point of view is called cessationism, for the cessation of the gifts. It is most prominent in those Churches having no outreach and whose attendance has been limited to Sunday services of a ritualistic flavor. Here there is no challenge requiring faith or courage, nor any exercise of selflessness or compassion. Here there is no manifestation of the Holy Spirit, not because the gifts have ceased, but because the Church has abandoned its fervent love of God.

The gifts of the Holy Spirit are as necessary today as they were in that Upper Room. Societies that have suppressed Christianity for decades and even centuries are re-awakening to Jesus' message. Their need to hear the Word of God is just as urgent as those societies of the First Century that had never heard the Gospel. In Africa and China, for example, the underground Church is spreading like wildfire, and multitudes of these repressed people are being harshly persecuted. But the Holy Spirit is working signs and wonders there, just as in the Book of Acts, and Churches continue to grow.

And the multitudes who are coming to God in the midst of their persecutions are growing in faith, courage, selflessness and compassion. They are well-pleasing to God and worthy of their future spiritual marriage to Jesus Christ.

We in societies in which Christians are comfortable may not be as fortunate as we think. Perhaps we should ask, even plead, for the Power of the Holy Spirit, even if it means our physical discomfort and danger. As Jesus said in Matthew 10:24,

> **The disciple is not above his master, nor the servant above his lord.**

If Jesus had to suffer for our sakes and was hated by the world, how should we expect not to encounter those same conditions? Perhaps, over the centuries, many sincere Christians were able to live out their lives in comfort and security. Perhaps they were fortunate, or perhaps not. But I know that personally, I'd like to have some things in common with Jesus. Provided, of course, that I am able to maintain my faith.

Three
Faith

Faith is the ability to understand that the God of Judeo-Christian Scripture truly exists, to *want* that God to exist, to the point that enough Scripture is read and digested to understand intuitively that God does, indeed, exist. Faith also accepts as real and welcome the work of the Holy Spirit, who indwells all believers. Moreover, faith involves the ability to appreciate that a better world exists, the spiritual one in which God plays such a vital and loving part. Faith includes the ability to value valor over wealth. Faith is explained in a noble manner in that great Hall of Faith chapter, Hebrews 11:

> **Now faith is the substance of things hoped for, the evidence of things not seen. For by it the elders received witness. Through faith we understand that the worlds were framed by the word of God, so that things which are seen were not made of things which do appear.**
>
> **By faith Abel offered to God a more excellent sacrifice than Cain, by which he obtained witness that he was righteous, God testifying of his gifts; and by it he being dead yet speaks. By faith Enoch was translated that he should not see death, and was not found, because God had translated him; for before his translation he had this testimony, that he pleased God.**
>
> **But without faith it is impossible to please him; for he who comes to God must believe that he is, and that he is a rewarder of those who diligently seek him.**
>
> **By faith Noah . . .By faith Abraham . . .By faith Isaac . . . By faith Jacob . . . By faith Joseph . . . By faith Moses . . .**
>
> **And what more shall I say? For the time would fail me**

to tell of Gideon, and of Barak, and of Samson, and of Jephthah; of David also, and Samuel, and of the prophets. Who, through faith, subdued kingdoms, wrought righteousness, obtained promises, stopped the mouths of lions, quenched the violence of fire, escaped the edge of the sword, out of weakness were made strong, became valiant in fight, turned to flight the armies of the aliens. Women received their dead raised to life again, and others were tortured, not accepting deliverance, that they might obtain a better resurrection: and others had trial of cruel mockings and scourgings, yea, moreover, of bonds and imprisonment; they were stoned, they were sawn asunder, were tested, were slain with the sword; they wandered about in sheepskins and goatskins; being destitute, afflicted, tormented (of whom the world was not worthy); they wandered in deserts, and in mountains, and in dens and caves of the earth.

And these all, having received witness through faith, received not the promise, God having provided some better thing for us, that they without us should not be made perfect.

Abel's offering to God was more excellent than Cain's because of his more noble understanding of what would be pleasing to God, which came from his greater faith. Even back then, Abel understood that God Himself would have to die sacrificially in the place of fallen and helpless mankind to bring him back into fellowship with God. He knew that and sacrificed an animal, one of God's creations, in honor of that future event, long before Abraham attempted to sacrifice Isaac and Moses instituted the Passover in commemoration of that same great sacrifice that Jesus made.

Cain failed to understand that same helplessness of man; he thought that he could please God through the fruit of his own labors. There are sects that attempt to do that today: storm the gates of heaven through their own efforts.

Enoch pleased God through his faith. His translation from Earth into Heaven without death was equivalent to what we look forward to today: the rapture of the Church, as described by Paul in 1 Corinthians 15:51-57 and 1 Thessalonians 4:13-18:

> **Behold, I show you a mystery: we shall not all sleep, but we shall all be changed, in a moment, in the twinkling of an eye, at the last trump; for the trumpet shall sound, and the dead shall be raised incorruptible, and we shall be changed. For this corruptible must put on incorruption, and this mortal must put on immortality. So, when this corruptible shall have put on incorruption, and this mortal shall put on immortality, then shall be brought to pass the saying that is written, Death is swallowed up in victory. O death, where is your sting? O grave, where is your victory? The sting of death is sin; and the strength of sin is the law. But thanks be to God, who gives us the victory though our Lord Jesus Christ.**
>
> **But I would not have you ignorant, brethren, concerning them who are asleep, that you sorrow not, even as others who have no hope. For if we believe that Jesus died and rose again, even so them also who sleep in Jesus God with bring with him. For this we say to you by the word of the Lord, that we who are alive and remain to the coming of the Lord shall not precede them who are asleep. For the Lord Himself shall descend from heaven with a shout, with the voice of the archangel, and with the trump of God; and the dead in Christ shall rise first; then we who are alive and remain shall be caught up together with them in the clouds, to meet the Lord in the air; and so shall we ever be with the Lord. Wherefore, comfort one another with these words.**

Jesus Himself stressed the importance of faith, often attributing the faith of those whom He healed to their restoration. In Luke 18:42, Jesus heals a man, and then tells him that he was saved through his faith:

> **And Jesus said to him, Receive your sight; your faith has saved you.**

Four
Courage

To fear the Lord is to understand His reality, and the greatness of His Being. That fear however, is tempered with a companion knowledge of His goodness, permitting that fear to banish from the mind the fear of anything else. According to Proverbs 1:7, it fosters wisdom.

> **The fear of the Lord is the beginning of knowledge, but fools despise wisdom and instruction.**

Fear of the Lord supports courage. God treasures that quality of character, as exemplified in Joshua 1:5-9, where God speaks to Joshua as he replaces Moses as leader of the Israelites in their journey into the land promised to Abraham by God.

> **There shall not any man be able to stand before you all the days of your life. As I was with Moses, so I will be with you; I will not fail you, nor forsake you. Be strong and of good courage; for unto this people shall you divide for an inheritance the land which I swore to their fathers to give them. Only be you strong and very courageous, that you may observe to do according to all the law, which Moses, my servant, commanded you; turn not from it to the right hand or to the left, that you may prosper wherever you go. This book of the law shall not depart out of your mouth, but you shall meditate therein day and night, that you may observe to do according to all that is written therein; for then you shall make your way prosperous, and then you shall have good success. Have not I commanded you? Be strong and of good courage; be not afraid, neither be you dismayed; for the Lord your God is with you wherever you go.**

Joshua of the tribe of Ephraim was given that position of leadership upon the passing of Moses because, through his faith in God, he stood with only Caleb of Judah in support of their entry into the Promised Land out of the twelve tribal representatives who went into the land to spy it out. When they returned from their venture, only Joshua and Caleb had the courage to recommend that they go into it and conquer it.

Two years into their wilderness wanderings, the Israelites stopped over at Kadesh-Barnea while the twelve tribal representatives went into the land of Canaan to spy out the produce and the people who inhabited it. They returned with news that the land was lush and productive, but the people there were giants. While Joshua and Caleb stood firm in their trust in God, the other ten were afraid and, weeping in abject terror, convinced the nation to hold back from entering the land. God did just that – He kept them in the wilderness for another thirty eight years, waiting for a full forty years from the exodus of the Israelites from Egypt, until the last of that generation died out save Joshua and Caleb. For his valor God awarded Caleb Hebron, the final resting place of the Patriarchs and their primary wives, and the location of David's first throne. For the valor of Joshua, God awarded him leadership over Israel upon the death of Moses.

The journey of the Israelites from Egypt to Canaan was a real event; it also was a type of every Christian's personal journey from sin to salvation and fellowship with God. Our individual journeys involve our development of character from the secular traits of self-service, avoidance of trouble, greed and indifference toward others to the more noble qualities set before Christians. This process of growth demands the heavy involvement of the Holy Spirit, but also asks of the individual personal courage and eventually results in the Christian's own possession of valor.

Jesus Himself set the standard for courage. Knowing that He was God and understanding with excruciating clarity what lay ahead, yet for our sakes He submitted Himself to disgrace and great suffering. In the Garden of Gethsemane, according to Matthew 26:36-39, He revealed His knowledge of the horror to come upon Him.

> **Then came Jesus with [His disciples] to a place called Gethsemane, and said to the disciples, Sit here, while I go and pray yonder. And he took with him Peter and the two sons of Zebedee, and began to be sorrowful and very depressed. Then he said to them, My Soul is exceedingly sorrowful, even to death; stay here, and watch with me. And he went a little further, and fell on his face, and prayed, saying, O my Father, it is be possible, let this cup pass from me; nevertheless, not as I will, but as you will.**

Faith and courage are very close in nature, but there is a subtle difference. Faith involves a willingness to believe, even in times of stress when it might be thought of as beneficial to give up that belief. Courage involves faith to the extent of casting out fear, but also requires the ability to do something unpleasant, of which the flesh protests.

Persecuted Christians everywhere must exercise courage to stand fast in their faith.

Five
Selflessness

In Israel's confrontation with the Philistines, David demonstrated a selfless nobility that was highly pleasing to God. The account begins in 1 Samuel 17:1-14:

> **Now the Philistines gathered together their armies to battle, and were gathered together at Socoh, which belonged to Judah, and encamped between Socoh and Azekah, in Ephesdammim. And Saul and the men of Israel were gathered together, and encamped by the valley of Elah, and set the battle in array against the Philistines. And the Philistines stood on a mountain on the one side, and Israel stood on a mountain on the other side, with a valley between them.**
>
> **And there went out a champion out of the camp of the Philistines, named Goliath, of Gath, whose height was almost ten feet. And he had a helmet of bronze upon his head, and he was armed with a coat of mail; and the weight of the coat was about one hundred pounds. And he had shin armor of bronze upon his legs, and carried a javelin of bronze between his shoulders. And the staff of his spear was like a weaver's beam; and his spear's head weighed ten pounds of iron: and one bearing a shield went before him. And he stood and cried to the armies of Israel, and said to them, Why are you come out to set your battle in array? Am not I a Philistine, and you servants to Saul? Choose you a man for you, and let him come down to me. If he be able to fight with me, and to kill me, then will we be your servants; but if I prevail against him, and kill**

> **him, then shall you be our servants, and serve us. And the Philistine said, I defy the armies of Israel this day; give me a man, that we may fight together.**
>
> **When Saul and all Israel heard those words of the Philistine, they were dismayed, and greatly afraid.**
>
> **Now David was the son of that Ephrathite of Bethlehem-judah,whose name was Jesse, who had eight sons; and the man went among men as an old man in the days of Saul. And the three eldest sons of Jesse went and followed Saul to the battle; and the names of his three sons who went to the battle were Eliab, the first-born, and next to him, Abinadab, and the third, Shammah. And David was the youngest; and the three eldest followed Saul.**

David was kept back from the challenge because of his youth and size. Instead, he was told to tend the family sheep. In modern terms, it was like he was told to stay in the car. But at one point Jesse told David to take some food to his brothers at the battleground, where Goliath held forth for forty days mocking the fearful Israelites, none of whom wanted to do battle with the giant of Gath. While he was with his brothers, Goliath was indulging in trash-speak about the Israelites and their God, while the Israelites continued to cower. The account continues with Saul offering a reward to anyone brave enough to face Goliath. In 1 Samuel 17:26 David responds:

> **And David spoke to the men who stood by him, saying, What shall be done for the man who kills this Philistine, and takes away the reproach from Israel? For who is this uncircumcised Philistine, that he should defy the armies of the living God?**

When Saul heard of David's response, he sent for him, whereupon David volunteered to face the giant. When Saul told him that he was too inexperienced to go against Goliath, David told him about how, during his shepherding duties, he had killed a lion and a bear that had threatened his flock. The record continues as David addresses Saul and then takes to the field in verses 36-50:

Your servant slew both the lion and the bear; and this uncircumcised Philistine shall be as one of them, seeing he hath defied the armies of the living God. David said, moreover, The Lord who delivered me out of the paw of the lion, and out of the paw of the bear, he will deliver me out of the hand of this Philistine. And Saul said to David, Go, and the Lord be with you. And Saul armed David with his armor, and he put a helmet of bronze upon his head; also he armed him with a coat of mail. And David girded his sword upon his armor, and he attempted to go; for he had not tested it. And David said to Saul, I cannot go with these; for I have not tested them. And David put them off.

And he took his staff in his hand, and chose five smooth stones out of the brook; and put them in a shepherd's bag which he had, even in a wallet; and his sling was in his hand: and he drew near the Philistine. And the Philistine came on and drew near to David; and the man who bore the shield went before him. And when the Philistine looked about, and saw David, he disdained him; for he was but a youth, and ruddy, and of a fair countenance. And the Philistine said to David, Am I a dog, that you come to me with staves? And the Philistine cursed David by his gods. And the Philistine said to David, Come to me, and I will give your flesh to the fowls of the air, and to the beasts of the field.

Then said David to the Philistine, You come to me with a sword, and with a spear, and with a shield; but I come to you in the name of the Lord of hosts, the God of the armies of Israel, whom you have defied. This day will the Lord deliver you into my hand; and I will smite you, and take your head from you; and I will give the carcasses of the host of the Philistines this day to the fowls of the air, and to the wild beasts of the earth, that all the earth may know that there is a God in Israel. And all this assembly shall know that the Lord saves not with sword and spear;

for the battle is the Lord's, and he will give you into our hands.

And it came to pass, when the Philistine arose, and came and drew near to meet David, that David hastened, and ran toward the army to meet the Philistine. And David put his hand in his bag, and took from there a stone, and slung it, and smote the Philistine in his forehead, that the stone sank into his forehead; and he fell upon his face to the earth. So David prevailed over the Philistine with a sling and with a stone, and smote the Philistine, and slew him; but there was no sword in the hand of David.

Some unbelievers are fond of pointing out what they think is a discrepancy in this account that renders it a fable, the mention of five stones when David only used one. Why five stones, they ask in contempt of the Word. The reason why David picked up five stones is because Goliath had four brothers. David was arming himself to do battle with all five.

In this account, David surely exercised his faith, and demonstrated an abundance of courage as well. But he did something else besides: he kept his eye on the Lord instead of himself, taking offense at the ease with which the Philistine denigrated his beloved God. In modern-day accounts of the recipients of the Congressional Medal of Honor for their valor on the field of battle, there continue to crop up the medals awarded posthumously to those who knew that they were to die in the process of saving others, but who did so willingly, their minds focused on their brothers' peril rather than their own.

Jesus spoke in John 15:13 of this selfless nobility:

Greater love has no man than this, that a man lay down his life for his friends.

Six
Compassion

God often chided the Israelites for adhering to ritual worship while foregoing the far more important compassion and mercy embedded in the spirit of the law. In Proverbs 21:3, Isaiah 11:1-17 and Malachi 3:5, for a small sample, God speaks about this issue:

> To do righteousness and justice is more acceptable to the Lord than sacrifice.
>
> To what purpose is the multitude of your sacrifices to me? Says the Lord; I am full of the burnt offerings of rams, and the fat of fed beasts, and I delight not in the blood of bullocks, or of lambs, or of he-goats. When you come to appear before me, who has required this at your hand, to tread my courts? Bring no more vain oblations; incense is an abomination to me; the new moons and Sabbaths, the calling of assemblies, I cannot bear; it is iniquity, even the solemn meeting. Your new moons and your appointed feasts my soul hates; they are a trouble to me, I am weary of bearing them. And when you spread forth your hands, I will hide my eyes from you; yea, when you make many prayers, I will not hear. Your hands are full of blood. Wash yourselves, make yourselves clean; but away the evil of your doings from before my eyes; cease to do evil. Learn to do well; seek justice, relieve the oppressed, judge the fatherless, plead for the widow.
>
> And I will come near to you to judgment; and I will be a swift witness against the sorcerers, and against the adulterers, and against false swearers, and against those who oppress the hireling in his wages, and widow, and the

fatherless, and that turn aside the stranger from his right, and fear not me, says the Lord of hosts.

Jesus displayed His honor of compassion in His parable of the good Samaritan, recounted in Luke 10:30-37. He added further depth to the account by having the compassionate person a Samaritan, one who was looked down upon by the Jews, contrasting him with Jewish religious elites, who failed to follow the spirit of Jewish law.

And Jesus, answering, said, A certain man went down from Jerusalem to Jericho, and fell among thieves, who stripped him of his clothing, and wounded him, and departed, leaving him half dead. And by chance there came down a certain priest that way; and when he saw him, he passed by on the other side. And likewise a Levite, when he was at the place, came and looked on him, and passed by on the other side.

But a certain Samaritan, as he journeyed, came where he was; and when he saw him, he had compassion on him, and went to him, and bound up his wounds, pouring in oil and wine, and set him on his own beast, and brought him to an inn, and took care of him. And on the next day, when he departed, he took out ten dollars, and gave them to the host, and said to him, Take care of him; and whatever you spend above that, when I come again, I will repay you.

Which, now, of these three, do you think was neighbor to him that fell among the thieves? And he said, He who showed mercy on him. Then said Jesus to him, Go, and do you likewise.

Jesus, of course, honored mercy and compassion in His own doing as well as His speaking by offering His own body as a substitutionary atonement for the wrongdoings of a helpless human race. He also showed compassion in other ways, such as His mercy toward Peter, who had denied Him three times during His incarceration. In John 21, Jesus forgave Peter three times for that, and Peter went on from there not only to fulfill Jesus' parting commandment to feed His sheep, but also to become a giant of a Christian in the process.

The account of Joseph in Genesis 37 through 45 is an early portrait of Jesus' compassionate nature. It foretells in detail the tender love that Jesus showed, even toward those who hated Him.

> **Then Joseph could not refrain himself before all them who stood by him; and he cried, Cause every man to go out from me. And there stood no man with him, while Joseph made himself known to his brethren. And he wept aloud: and the Egyptians and the house of Pharaoh heard. And Joseph said to his brethren, I am Joseph; does my father yet live? And his brethren could not answer him; for they were terrified at his presence. And Joseph said to his brethren, Come near to me, I ask you. And they came near. And he said, I am Joseph, your brother, whom you sold into Egypt.**
>
> **Now therefore be not grieved, nor angry with yourselves, that you sold me here; for God did send me before you to preserve life. For these two years has the famine been in the land: and yet there are five years, in which there shall neither be plowing nor harvest. And God sent me before you to preserve you a posterity in the earth, and to save your lives by a great deliverance. So now it was not you that sent me here, but God: and he has made me a father to Pharaoh, and lord of all his house, and a ruler throughout all the land of Egypt.**

But the account of Joseph involves more than this central character. Joseph's revelation of himself before his brothers was triggered by another compassionate event that pointed to Jesus as well, the offer of Judah, Jesus' forefather, to offer his substitutional enslavement in place of his youngest brother Benjamin, just as Jesus died in our place on the cross.

God's focus on compassion often links it with selflessness. But there is another factor in compassion: in its concern for others, it involves love of pure selflessness.

Seven
Otherness

The various Christian creeds have a number of things in common, one of which is that while for the most part they conform well to the essence of Scripture, they are in fact extra-Scriptural. They make some statements that don't quite match up with Bible teachings. In one major issue, in fact, they oppose the clear teaching of Scripture. This issue is time, or sequence.

In this issue of time, the Nicene Creed and others like it claim that Father, Son and Holy Spirit coexisted from eternity past. The implication is that they coexisted forever, or to state it in a firmer way, there was never an occasion where they didn't exist apart from each other. But that implication runs against the grain of Genesis in general and Revelation 3:14 specifically, in which Jesus asserts that He is the beginning of creation. This assertion of Jesus is a claim that harmonizes with Genesis 1 and John's Prologue, in which Jesus is the first light of the spoken Word.

Paul, speaking of Jesus in Colossians 1:15, echoes that assertion:

> **Who is the image of the invisible God, the first-born of all creation;**

This issue is anything but trivial. As co-existing Entities, and either genderless or weakly-gendered as well, each Member of the Godhead in the eyes of the creeds is self-sufficient with regard to attributes, powers and commitment to the others, and fully God in a manner identical with the others. This perceived self-sufficiency creates a situation that profoundly opposes the intrinsic nature of God.

Scripture often speaks out against the sin of pride. Proverbs, for example, has much to say against pride, as exemplified in Proverbs 8:13, 11:2, 13:10, 14:3 and 16:18:

> **The fear of the Lord is to hate evil; pride, and arrogance, and the evil way, and the perverse mouth, do I hate.**
>
> **When pride comes, then comes shame; but with the lowly is wisdom.**
>
> **Only by pride comes contention, but with the well-advised is wisdom.**
>
> **In the mouth of the foolish is a rod of pride, but the lips of the wise shall preserve them.**
>
> **Pride goes before destruction, and a haughty spirit before a fall.**

Despite the numerous instances in Scripture where God speaks out against the sin of pride, an eternally coexistent, individually self-sufficient Godhead renders it difficult for the Christian to understand and appreciate the unity in love implicit in Jesus' Great Commandment, Mark 12:28-30, which echoed God's Word through Moses in Deuteronomy 6:4 and 5:

> **And one of the scribes came, and having heard them reasoning together, and perceiving that he had answered them well, asked him, Which is the first commandment of all? And Jesus answered him, The first of all the commandments is: Hear, O Israel: the Lord our God is one Lord; and you shall love the Lord your God with all your heart, and with all your soul, and with all your mind, and all your strength: this is the first commandment.**

In attempting to maximize the majestic attributes of God, the founders of the creeds minimized the attributes of God of most importance, their selflessness and humble nature. Earlier, in Mark 7:6-9, Jesus spoke out against teaching doctrines of men in the place of Scripture:

> **[Jesus] answered and said to [the Pharisees], Well has**

> **Isaiah prophesied of you hypocrites, as it is written, This people honors me with their lips, but their heart is far from me. However, in vain do they worship me, teaching for doctrines the commandments of men. For laying aside the commandment of God, you hold the tradition of men, as the washing of pots and cups; and many other such things you do. And he said to them, Full well you reject the commandment of God, that you may keep your own tradition.**

Apparently not much was changed from the time of the Pharisees to the time that Christianity became legal and began taking over the affairs of men.

The problem of eternally co-existent, self-sufficient Members of the Godhead is that such an arrangement would support the narcissim of each Member. Moreover, that situation would tend to convey to Christians that same self-centered characteristic within the Godhead.

For that reason, otherness within the Godhead is an absolutely necessary feature. How much more representative of the tenor of Scripture to impute complementary otherness between Father and Holy Spirit, where they are strongly bound together by love, a love that bears fruit in Jesus Christ, their only-begotten Son!

Eight
The First Light of Creation

In Revelation 3, the risen Jesus delivers to John an admonishment regarding the seventh Church of His concern, the Church of Laodicea. In His description of that Church, He bypasses His usual format by omitting any mention of commendation. Of the seven Churches over which Jesus prophesied, only Sardis and Laodicea received that implicit chastisement. The Church of Laodicea, in fact is often cited by scholars of the Bible as representative of the fallen state of the Church at the time of the end of the age.

Focused on the characteristics of the Laodicean Church, scholars typically overlook the nature of the label that Jesus applied to Himself in verse 14, which is odd because that statement contradicts the traditional doctrine of the mainstream Christian Church in a very important area.

> **And unto the angel of the church of the Laodiceans write: These things saith the Amen, the faithful and true witness, the beginning of the creation of God.**

According to the Athanasian Creed and implicit in the others, including the Nicean Creed, Jesus had no beginning in time. The Father, the Son and the Holy Spirit were supposedly co-existent throughout eternity, none having been created. While in one sense that may be true, if one considers the pre-existence of one to include presence within another Being, that is not the usual interpretation of the creed as understood by the mainstream Churches, both Catholic and Protestant: Jesus and the Holy Spirit existed forever as separate Entities alongside the Father.

Yet there in Revelation 3:14 Jesus directly claims the opposite. If one must choose between a creed, which itself is extra-Scriptural, and Jesus, the very embodiment of truth, the obvious choice is Jesus.

The understanding that Jesus was created carries with it some very important collateral implications. In opposition to the mainstream Church's insistence upon God being genderless, which itself implies that procreation is a non-existent feature of the heavenly realm, this contradictory understanding implicit in Revelation 3:14 solidifies the notion of the Holy Spirit's femininity, which, in turn, supports the characterization of the Holy Trinity as the embodiment of Family, complete with the function of procreation. The procreated Entity, in that context, is none other than Jesus Christ, the Son of the Father and of the Holy Spirit.

This identification clarifies a functional issue: do the members of the Holy Trinity have the same or different functions, and if they are different, what are they? In the family context, with procreation on the table, the functions are indeed different, much as in an earthly family. Scripture itself identifies the Holy Father as embodying the divine Will. Scripture in John 6:38-40 exemplifies this association:

> **For I came down from heaven, not to do mine own will but the will of him who sent me. And this is the Father's will who hath sent me, that of all that he hath given me, I should lose nothing, but should raise it up again at the last day. And this is the will of him who sent me, that everyone who seeth the Son, and believeth on him, may have everlasting life; and I will raise him up at the last day.**

As divine spouse of the Father within the divine Family, the Holy Spirit must not only be feminine but must embody a function that represents the perfect complement in the procreative sense. That would necessarily define the functional attribute of the Holy Spirit as one which would enable the implementation of the Father's will. A word for this enabling function would be "means". Thus the divine will, in union with the divine means, creates the Holy Son, the divine actuality Jesus Christ. It is Jesus, the divine implementation resulting from the union of will and means, who came into the created universe and represents the actuality of creation. John's

Prologue, verses one through eighteen of John 1, says nothing less:

> **In the beginning was the Word, and the Word was with God, and the Word was God. The same was in the beginning with God. All things were made by him; and without him was not anything made that was made. In him was life; and the life was the light of men. And the light shone in darkness; and the darkness comprehended it not.**
>
> **There was a man sent from God, whose name was John. The same came for a witness, to bear witness of the Light, that all men though him might believe. He was not that Light, but was sent to bear witness to that Light.**
>
> **That was the true Light, which lights every man that comes into the world. He was in the world, and the world was made by him, and the world knew him not. He came to his own, and his own received him not. But as many as received him, to them gave he power to become the children of God, even to them who believe on his name; who were born, not of blood, nor of the will of the flesh, nor of the will of man, but of God. And the Word was made flesh, and dwelt among us (and we beheld his glory, the glory as of the only begotten of the Father), full of grace and truth.**
>
> **John bore witness of him, and cried, saying, This was he of whom I spoke, He that comes after me is preferred before me; for he was before me. And of his fullness have all we received, and grace for grace. For the law was given by Moses, but grace and truth came by Jesus Christ.**
>
> **No man has seen God at any time; the only begotten Son, who is in the bosom of the Father, he has declared him.**

In addition to declaring Him to be the actuality of creation, John's Prologue equates Jesus to both the Word and the Light. Given the nature of Jesus in this passage that is so fundamental to creation itself, is there a context within the creation epic of Genesis in which

Jesus is both the Word and the Light? The account in Genesis 1:14-19 that the sun and moon were created on the fourth day of creation places these bodies as having been created later than other events; while it doesn't implicate Jesus as the Word and the Light, an earlier passage does, that of Genesis 1:3-5, and it is the first act of creation, following references to God and the Spirit working together:

> **And God said, Let there be light; and there was light. And God saw the light, that it was good: and God divided the light from the darkness. And God called the light Day, and the darkness he called Night. And the evening and the morning were the first day.**

In this passage God speaks. His first Word is the will for Light. We can assume from this that the Holy Spirit responded with the birth of the Light, the implementation of the Word of God – Jesus Christ, who acknowledged His birth in Revelation 3:14.

Is the Holy Spirit associated with birth elsewhere in Scripture? Yes, and directly indeed, from John 3:3-8 and Colossians 1:15:

> **Jesus answered, and said unto [Nicodemus], Truly, truly, I say unto you, Except a man be born again, he cannot see the kingdom of God. Nicodemus said to him, How can a man be born when he is old? Can he enter the second time unto his mother's womb, and be born? Jesus answered, Truly, truly, I say to you, Except a man be born of water and of the Spirit, he cannot enter into the kingdom of God. That which is born of the flesh is flesh; and that which is born of the Spirit is spirit. Marvel not that I said to you, You must be born again. The wind blows where it wills, and you hear the sound of it, but can not tell from where it comes, and where it goes; so is every one who is born of the Spirit.**

> **[Jesus], who is the image of the invisible God, the first-born of all creation;**

Given the obvious nature of birth as a feminine function, Jesus and Paul here directly identify the Holy Spirit as feminine. Proverbs

8:22-31 is a more detailed and beautifully intimate narrative, delivered from the perspective of a feminine source, of the Holy Spirit's function as complementary to the Father's:

> **The Lord possessed me in the beginning of his way, before his works of old. I was set up from everlasting, from the beginning, or ever the earth was. When there were no depths, I was brought forth – when there were no fountains abounding with water. Before the mountains were settled, before the hills, was I brought forth; while as yet he had not made the earth, nor the fields, nor the highest part of the dust of the world. When he prepared the heavens, I was there; when he set a compass upon the face of the depth; when he established the clouds above; when he strengthened the fountains of the deep; when he gave to the sea its decree, that the waters should not pass his commandment; when he appointed the foundations of the earth.**
>
> **Then I was by him, as one brought up with him; and I was daily his delight, rejoicing always before him, rejoicing in the habitable part of his earth; and my delight was with the sons of men.**

Nine
Family

The beauty of complementary otherness within the Godhead shines forth in its ideal representation of family. I attempted to capture the essence of that beauty in my novel *Buddy,* where in Chapter 20 I repeated a blog that I had posted on my site *friendofthefamily.wordpress.com* entitled *The Marriage of God with God.* Excerpts are presented below.

> **In previous postings I have raised the question of why God's Trinitarian nature, a facet of Him that is accepted without question by mainstream Christianity, is so vaguely defined in Scripture. I also raised a companion question as to why, in the face of this apparently feeble portrayal of the Trinity, both Moses and Jesus declared with passion the oneness of God. I then presented the obvious answer, which was that the loving union of male and complementary female produces unity from multiplicity, a unity that continues with the fruit of the union. In this context and only in it, the description of the Trinity in Scripture isn't feeble at all; it's quite strong. Given that basic understanding, the wonderful truth about the Holy Trinity is expressed openly throughout Scripture beginning in Genesis 2:23 and 24:**
>
> > **And Adam said, This is now bone of my bones, and flesh of my flesh: she shall be called Woman, because she was taken out of man.**
> >
> > **Therefore shall a man leave his father and his mother, and shall cleave to his wife, and they shall be one flesh.**

To the above I add the following:

God Himself through Scripture has provided man with certain specific images of His nature by which He apparently wishes us to understand and appreciate Him. First among these is His ability to give and to receive love. Fundamental to the exercise of that ability is the family structure, within which we have the ability to intuitively understand a corresponding relationship among the Members of the Godhead itself as well as of the relationship between God and mankind. The family is the singular means within our comprehension by which separate individuals may become component elements of a greater whole, a oneness in love that both transcends the individual person and extends his own significance.

As the communication and functional harmony within the family approach the highest ideal of which humans are capable, in the setting of selfless love at an equally ideal level, the individuality of its component members blurs. All become subordinate to but vital elements of the greater entity called family, which itself takes on a life of its own. If the love, communication and harmony within this entity are perfect, an impossibility with mankind but perhaps a defining quality for God, one would expect a spiritual unity and mutual identification so complete that the component members could no longer rightly be thought of as separate individuals. The divine Family, in which the various Members would identify perfectly with each other as if the individual boundaries did not exist, would have its own unique identity and life.

God, in this context, is truly one God.

Given the family nature of the Godhead, the commandment to love this God fervently becomes natural and effortless. Indeed, as I had commented in Part 2, Chapter 2 of *Family of God,* within our own families we see positive attributes of our own that arise from the family relationship.

Under the extraordinary circumstances of disaster or

war, a man might bond with his companions through the sharing of hardships and fear. In some cases, this bond may become so close that he will lay down his life for them. But the individual character and the conditions that might bring this about are so unique that medals are granted for altruism of this order. More typically, man is, at best, indifferent to the welfare of his neighbors and acquaintances. At his worst, he regularly places those with whom he is in contact at a disadvantage for his own profit, caring little about his victims' consequent loss and discomfort. He lies, cheats, covets, and steals, doing these things with impunity under a pragmatic and often twisted legal system. He may do them with little sense of wrongdoing. Hidden behind the mask of a false face or the tinted glass of his automobile, he often indulges in nasty, mean-spirited thoughts: he hates; he is quick to take offense and visualize a bad end for the offender. In this manner he might, in his mind, break most of God's commandments without hesitation during a simple drive from home to work.

But there is a unique relationship in which that same individual will often behave in an altogether more altruistic manner. That relationship is with his family, his spouse and children. Historically, most people on earth have willingly belonged to this unit, exercising their responsibilities to it and taking pleasure and comfort from it. The individual intuitively understands and accepts the principle that while every member of the family unit deeply and permanently belongs to him, he also belongs to them in the same way. He accepts as natural the principle of sharing: of shared responsibilities, shared activities and recreation, shared possessions and, most importantly, shared intimacy. Within the impositions and limitations of the larger society to which he belongs, the individual will also usually accept as natural and beneficial that particular division of function and labor which will result in the most secure and orderly

> **maintenance of the family unit. Beyond that, he will often behave as nobly as the heroic soldier in the protection of his family members from harm.**

In thinking of our Judeo-Christian God as a Divine Family as Scripture suggests, I gladly and without reservation worship Him with the fervor of the Great Commandment.

Ten
Paul

Perhaps, when Paul, known as Saul, was so down on Christians, he had an attitude toward God much like what the nominal Christian has today. Possibly, governed by what he had learned about God through the Jewish religion of the day, he saw God as rather remote, even alien, His attribute of transcendent majesty may have taken front place over any alternative understanding.

Paul in his unregenerate state was, in the words of modern conservatives, a defender of the faith. Zealous in his protection of God from the intruding Christian faith, he managed through this very devotion to see in himself a man worthy of the favor of God and the ultimate prize, heaven.

In his amazing transformation on the road to Damascus as described in Acts 9, Paul must have received from Jesus some profound insights into the real nature of God. Only an enormous shift in understanding could have led him to follow Jesus in such humble adoration thereafter. There is some evidence in Scripture that Paul was given an incredibly detailed picture of God that went way beyond what he had learned at the hands of men. It is generally accepted that when Paul spoke of a man who went to heaven in 2 Corinthians 12:2-4, he was speaking of himself, probably during the time after Jesus had approached him that he was temporarily blinded:

> **I knew a man in Christ above fourteen years ago (whether in the body, I cannot tell; or whether out of the body, I cannot tell: God knows) – such a one caught up to the third heaven. And I knew such a man (whether in the body or out of the body, I cannot tell: God knows) – How he was caught up into paradise and heard unspeakable words,**

which it is not lawful for a man to utter.

The most prominent feature of the Godhead must have changed in Paul's mind and heart from magnificence to valor. What else could have led him to dote upon his baby Church so lovingly, and to willingly endure such trials as Jesus had promised him when He appeared to him on that road, becoming perhaps the greatest Christian outside of Jesus who ever lived?

And Saul, yet breathing out threatenings and slaughter against the disciples of the Lord, went to the high priest, and desired of him letters to Damascus to the synagogues, that if he found any of this way, whether they were men or women, he might bring them under arrest to Jerusalem. And as he journeyed, he came near Damascus, and suddenly there shone round about him a light from heaven; and he fell to the earth, and heard a voice saying to him, Saul, Saul, why do you persecute me? And he said, Who are you, Lord? And the Lord said, I am Jesus, whom you persecute; it is hard to you to kick against the goads. And he, trembling and astonished, said, Lord what will you have me to do? And the Lord said to him, Arise and go into the city, and it shall be told you there what you must do. And the men who journeyed with him stood speechless, hearing a voice, but seeing no man.

And Saul arose from the earth, and when his eyes were opened, he saw no man; but they led him by the hand, and brought him into Damascus. And he was three days without sight, and neither did eat nor drink. And there was a certain disciple at Damascus, named Ananias; and to him said the Lord in a vision, Ananias. And he said, behold, I am here, Lord. And the Lord said to him, Arise, and go into the street which is called Straight, and inquire in the house of Judas for one called Saul of Tarsus; for, behold, he is praying, and has seen in a vision a man, named Ananias, coming in and putting his hand on him, that he might receive his sight. Then Ananias answered,

Lord, I have heard by many of this man, how much evil he has done to your saints at Jerusalem; and here he has authority from the chief priests to bind all that call on your name.

But the Lord said to him, Go your way; for he is a chosen vessel to me, to bear my name before the Gentiles, and kings, and the children of Israel; for I will show him how great things he must suffer for my name's sake.

Paul did suffer, and willingly, for a God whom he truly loved with all his heart. As he recalled in 2 Corinthians 11:22-31:

Are they Hebrews? So am I. Are they Israelites? So am I. Are they the seed of Abraham? So am I. Are they ministers of Christ? (I speak as a fool) I am more; in labors more abundant, in stripes above measure, in prisons more frequently, in deaths often. Of the Jews five times I received forty stripes, save one. Thrice I was beaten with rods, once I was stoned, thrice I suffered shipwreck, a night and a day I have been in the deep; in journeyings often, in perils of waters, in perils of robbers, in perils by my own countrymen, in perils by the Gentiles, in perils in the city, in perils in the wilderness, in perils in the sea, in perils among false brethren; in weariness and painfulness, in watchings often, in fastings often, in cold and nakedness. Beside those things that are without, that which comes upon me daily, the care of all the churches. Who is weak, and I am not weak? Who is offended, and I am not indignant? If I must needs glory I will glory in the things which concern my infirmities. The God and Father of our Lord Jesus Christ, who is blessed for evermore, knows that I lie not.

Eleven
Perpetua

I'd often wondered where the unusual and strikingly noble name of Perpetua originated. There is a promontory on the Oregon Coast that first brought the name to my attention. The only other time I've seen it is in John Foxe's *Christian Martyrs of the World.* I'd very much like to think that it was this Perpetua, born around 181 A.D. and who lived in Carthage in the Roman province of Africa, who inspired the name of that beautiful Oregon cape.

Perpetua suffered under the persecution which began in A.D. 200. According to Foxe, this was the fifth of ten persecutions foretold by Jesus in His message to the Church at Smyrna, Revelation 2:8-11:

> **And unto the angel of the church in Smyrna write: These things say the first and the last, who was dead, and is alive. I know your works, and tribulation, and poverty (but you are rich); and I know the blasphemy of them who say they are Jews, and are not, but are of the synagogue of Satan. Fear none of those things which you shall suffer. Behold, the devil shall cast some of you into prison, that you may be tried, and you shall have tribulation ten days; be you faithful unto death, and I will give you a crown of life. He who has an ear, let him hear what the Spirit says to the churches: he who overcomes shall not be hurt of the second death.**

The Church at Smyrna was the second of the seven Churches addressed by Jesus in Revelation Chapters 2 and 3. Of these Churches, Smyrna and Philadelphia were the only two for which Jesus had nothing negative to say. It has been broadly recognized as the persecuted Church. According to Foxe and other theologians the ten "days" spoken of by Jesus were ten periods of overt, usually intense persecution. Foxe listed them all in his book, which is considered to be one of the three greatest Christian works outside the Bible ever written. The following is his entry regarding Perpetua:

> **During the reign of Severus, the Christians had several years of rest and could worship God without fear of punishment. But after a time, the hatred of the ignorant mob again prevailed, and the old laws were remembered and put in force against them. Fire, sword, wild beasts, and imprisonment were resorted to again, and even the dead bodies of Christians were stolen from their graves and mutilated. Yet the faithful continued to multiply. Tertullian, who lived at this time, said that if the Christians had all gone away from the Roman territories, the empire would have been greatly weakened.**
>
> **By now, the persecutions had extended to northern Africa, which was a Roman province, and many were murdered in that area. One of these was Perpetua, a married lady twenty-six years old with a baby at her breast. On being taken before the proconsul Minutius, Perpetua was commanded to sacrifice to the idols. Refusing to do so, she was put in a dark dungeon and deprived of her child, but two of her keepers, Tertius and Pomponius, allowed her out in the fresh air several hours a day, during which time she was allowed to nurse her child.**
>
> **Finally the Christians were summoned to appear before the judge and urged to deny their Lord, but all remained firm. When Perpetua's turn came, her father suddenly appeared, carrying her infant in his arms, and begged her to save her own life for the sake of her child. Even the judge seemed to be moved. "Spare the gray hairs of your father," he said. "Spare your child. Offer sacrifice for the welfare of the emperor."**
>
> **Perpetua answered, "I will not sacrifice."**

"Are you a Christian?" demanded Hilarianus, the judge.

"I am a Christian," was her answer.

Perpetua and all the other Christians tried with her that day were ordered killed by wild beasts as a show for the crowd on the next holiday. They entered the place of execution clad in the simplest of robes, Perpetua singing a hymn of triumph. The men were to be torn to pieces by leopards and bears. Perpetua and a young woman named Felicitas were hung up in nets, at first naked, but the crowd demanded that they should be allowed their clothing.

When they were again returned to the arena, a bull was let loose on them. Felicitas fell, seriously wounded. Perpetua was tossed, her loose robe torn and her hair falling loose, but she hastened to the side of the dying Felicitas and gently raised her from the ground. When the bull refused to attack them again, they were dragged out of the arena, to the disappointment of the crowd, which wanted to see their deaths. Finally brought back in to be killed by gladiators, Perpetua was assigned to a trembling young man who stabbed her weakly several times, not being used to such scenes of violence. When she saw how upset the young man was, Perpetua guided his sword to a vital area and died.

Additional material on Perpetua can be found on the Internet by Googling "Perpetua." The Wikipedia entry differs in some minor details from Foxe's, but also adds some useful information. Perpetua, for example, is identified there as of noble heritage. Felicitas (Felicity), was supposedly her slave. The Catholic Church has canonized her, along with Felicity, as a saint. Her feast day is March 7, the date of her execution.

The perceived nobility of her name has a factual basis in the circumstance of her birth. But her high birth is of little consequence compared to the nobility of her faith and the beautiful manner in which she chose to exercise it. In her nobility, Perpetua reflected that same quality of Jesus' character.

Volume Seven

Israel

Contents

Preface 323
One: Israel's Captivities and Dispersions 325
Two: Restoration of the Land 329
Three: Making Aliyah 333
Four: Esther 337
Five: Hebron 342
Six: Parting the Land 345
Seven: The War of Psalm 83 348
Eight: The War of Ezekiel 38 352
Nine: Gideon 356

Preface

The integrating theme for the present volume, Volume Seven, is the nation of Israel, the only country in history that God has called His own, and of God's everlasting love for its people.

Far from being rejected of God, the nation of Israel remains beloved to God. That it has been severely chastised in the past is a token of God's love for it, and of His desire to return the nation into fellowship with Him. Israel stands apart as an incredibly accurate timepiece by which we as Christians can discern where we stand in the grand sweep of history described by God in Scripture. Moreover, we as Christians owe much to Israel: from there came our Scripture; from there came our Savior Jesus Christ; and from there we still see the unfolding of God's plan for the world. The promise of God to Abraham through Moses in Genesis 12:1-3 remains as valid today as the day that it was spoken:

> **Now the Lord had said to Abram, Get you out of your country, and from your kindred, and from your father's house, to a land that I will show you; and I will make of you a great nation, and I will bless you, and make your name great; and you shall be a blessing.**
>
> **And I will bless them who bless you, and curse him who curses you: and in you shall all families of the earth be blessed.**

According to Hebrews 13:8, Jesus Christ is the same yesterday, and today, and forever. As Jesus is the living Word of God, this statement applies to Scripture as well, and Scripture favors the continued existence of Israel under the unilateral and everlasting covenants of God. Despite what the world may think about Israel or attempt to do toward her destruction, Israel shall remain as the apple of God's eye, and shall be a blessing to those who bless her.

One
Israel's Captivities and Dispersions

Moses foretold in Deuteronomy 28 two separate instances where Israel would be removed from her land as punishment for willful, prolonged disobedience to God's commandments, particularly for turning away from Abraham's God to the false gods of other nations. The first instance is highlighted in two parts: Deuteronomy 28:32-34 and Deuteronomy 28:36.

According to Deuteronomy 28:32-34,

> **Your sons and your daughters shall be given unto another people, and your eyes shall look, and fail with longing for them all the day long: and there shall be no might in your hand. The fruit of your land, and all your labors, shall a nation which you know not eat up; and you shall be only oppressed and crushed always: so that you shall be mad for the sight of your eyes which you shall see.**

Quoting next from Deuteronomy 28:36,

> **The Lord shall bring you, and your king which you shall set over yourselves, to a nation which neither you nor your fathers have known; and there shall you serve other gods, wood and stone.**

The second instance, which is highlighted in Deuteronomy 28:64-67, is more severe and lengthy, wherein the Jews are to be scattered among all the nations of the earth:

> **And the Lord shall scatter you among all people, from the**

> **one end of the earth, even to the other; and there you shall serve other gods, which neither you nor your fathers have known, even wood and stone. And among these nations shall you find no ease, neither shall the sole of your foot have rest: but the Lord shall give you there a trembling heart, and failing of eyes, and sorrow of mind: and your life shall hang in doubt before you; and you shall fear day and night, and shall have none assurance of your life: in the morning you shall say, Would God it were evening! And at evening you shall say, Would God it were morning! For the fear of your heart wherewith you shall fear, and for the sight of your eyes which you shall see.**

The prophecies do not end here. In Deuteronomy Chapter 30, God shows His mercy toward Israel with the promise that they will not remain scattered among the nations. Instead, they eventually will be regathered and returned to their land.

The first instance of Israel's removal from her land is in two parts because following the reign of Solomon around 950 B.C., Israel broke up into two separate kingdoms (1 Kings 12) wherein Israel (later known as Samaria) consisted of the northern ten tribes and Judah consisted of southern two tribes of Judah and Benjamin. Each of these kingdoms suffered defeat at separate times. The northern kingdom of Samaria was overthrown by the Assyrians under Shalmaneser around 730 B.C. (2 Kings 17 and 18). A few years later Shalmaneser's son Sennacherib attempted to besiege Judah also (2 Kings 18-20) but his troops were wiped out by an odd natural catastrophe; Sennacherib's attempt simply didn't conform to the Lord's timing. Judah would still be subject to the reign of good kings among the bad who would remain somewhat loyal to Abraham's God. The kingdom of Judah was later taken captive by Nebudchadnezzar around 605 B.C., a little more than a hundred years after the fall of Samaria. The Books of 1 and 2 Kings are replete with the sordid details of this first falling away from God of Samaria and Judah following the reigns of David and his son Solomon.

As foretold by the prophet Jeremiah in Jeremiah 25:12, the captivity of Judah lasted for seventy years until 535 B.C. Samaria didn't fare so well, as the people of the northern kingdom who remained behind after Assyria relocated a large group of Israelites, as noted in 2 Kings 17:6, were forced to intermarry, thus diluting and confusing their Hebrew bloodline. It was for that reason that, at the time of Jesus, the Jews looked down upon the Samaritans, having little to do with them. Most interestingly, the tribe of Judah was not subjected to this forced intermarriage, thus preserving the bloodline to Jesus.

Another interesting side issue is the nature of the blast that killed 185,000 of Sennacherib's troops during his attempt to besiege Jerusalem. At the time of the blast the sun moved about ten degrees, indicating a planetwide catastrophe so enormous as to alter the rotation of the earth. Immanuel Velikovsky (*Worlds in Collision*, 1950 and *Earth in Upheaval*, 1955) and others have surmised that the cause of this disaster was a near collision of the earth with a planet-sized mass, probably Mars. He thought that it was this same event that evoked Homer's *Iliad* (possibly an eyewitness account rather than myth) and reinforced the gentile practice of associating planets with gods. Recently-acquired data regarding the devastation of Mars, as well as the discovery in the Antarctic continent of meteorite ALH84001 that originated in Mars, the juvenile Argon-36 in the Martian atmosphere, and the synchronous kinematic features between Earth and Mars tend to support this hypothesis.

Two important events accompanied the end of the first captivity of the Israelites. The first of these was the proclamation of Cyrus, king of Persia around 535 B.C. under which a number of Israelites under Ezra were permitted to return to Jerusalem for the purpose of rebuilding the temple there. This event is recorded in the Book of Ezra.

Another interesting side point is that the prophet Isaiah (Isaiah 44:28, 45:1) over 150 years earlier had called Cyrus by name as God's servant in association with the rebuilding of the temple.

The second event associated with the end of the Israelites'

captivity was the decree by the Persian King Artaxerxes Longimanus allowing the Israelites under Nehemiah to return to Jerusalem to rebuild the city itself. This decree was issued in 445 B.C. and is the same decree predicted by the Prophet Daniel (Daniel 9:25) that was to initiate the countdown to the coming of Messiah after 69 weeks of (prophetic) years. Jesus made his triumphal entry into Jerusalem 173,880 days later, 69 weeks from the decree *to the very day.*

The second instance of the removal of Israel from her land occurred was also foretold by Jesus in Matthew 24:2 and occurred in 70 A.D., about 37 years after Jesus' crucifixion and resurrection. The destruction was led by the Roman General Titus, but was accomplished with the use of soldiers recruited locally, which were presumably of Arab stock. The event indeed left not one stone upon another because of the soldiers' furious scramble for the gold within, melted by the burning of the temple and which spilled into the cracks between the stones.

This time the dispersion of the Jews, called the Great Diaspora, was worldwide. But it, too, ended as foretold by Ezekiel (Ezekiel 36 and 37) as well as Moses (Deuteronomy 30) some eighteen centuries later with the creation of the state of Israel on May 15, 1948. This date also was foretold by both Hosea and Ezekiel, as was detailed in Volume 2, Chapter 5, entitled *Ezekiel's Prophecy of Israel's Return.*

Two
Restoration of the Land

When God gave his everlasting covenant of land to Abraham, as first described in Genesis 15:18 and later reaffirmed to Isaac and still later to Jacob, it amounted to the only land grant that ever came from God Himself. But the promise extended beyond mere land: the land was to be filled with the riches of life. Much later, when God appeared to Moses out of the burning bush, He spoke again about that land, as described in Exodus 3:7 and 8:

> **And the Lord said, I have surely seen the affliction of my people who are in Egypt, and have heard their cry by reason of their taskmasters; for I know their sorrows; and I am come down to deliver them out of the hand of the Egyptians, and to bring them up out of that land to a large and good land, to a land flowing with milk and honey; to the place of the Canaanites, and the Hittites, and the Amorites, and the Perizzites, and the Hivites and the Jebusites.**

After the Fifteenth Roman Legion under the command of General Titus destroyed the Jewish temple in 70 A.D., much of the land fell into disuse. Moreover, there came an extended period of drought that transformed many of the lush regions into barren wastelands.

That was the environment that greeted the first modern settlers out of the Zionist movement of the nineteenth century as they trickled back into their old homeland. They formed *kibbutzim,* farming communities wherein they struggled to restore small areas back to life, hoping for the restoration of the land that God Himself promised them in Joel 3:18:

And it shall come to pass, in that day, that the mountains shall drop down new wine, and the hills shall flow with milk, and all the rivers of Judah shall flow with waters, and a fountain shall come forth from the house of the Lord, and shall water the valley of Shittim.

That promise of Joel's is not yet fulfilled in every detail. But it has been realized to an amazing extent. God Himself had a big hand in the land's restoration, for when the Israelites came back to the land, the centuries-long drought came to an end. After 1800 years, from the first century to the twentieth, it began to rain again. The heaviest rainfall to date came in 1948, when Israel was restored as a nation, and in 1967, when Israel reclaimed Jerusalem. Adding to the rainfall, the Israelis have created a vast irrigation system, restoring much of what once was wasteland into extremely productive farms. The country now is a major exporter of food and flowers to Europe, and is considered a world leader in the production of milk. Its cows produce more milk per year than cows in America and Europe.

Recognizing the promise of Ezekiel 36:4-8, the settlers began to plant trees with a fervor.

Therefore, you mountains of Israel, hear the word of the Lord God, Thus says the Lord God to the mountains, and to the hills, to the rivers, and to the valleys, to the desolate wastes, and to the cities that are forsaken, which became a prey and derision to the residue of the nations that are round about; therefore, thus says the Lord God: Surely in the fire of my jealousy have I spoken against the residue of the nations, and against all Edom, who have appointed my land into their possession with the joy of all their heart, with despiteful minds, to cast it out for a prey. Prophecy, therefore, concerning the land of Israel, and say to the mountains, and to the hills, to the rivers, and to the valleys, Thus says the Lord God: Behold, I have spoken in my jealousy and in my fury, because you have borne the shame of the nations; therefore, thus says the Lord god: I have lifted up my hand. Surely the nations that are about you,

they shall bear their shame.

But you, O mountains of Israel, you shall shoot forth your branches, and yield your fruit to my people of Israel, for they are soon to come home.

Israel now boasts two hundred million trees. Thousands of acres are devoted to date palms, the ancient source of honey production from bees. Each tree is highly productive, yielding over three hundred pounds of dates per year. Over ten thousand tons of dates are exported each year.

Scripture links the fig tree to the nation of Israel. In *His Olivet Discourse* (Matthew 24), Jesus tells His followers to watch for the budding of the fig tree as a sign that the end of the age is very close. Many Christians consider the budding of the fig tree as a metaphor for either the reestablishment of Israel as a nation in 1948 or the retaking of Jerusalem in 1967. But there is a natural element as well to Jesus' assertion: fig production in modern Israel amounts to five thousand tons – not a huge amount, but not insignificant, either, and growing.

Orchards of olive trees occupy eighty thousand acres in Israel. Olives and olive oil are major export items.

In Ezekiel 36:29, 30, 34 and 35, God promises to make the land productive again:

I will also save you from all your uncleanness, and I will call for the grain, and will increase it, and lay no famine upon you. . . And the desolate land shall be tilled, whereas it lay desolate in the sight of all that passed by. And they shall say, This land that was desolate is become like the garden of Eden, and the waste and desolate and ruined cities are become fortified, and are inhabited.

As of 2013, Israel grew 95% of its own food and exported $2.4 billion in food to other countries.

Now there's talk of oil. Surely there's incentive here, with all of Israel's modern riches, for Russia to come into the land to take a spoil, as foretold in Ezekiel 38. Nevertheless, as noted by evangelist David Reagan, the burning bush from which God spoke to Moses was itself prophetic of the indestructibility of the Jewish people in the face of the flames of hatred and violence against them.

Three
Making Aliyah

The Hebrew word *Aliyah* means to go up, to ascend. Jerusalem was situated on a hill above the lower cities that surrounded it, so in ancient Israel the process of going to the holy city Jerusalem was associated with ascension. Eventually the land itself was associated with holiness, particularly to those of the great dispersion, and the return of Jews to the land was spoken of as *making aliyah.*

The ingathering of the Jews back to their homeland began in earnest toward the end of the nineteenth century, but the hundreds of thousands of immigrants turned into a flood of millions after the formal declaration of Israeli statehood in 1948.

The prophet Ezekiel, in Chapters 36 and 37, makes an astonishingly accurate and detailed forecast of the return of the Jews to their homeland following the holocaust of Hitler's Germany during World War II.

The Word of God in Ezekiel 36:17-28, 37 and 38 reverses the pronouncement of God to the Israelites in Deuteronomy 28 that He will punish the nation for turning away from Him and banish them to other lands:

> **Son of man, when the house of Israel dwelt in their own land, they defiled it by their own way and by their doings; their way was before me as the uncleanness of a removed woman. Wherefore I poured my fury upon them for the blood that they had shed upon the land, and for their idols by which they had polluted it; and I scattered them among the nations, and they were dispersed through the countries; according to their way and according to their doings, I**

> **judged them. And when they entered to the nations to which they went, they profaned my holy name, when they said to them, These are the people of the Lord, and are gone forth out of his land.**
>
> **But I had pity for my holy name, which the house of Israel had profaned among the nations, to which they went. Therefore, say to the house of Israel, Thus says the Lord God: I do not this for your sakes, O house of Israel, but for my holy name's sake, which you have profaned among the nations to which you went. And I will sanctify my great name, which was profaned among the nations, which you have profaned in the midst of them, and the nations shall know that I am the Lord, says the Lord God, which I shall be sanctified in you before their eyes.**
>
> **For I will take you from among the nations, and gather you out of all countries, and will bring you into your own land. Then will I sprinkle clean water upon you, and you shall be clean; from all your filthiness, and from all your idols, will I cleanse you. A new heart also will I give you, and a new spirit will I put within you; and I will take away the stony heart out of your flesh, and I will give you a heart of flesh. And I will put my Spirit within you, and cause you to walk in my statutes, and you shall keep my ordinances, and do them. And you shall dwell in the land that I gave to your fathers; and you shall be my people, and I will be your God. . . Thus says the Lord God, I will yet for this be inquired of by the house of Israel, to do it for them; I will increase them with men like a flock. As the holy flock, as the flock of Jerusalem in her solemn feasts, so shall the waste cities be filled with the flocks of men; and they shall know that I am the Lord.**

I have heard a Christian say that since the majority of Israelites still don't believe that Jesus is their Messiah, that nation is not from God. That statement, besides being untrue, represents an attempt to reassert the very un-Christian and anti-Semitic notion of replacement theology. Beyond that, the notion blatantly contradicts the fulfillment to the year of Scripture's prophecy in Ezekiel 4:3-6 and Leviticus 26 as noted in Volume 2, Chapter 5, entitled *Ezekiel's Prophecy of Israel's Return.* Notice in the passage above, written half a millennium before Jesus' first advent, that God specifically states that Israel will return in unbelief. The belief in Jesus as Messiah would come afterward.

In Ezekiel 37, the prophet was given a vision of a valley full of dry bones. God asks Ezekiel a question: can the bones live? He then proceeds to answer His own question, saying that He will put flesh and skin upon the bones and breathe life back into them. God asserts that these bones represent the whole house of Israel, who had lost their hope, and promises them that He will return them to their homeland. Christians commonly view this prophecy as a restoration of the people of Israel following the Holocaust of Hitler's Germany, in which six million Jews, a third of the world's Jewry, perished in the Nazi concentration camps.

God becomes more specific about the restoration. For centuries the nation of Israel was divided into to houses: Israel and Judah. God asserts in Ezekiel 37 that in the restoration the nation would again be unified, as it was under David and Solomon. That is indeed what has taken place in modern Israel. Moreover, the new nation has taken its ancient name of Israel, and the common language is Hebrew, as it was before the dispersion.

Isaiah, in verses 5-7 of Chapter 43, spoke of the latter-day ingathering of Jews as well.

> **Fear not; for I am with you. I will bring your seed from the east, and gather you from the west. I will say to the north, Give up; and to the south, Keep not back; bring my sons from afar, and my daughters from the ends of the earth.**

To date, Jews have returned from a multitude of nations throughout the world, fulfilling God's promise to bring them back from all four directions of the compass. With respect to the north and the south the promise in Isaiah is forceful, with the implication that these countries would release their Jews reluctantly. Indeed, Russia of the North and Ethiopia of the south refused to let them go, but did so eventually as the pressure increased.

As of this writing, there is one group of people from the Assyrian conquest of Israel in the eighth century B.C. that has not yet returned to Israel. The group is well-known, but certainly not understood to be Jewish. I speculate about their identity and their return in my novel *Home, Sweet Heaven.*

Four
Esther

The Book of Esther describes the peril of the Jews who, after having been captured and removed from their homeland of Israel to Babylon under King Nebudchadnezzar around 605 B.C., find themselves on the brink of extermination a century later.

In the book of Esther a new world power has emerged, Babylon having been conquered by the Medes and the Persians. From his Persian throne King Ahasuerus controls a vast kingdom consisting of 127 provinces.

To administer this grand domain he has appointed Haman as his chief executive officer. Haman, a descendent of Amalekite King Agag, has been granted such sweeping powers that in his haughtiness he expects obeisance from the king's subjects not very far removed from that expected by the king himself. Mordecai, a devout Jew who served the king in the palace, in his insistence upon worshiping God alone as did Daniel before him, refuses to bow to Haman. This act of disrespect enrages Haman who, as an Edomite (Genesis 36:1,12) harbors an historic ill-will toward the Jews. In response, Haman requests of the king and is granted the ability to rid the kingdom of the Jews through a mass execution, to be conducted on a single day as to be determined by lot (Pur).

As these events are taking place, another drama is unfolding in the palace. In the midst of a long-lasting party King Ahasuerus has commanded his queen Vashti to come to his side so that he can show her off to his companions. She refuses his humiliating request, after which he casts her out in anger. Responding to advice from his guests, he conducts a search for the prettiest maidens in the kingdom, from whom he shall pick a queen to replace the banished

Vashti. He eventually selects a beautiful lady whose name is Esther.

Esther, it turns out, had been put into the mix by her uncle Mordecai, the same Jew who was the object of Haman's wrath. Orphaned at an early age, she had been Mordecai's ward ever since. Knowing of the anti-Semitism in high places, Mordecai had cautioned her against exposing her Jewish roots during the process of being selected as the next queen. She was indeed chosen.

As the threat of extermination approached ever closer, Mordecai asked the new Queen Esther to intervene with the king on behalf of her Jewish people. There was an obstacle to her ability to carry this out: it was customary for the queen to enter the king's chamber only in response to his specific request. Violations to this sort of custom were usually appeased by the death of the offender. The king had not summoned Esther, so to approach him would be to invite her death. Nevertheless, her uncle Mordecai's comment that *". . .who knows whether you are come to the kingdom for such a time as this?"* lay heavy on her heart. Speaking her famous line *". . .if I perish, I perish,"* she braved the king's wrath and approached him after fasting for three days.

Inviting the king and Haman to a special feast, she exploited the occasion to inform the king of her own Jewish roots, after which she exposed Haman's evil plans for genocide which would naturally include the deaths of both Mordecai (for whom Haman was preparing a gallows) and Esther. In response to this information, King Ahasuerus reversed the commandment to kill the Jews and ordered that Haman be hanged on the very gallows that he had prepared for Mordecai. Thus did God through Queen Esther save the Jews from extermination.

The story doesn't end there. The feast of Purim (lots) is observed to this day as a yearly celebration of Esther's brave deed. Purim, a happy Mardi Gras-like revelry, is held in Springtime a month before Passover. To this day stands a memorial to Esther and Mordecai in Iran of all places, in the city of Hamadan. As would be expected, Iranian officials are in the process of revising the history of Esther and Mordecai; they are calling her salvation of the Jews a genocidal act against the Persians and have removed the sign that identifies the mausoleum as associated with Esther and Mordecai.

There is the possibility of an intimate involvement of Esther in an intersection with the prophet Daniel, the Babylonian captive who preceded Esther by about a century. In Chapter 9 of the Book of Daniel, he delivers a prophetic message that is still being studied intently by both Jews and Christians as containing important information regarding the end of the age as noted by Jesus in His Olivet Discourse (Matthew 24 and Mark 13), His Temple Discourse (Luke 21) and His Revelation to John. God, in responding to Daniel's plea for mercy upon the captive nation of Israel, gives His beloved Daniel a message for the future through the angel Gabriel:

> **Seventy weeks are determined upon your people and upon your holy city, to finish the transgression, and to make an end of sins, and to make reconciliation for iniquity, and to bring in everlasting righteousness, and to seal up the vision and prophecy, and to anoint the most Holy.**
>
> **Know therefore, and understand, that from the going forth of the commandment to restore and to build Jerusalem to the Messiah the Prince shall be seven weeks, and threescore and two weeks: the street shall be built again, and the wall, even in troublous times. [Daniel 9:25]**
>
> **And after threescore and two weeks shall Messiah be cut off, but not for himself; and the people of the prince that shall come shall destroy the city and the sanctuary; and the end thereof shall be with a flood, and to the end of the war desolations are determined. And he shall confirm the covenant with many for one week: and in the midst of the week he shall cause the sacrifice and the oblation to cease, and for the overspreading of abominations he shall make it desolate, even until the consummation, and that determined shall be poured upon the desolate.**

The astonishing precision with which Daniel's prophecies have been fulfilled so far include that given in Daniel 9:25 above. The details of this particular fulfillment, in which during the first seven weeks of Daniel's prophecy the city of Jerusalem is rebuilt, are given in the Book of Nehemiah, a portion of which (Nehemiah 1:11 through 2:8) is repeated below:

> **O Lord, I beseech thee, let now your ear be attentive to the prayer of your servant, and to the prayer of your servants, who desire to fear your name: and prosper, I pray to you, your servant this day, and grant him mercy in the sight of this man. For I was the king's cupbearer.**
>
> **And it came to pass in the month Nisan, in the twentieth year of Artaxerxes the king, that wine was before him: and I took up the wine, and gave it to the king. Now I had not been beforetime sad in his presence. Wherefore the king said unto me, Why is your countenance sad, seeing that you art not sick? This is nothing else but sorrow of the heart. Then I was very sore afraid, and said to the king, Let the king live for ever: why should not my countenance be sad, when the city, the place of my fathers' sepulchers, lies waste, and the gates thereof are consumed with fire? Then the king said to me, For what do you make request? So I prayed to the God of heaven. And I said to the king, If it please the king, and if your servant has found favor in your sight, that you would send me to Judah, to the city of my fathers' sepulchers, that I may build it.**
>
> **And the king said to me, (the queen also sitting by him,) For how long shall your journey be? And when will you return? So it pleased the king to send me; and I set him a time. Moreover I said to the king, If it please the king, let letters be given me to the governors beyond the river, that they may convey me over till I come to Judah; And a letter to Asaph the keeper of the king's forest, that he may give me timber to make beams for the gates of the palace which appertained to the house, and for the wall of the city, and for the house that I shall enter into. And the king granted me, according to the good hand of my God upon me."**

Good hand of God indeed. There is a special reason why the Persian King Artaxerxes Longimanus was so amenable to Nehemiah's request and so readily granted the event that in fulfillment of verse 25 of Daniel's prophecy began the countdown to the triumphal appearance of Messiah in Jerusalem exactly 69 weeks later. Jerusalem was dear to him also, for he was half Jewish. His mother was Esther.

The Book of Esther is also prophetic, with Haman forecasting the intent exercised by Adolph Hitler to eliminate the Jewish race. This same intent is harbored now by Israel's neighbors.

Five
Hebron

There is a town on the west bank of the Jordan River, part of territory occupied by the Israelis after the 1967 war but now, thanks to pressure applied to Israel by the United States under several administrations from Clinton to Obama, is an integral part of territory claimed by Palestinian militants. The name of the town is Hebron. Hebron and the surrounding West Bank territory are frequently in the news as elements of animosity between Palestinians and Israelis. America under the leadership of Barack Obama had again joined the world in siding with Palestinian claims on this sacred territory, as if the region would finally be blessed with peace if only Israel will have the good sense to acquiesce to the demand for a two-state solution, under the terms of which Hebron would almost certainly be offered to the Islamic militants who clamor for it as their rightful due.

The world forgets Hebron and its rich Biblical history associated with Israel. That was in the region, according to Genesis 12 and 13, where, as far back in time as when the nation of Israel was still but a promise from God, Abraham stood as God first gave him the promise:

> **Now the Lord had said unto Abram, Get you out of your country, and from your kindred, and from your father's house, into a land that I will show you: And I will make of you a great nation, and I will bless you, and make your name great; and you shall be a blessing: And I will bless those who bless you, and curse him who curses you: and in you shall all families of the earth be blessed. . .**
>
> **And the Lord said to Abram, after that Lot was separated**

from him, Lift up now your eyes, and look from the place where you art northward, and southward, and eastward, and westward: For all the land which you see, to you will I give it, and to your seed for ever. And I will make your seed as the dust of the earth: so that if a man can number the dust of the earth, then shall your seed also be numbered. Arise, walk through the land in the length of it and in the breadth of it; for I will give it to you. Then Abram removed his tent, and came and dwelt in the plain of Mamre, which is in Hebron, and built there an altar to the Lord.

God later formalized this promise by a unilateral, everlasting covenant which also established specific boundaries for the land of Israel, the borders of which extended far beyond both the region of Hebron and the present-day borders established by modern statesmen.

Abraham, Isaac, and Jacob are often referred to as Israel's Partriarchs. Abraham's wife Sarah died, at the age of 127, in Hebron. Abraham purchased a grave for her there, in the cave in Machpelah near Mamre, from Ephron the Hittite. He paid four hundred shekels of silver for it. When he died at the age of 175 he was also buried there, as were his son Isaac and his wife Rebekah, and his grandson Jacob and his primary wife Leah, the mother of Judah, out of whose seed was born Mary, the mother of Jesus.

When Moses told representatives from each of the twelve tribes of Israel to spy out the Promised Land, ten of the twelve came back with words of fear and discouragement. Two retained their courage in their faith in God: Joshua, of the tribe of Ephraim, and Caleb, of the tribe of Judah. God rewarded Joshua as successor to Moses with leadership over the nation of Israel as they went in to claim the Promised Land for their own; He rewarded Caleb with Judah's ownership of Hebron for an everlasting possession.

David reigned first over Judah for seven years, and then over the combined nation representing all twelve tribes of Israel for thirty three additional years. In the latter reign his seat of government was Jerusalem; in the former, it was Hebron.

Of some things we can be certain: Hebron belongs to Israel, first, because the city lies within the boundaries of God's land grant to Jacob through Abraham, second, because God specifically gave it as a reward for valor to Caleb of the tribe of Judah, and third because of the prominence of the city in Israel's history including the graves of the Patriarchs and the first location of David's throne; moreover, despite what the leaders of the world intend to do with Hebron, God will have the last word in restoring it to the tribe of Judah.

Six

Parting the Land

Years afterward, whenever I recall the incident on our boat where my daughter's boyfriend "Bob" shook his fist at God for the benign movement of the wind, shouted "Is this all You can give me?" and reaped a terrifying windstorm, I can't help but laugh.

A later incident that brought it back to mind again was less laughable. It was a television broadcast that noted a few "coincidental" occurrences during the tenures of our past several U.S. Presidents. The key factor among the noted incidents was the ill-conceived "Roadmap for Peace", by means of which our government insists that Israel give up big chunks of its already tiny territory to its Palestinian enemies in exchange for "guarantees" of peace. There are several things that are terribly wrong with the idea. First, Israel has already given up land for "peace" in the past with no demonstrable "peace" having resulted. Second, there can't be any lasting "peace", because the Palestinians will continue to hate Israel until it no longer exists (if that were possible). Third, and most important, the Bible states most emphatically that not only will there be no peace, but that God doesn't like the idea of Israel giving up her land, which He gave to them as an everlasting possession. In Genesis 12:3, God promises to bless those who bless Israel, and to curse him that curses Israel. The prophet Joel, for another example, speaks on behalf of God against those nations who have scattered His people among other nations and parted His land:

> **For, behold, in those days, and in that time, when I shall bring again the captivity of Judah and Jerusalem, I will also gather all nations, and will bring them down into the Valley of Jeshoshaphat, and will judge them there for**

my people and for my heritage, Israel, whom they have scattered among the nations, and parted my land.

The prophet Obadiah foretells as well of a coming judgment against those who attempt to weaken that nation. Other prophets, besides, wrote of judgment against those who attempt to come against Israel, including Ezekiel, who very specifically described a future war that would decimate Israel's aggressors.

On October 30, 1991, the television broadcast recalled, George Bush senior spoke in favor of parting Israel's land to those attending the Madrid Peace Process. It was the first time that the U.S. had departed from its previous policy of firmly and uncompromisingly supporting Israel. That same day a freak storm of hurricane proportions that had developed in the North Atlantic and was heading in the wrong direction happened to create a huge, 30-foot wave that crashed ashore on a little spit of land in Maine and trashed the mansion that was located there. The ill winds became known as "The Perfect Storm", and the estate was the Kennebunkport home of George Bush senior. The broadcast continued to link other "Roadmap to Peace" speeches by U.S. Presidents with corresponding shots over our bow, most of which also were same-day events. Thus, when the Madrid Peace Process came to the U.S. and we continued to demand Israel's removal of settlements from Gaza, we were hit by Hurricane Andrew. In 1994, as then-President Clinton met with Syria's Assad to discuss Israel's abandonment of the Golan Heights in return for pledges for peace, the devastating Northridge Earthquake hit Southern California. As George Bush junior was attempting to get Ariel Sharon to unilaterally give up the Gaza Strip, Hurricane Katrina was getting ready to pounce. As Israeli citizens began to evacuate Gaza, our own evacuation of New Orleans and its neighboring cities was occurring in lockstep with it. More recent links associate similar political events with significant stages of our recent economic meltdown. The three worst market freefalls occurred on three of Israel's major feast days.

Maybe it *is* just coincidence that Obama's continuation of that policy along with his irritation with Israel and her Prime Minister

Benjamin Netanyahu had paralleled our economic doldrums and the large number of natural disasters with which our nation has had to contend during his administration. But then again, maybe it isn't.

Seven
The War of Psalm 83

Through Abraham's long and otherwise happy marriage to Sarah, they remained without children. This bothered them both, because God had already promised Abraham that his seed would be as plentiful as the stars. When Abraham was about eighty five years old, they decided to take matters into their own hands. Sarah gave her handmaid Hagar to Abraham to bear a child in their name.

This almost immediately caused a problem, as Abraham's new mistress Hagar became arrogant toward Sarah, while Sarah was jealous of Hagar. In an attempt to prune Hagar back, Sarah treated her harshly, causing Hagar to flee from them. An angel of the Lord found Hagar in the wilderness and spoke to her, as recorded in Genesis 16:7-12:

> **And the angel of the Lord found [Hagar] by a fountain of water in the wilderness, by the fountain in the way to Shur. And he said, Hagar, [Sarah's] maid, from where did you come? And where will you go? And she said, I flee from the face of my mistress, [Sarah]. And the angel of the Lord said to her, Return to your mistress, and submit yourself under her hands. And the angel of the Lord said to her, I will multiply your seed exceedingly, that it shall not be numbered for multitude. And the angel of the Lord said to her, behold, you are with child, and shall bear a son, and shall call his name Ishmael; because the Lord has heard your affliction. And he will be a wild man; his hand will be against every man, and every man's hand will be against him; and he shall dwell in the presence of all his brothers.**

Years passed, and Ishmael grew to be a teenager. At that point several major events took place in Abraham's life. God commanded all the males of Abraham's household to be circumcised, and Abraham himself was circumcised at the age of 99. At the same time, God destroyed Sodom and Gomorrah.

God also told Abraham that he would have a son through his wife Sarah, telling Abraham that it would be through this other son Isaac that he would continue His everlasting covenant with Abraham. The next year, when Abraham was 100 years old, Sarah gave birth to Isaac, who was to be the son of promise.

While Ishmael was not the son of promise, God did not leave him destitute. In Genesis 17:20 and 21, God told Abraham His plans for Ishmael:

> **And as for Ishmael, I have heard you: behold, I have blessed him, and will make him fruitful, and will multiply him exceedingly; twelve princes shall he beget, and I will make him a great nation. But my covenant will I establish with Isaac, whom Sarah shall bear to you at this set time in the next year.**

The old rivalry between Sarah and Hagar re-emerged with the birth of Isaac, causing Sarah to demand that Abraham cast Hagar and Ishmael away from the family. Hagar fled again into the desert, this time with insufficient water and finding herself in a survival situation. The event plays out in Genesis 21:14-21:

> **And Abraham rose up early in the morning, and took bread, and a skin of water, and gave them to Hagar, putting the water on her shoulder, and gave her the child [Ismael], and sent her away: and she departed, and wandered in the wilderness of Beersheba. And the water was spent in the skin, and she cast the child under one of the shrubs. And she went, and sat down apart from him a good way off, as it were a bowshot; for she said, Let me not see the death of the child. And she sat apart from him, and lifted up her voice, and wept. And God heard the voice of the lad; and**

the angel of God called to Hagar out of heaven, and said to her, What ails you, Hagar? Fear not, for God has heard the voice of the lad where he is. Arise, lift up the lad, and hold him in your hand; for I will make him a great nation. And God opened her eyes, and she saw a well of water; and she went, and filled the skin with water, and gave the lad drink. And God was with the lad; and he grew, and dwelt in the wilderness, and became an archer. And he dwelt in the wilderness of Paran: and his mother took him a wife out of the land of Egypt.

Starting with this issue way back at the time of Abraham, there has been contention between the people of Israel and her surrounding neighbors. Upon the restoration of Israel as a nation in 1948, there have been several bitter, end-game wars with her neighbors in which Israel, while being greatly outnumbered, not only managed to maintain her existence, but emerged victorious.

This animosity was prophetically expressed in Psalm 83, written by Asaph, a contemporary of King David:

Keep not your silence, O God; hold not your peace, and be not still, O God. For, lo, your enemies make a tumult, and they who hate you have lifted up the head. They have taken crafty counsel against your people, and consulted against your hidden ones.

They have said, Come, and let us cut them off from being a nation; that the name of Israel may be no more in remembrance. For they have consulted together with one consent; they are confederate against you.

The tabernacles of Edom, and the Ishmaelites; of Moab, and the Hararenes; Gebal, and Ammon, and Amalek; the Philistines with the inhabitants of Tyre; Assyria also is joined with them; they have helped the children of Lot. Selah.

Do to them as to the Midianites; as to Sisera, as to Jabin, at the brook of Kishon, who perished at Endor; they became

as dung for the earth. Make their nobles like Oreb, and like Zeeb: yea, all their princes as Zebah, and as Zalmunna, who said, Let us take to ourselves the houses of God in possession.

O my God, make them like a wheel, like the stubble before the wind. As the fire burns a forest, and as the flame sets the mountains on fire, so persecute them with your tempest, and make them afraid with your storm. Fill their faces with shame, that they may seek your name, O Lord. Let them be confounded and troubled forever; yea, let them be put to shame, and perish, that men may know that you, whose name alone is the Lord, are the Most High over all the earth.

The expectation among many theologians is that this Psalm has not yet been completely fulfilled, but will be in the very near future.

Eight
The War of Ezekiel 38

The Psalm 83 War pits Israel against her inner circle of neighbors. In Ezekiel 38, an outer ring of neighboring countries bands together to invade Israel and destroy her as a nation. According to Ezekiel, who lived a half millennium before Christ, the major players in this other war will include Russia (Magog), Iran (Persia), Libya, and Turkey (Togarmah). The perceived connection with Russia and the others is not trivial; it involves much scholarly research into the peoples of the Bible and of where they settled. The prophecy, the basics of which are in Ezekiel 38 and 39:2-4 and 11-15, is presented:

Ezekiel 38:

> **And the word of the Lord came to me, saying, Son of man, set your face against Gog, of the land of Magog, the chief prince of Meshech and Tubal, and prophecy against him, and say, Thus says the Lord God: Behold, I am against you, O Gog, the chief prince of Meshech and Tubal, and I will turn you back, and put hooks into your jaws, and I will bring you forth, and all your army, horses, and horsemen, all of them clothed with all sorts of armor, even a great company with bucklers and shields, all of them handling swords: Persia, Ethiopia and Libya with them; all of them with shield and helmet; Gomer, and all its bands; the house of Togarmah of the north quarters, and all its bands; and many peoples with you. Be you prepared, and prepare for yourself, you, and all your company that are assembled to you, and be you a guard to them.**
>
> **After many days you shall be visited; in the latter years you shall come into the land that is brought back from**

the sword, and is gathered out of many peoples, against the mountains of Israel, which have been always waste; but it is brought forth out of the nations, and they shall dwell safely, all of them. You shall ascend and come like a storm; you shall be like a cloud to cover the land, you, and all your bands, and many peoples with you. Thus says the lord God: It shall also come to pass that at the same time shall things come into your mind, and you shall think an evil thought; and you shall say, I will go up to the land of unwalled villages; I will go to those who are at rest, who dwell safely, all of them dwelling without walls, and having neither bars nor gates, to take a spoil, and to take a prey; to turn your hand upon the desolate places that now are inhabited, and upon the people who are gathered out of the nations, who have gotten cattle and goods, who dwell in the midst of the land. Sheba and Dedan, and the merchants of GTarshish, with all its young lions, shall say to you, Are you come to take a spoil? Have you gathered your company to take a prey, to carry away silver and gold, to take away cattle and goods, to take a great spoil?

Therefore, son of man, prophesy and say to God, Thus says the Lord God: In that day when my people of Israel dwell safely, shall you not know it? And you shall come from your place out of uttermost parts of the north, you, and many peoples with you, all of them riding upon horses, a great company, and a mighty army; and you shall come up against my people of Israel, like a cloud to cover the land; it shall be in the latter days, and I will bring you against my land, that the nations may know me, when I shall be sanctified in you, O Gog, before their eyes.

Thus says the Lord God: Are you he of whom I have spoken in old time by my servants, the prophets of Israel, who prophesied in those days many years that I would bring you against them? And it shall come to pass at the same time when Gog shall come against the land of Israel, says the Lord God, thay my fury shall come up in my face. For

> in my jealousy and in the fire of my wrath have I spoken, Surely in that day there shall be a great shaking in the land of Israel, so that the fish of the sea, and the fowls of the heavens, and the beasts of the field, and all creeping things that creep upon the earth, and all the men that are upon the face of the earth, shall shake at my presence, and the mountains shall be thrown down, and the steep places shall fall, and every wall shall fall to the ground. And I will call for a sword against him throughout all my mountains, says the Lord God; every man's sword shall be against his brother. And I will enter into judgment against him with pestilence and with blood; and I will rain upon him, and upon his bands, and upon the many peoples that are with him, an overflowing rain, and great hailstones, fire, and brimstone. Thus will I magnify myself, and sanctify myself; and I will be known in the eyes of many nations, and they shall know that I am the Lord.

Ezekiel 39:2-4:

> And I will turn you back, and leave but the sixth part of you, and will cause you to come up from the north parts and will bring you upon the mountains of Israel. And I will smite your bow out of your left hand, and will cause your arrows to fall out of your right hand. You shall fall upon the mountains of Israel, you, and all the bands, and all the peoples that are with you; I will give you to the ravenous birds of every sort, and to the beasts of the field to be devoured.

Ezekiel 39:11-15:

> And it shall come to pass in that day, that I will give to Gog a place there of graves in Israel, the valley of the passengers on the east of the sea; and it shall stop the noses of the passengers, and thee shall they bury Gog and all his multitude; and they shall call it the Valley of Hamon-gog.
>
> And seven months shall the house of Israel be burying

them, that they may cleanse the land. Yea, all the people of the land shall bury them; and it shall be to their renown on the day that I shall be glorified, says the Lord God. And they shall set apart men for the continual task of passing through the land to bury, with the help of the passengers, those who remain upon the face of the earth, to cleanse it; after the end of seven months shall they make their search. And the passengers who pass through the land, when any sees a man's bone, then shall he set up of sign by it, till the buriers have buried it in the Valley of Hamon-gog.

When the Soviet Union collapsed in 1991 without the fulfillment of this prophecy of war, the weaker in faith among Christian eschatologists began to question whether it would ever come to pass. They also spoke of Turkey's secular government and her alignment with the West and her participation in NATO, a defense alliance of Western nations. There would have to be radical changes in the lineup of nations for things to happen according to Ezekiel 38.

Radical changes have indeed come to pass, and in an astonishingly short time. In little more than a decade, Russia under Vladimir Putin is flexing her military muscles, showing belligerence against her neighbors in the former Soviet Union, rebuilding a mighty military engine, and making pacts with Iran and Turkey. In the meantime, Turkey under Recep Erdogan is returning to her Islamic roots and is distancing herself from the West. Both Turkey and Russia are now heavily involved in Syria's civil war, and operate at cross purposes to America's limited and largely ineffectual involvement. Israel's agricultural productivity is substantial; with oil now in the picture, she represents a ripe plum that Russia and her allies might be willing to pick in the very near future.

This prophecy is astonishingly precise. In verse 38:15, God places Russia as the land to the uttermost north. If one draws a line due north from Jerusalem, the line will pass very close to Moscow, the closest to the North Pole of any city near that line. Note also the hints, in the cleanup process in the aftermath of the war, of the involvement of nuclear weapons.

Nine
Gideon

Back in Deuteronomy 28 God through Moses forewarned the nation of Israel that its unique status as the beloved of God and its blessings from it involved the nation's loyal obedience to His commandments. He then set out in detail the penalty for their unfaithfulness to Him. It makes for grim reading, the harshest element being their separation from Him and from their homeland. History records the fact that Israel did eventually reach the point where God did take them from their homeland and scatter them throughout the earth. This lamentable and very lengthy situation is called the dispersion, or the *diaspora.* But before the *diaspora*, God gave them several wake-up calls in an attempt to get them to realize that the nation was heading in the wrong direction. These amounted to times of trouble of increasing severity, but less than the more final removal of the Israelites from their land.

During one of these times God involved Gideon. According to Judges 6:1-10, the children of Israel did evil in the sight of the Lord, who responded by bringing the Midianites into the land and allowing them to bully the Israelites and take over their fields and cattle, causing a situation of misery and near-starvation. He also sent a prophet to explain to the nation that through their disobedience to Him they had brought this trouble on by themselves.

But God was also using this trouble to give the Israelites a prophetic promise, that at a time in the distant future under another apparently hopeless situation He would supernaturally deliver the Jews.

Gideon, like many Jewish lads at the time, was attempting to thresh wheat out of the eyes of the Midianites when he saw an angel of the

Lord sitting under an oak, probably appearing as a hayseed with a stalk of wheat sticking out from between his front teeth. He spoke to Gideon, calling him a mighty man of valor, the man who would save Israel from the Midianites. I can visualize Gideon stepping back in shock, pointing a finger at himself, and asking "Who, me?"

The angel gave Gideon his credentials in the form of a small miracle, then demanded of Gideon that he tear down the altar to Baal that his father had built. After Gideon met that request, the Lord got down to the business of tasking Gideon to clear the land of Midianites, which required of Gideon a stronger measure of courage. Gideon wanted further proof that the God was indeed behind the request. He put a tuft of wool, which is called a fleece, on the floor, saying to the Lord that if the fleece was wet with dew in the morning while the surrounding floor was dry, he would know that it was truly God who was behind this audacious plan. When that came to pass, Gideon was not yet content with the outcome; he asked the Lord for one more sign. He put a fleece on the floor again the next night, asking the Lord this second time to do the reverse: make the fleece dry and the floor wet with dew. The Lord graciously gave Gideon that sign, and Gideon believed.

Gideon gathered together fighting men scattered throughout Israel, coming up with an army of thirty two thousand people. But God wasn't content with that number: so many people were involved that if Israel succeeded in thrusting the Midianites out of the land with them, they would point to their own selves as the victors rather than God. Therefore, God demanded Gideon to release from the upcoming battle those who didn't want to fight. That got rid of twenty two thousand people, leaving only ten thousand who remained. That still was too many for God's liking. He told Gideon to let the men drink from a nearby stream; those who got on their knees to drink instead of lapping water with their tongues would also be released from the upcoming action. This left only three hundred men to fight out of the original thirty two thousand. This number was so ridiculously small that any victory the Israelites would achieve over the Midianites would obviously be God's doing.

God instructed these three hundred men under Gideon's leadership to arm themselves with trumpets and empty pitchers with lamps inside and to separate themselves into three companies of one hundred each. Opposing them was the encampment of the Midianites, described as a horde in Judges 7:12:

> **And the Midianites and the Amalekites and all the children of the east lay along in the valley like grasshoppers for multitude; and their camels were without number, as the sand by the seaside for multitude.**

The Israelites were to approach them in the night, their lamps lit. When Gideon blew his horn they did likewise and broke the pitchers in their hands, shouting "The sword of the Lord, and of Gideon." As they did so, the Midianites fled in terror. The Israelites pursued them, and slew their kings Oreb, Zeeb, Zebah and Zalmunna.

Of course the Israelites had help. In a similar incident several hundred years later involving the prophet Elisha, the Israelites again were drastically outnumbered. God again came to the rescue, as described in 2 Kings 6:15-17:

> **And when the servant of the man of God was risen early, and gone forth, behold, a host compassed the city, both with horses and chariots. And his servant said to him, Alas, my master! What shall we do? And he answered, Fear not; for they who are with us are more than they who are with them. And Elisha prayed, and said, Lord, I pray you, open his eyes, that he may see. And the Lord opened the eyes of the young man, and he saw; and, behold, the mountain was full of horses and chariots of fire round about Elisha.**

Gideon's victory was prophetic of another event yet in the future, at a time, perhaps now, when the nation of Israel would stand alone, vastly outnumbered against a world that hated it and wanted to destroy it. It would be the time spoken of by the prophet Zechariah in Zechariah 12:1-9:

> **The burden of the word of the Lord for Israel, says the Lord, who stretched forth the heavens, and laid the foundation**

of the earth, and formed the spirit of man within him. Behold, I will make Jerusalem a cup of trembling to all the peoples round about, when they shall be in the siege both against Judah and against Jerusalem. And in that day will I make Jerusalem a burdensome stone for all peoples; all who burden themselves with it shall be cut in pieces, though all the nations of the earth be gathered together against it. In that day, says the Lord, I will smite every horse with terror, and his rider with madness; and I will open my eyes upon the house of Judah, and will smite every horse of the peoples with blindness. And the governors of Judah shall say in their heart, The inhabitants of Jerusalem shall be my strength in the Lord of hosts, their God. In that day will I make the governors of Judah like a hearth of fire among the wood, and like a torch of fire in a sheaf; and they shall devour all the peoples round about, on the right hand and on the left; and Jerusalem shall be inhabited again in her own place, even in Jerusalem. The Lord shall also save the tents of Judah first, that the glory of the house of David and the glory of the inhabitants of Jerusalem do not magnify themselves against Judah. In that day shall the Lord defend the inhabitants of Jerusalem; and he who is feeble among them at that day shall be like David; and the house of David shall be like God, like the angel of the Lord before them. And it shall come to pass, in that day, that I will seek to destroy all the nations that come against Jerusalem.

It is my humble opinion, subject to being overtaken by events, that the Judah that Zechariah refers to here is primarily the disputed West Bank, which includes the city of Hebron.

About the Author

Arthur Perkins is an electrical engineer by training and a Christian at heart who takes seriously the commandment of Moses, repeated by Jesus, to "Love our God with all our hearts, souls and might." In honor of that love, Art and his wife Carolyn have devoted time to sharing Scripture with others in nursing and assisted-living homes. Art and Carolyn live in the foothills of Mount Rainier in rural Western Washington.

In the course of the nursing home activity, Art met the key figure in *Buddy*, whose cheerful outlook in the face of the painful and seriously limiting affliction of cerebral palsy inspired him to write of their shared adventure of flight in that novel. *Buddy* was followed by three other novels, *Cathy*, *Jacob*, and *Home, Sweet Heaven* involving the fictional character Earl Cook and his wife Joyce. A unifying theme of this series is Christian service, first toward the handicapped and, expanding outward, toward the unsaved and to the faithful adherents of Christianity's beloved mother religion, Judaism, and ultimately to God's spiritual domain. Along with the adventures that Earl and Joyce encounter, they share with the reader topics of the Bible and the nature of God that are not commonly presented to the average Churchgoer, enriching the readers' understanding of the faith they have embraced and which are of significance in today's chaotic world. In addition to the novels, Art has written a Christian nonfiction book entitled *Marching to a Worthy Drummer*, in which he addresses the true nature of the Holy Spirit who, unfortunately, has been misrepresented by the Church for a distressingly long time.

Art and his wife Carolyn have shared together many of the experiences described in his novels. Since their retirement, they continue to build a repertoire of treasured memories out of their mutual interests and incredible adventures.

Residing above the unifying themes of Christian service and the understanding of Scripture dwells the all-important subject of love: the love of God toward us and the possibility of its return to Him by us. On top of that love between God and the human race is the amazing love that exists within the Godhead Itself.

It is the profound love that exists within the Godhead between its Divine Members that drives this nonfiction work, motivating the author to share in its appreciation with readers who wish to experience the love of God in the fullness that He intended.

www.ingramcontent.com/pod-product-compliance
Lightning Source LLC
Chambersburg PA
CBHW071404090426
42737CB00011B/1344
* 9 7 8 1 9 4 0 1 4 5 7 9 2 *